Working

with children

in the early years

Edited by Jane Devereux and Linda Miller

David Fulton Publishers
London

in association with

The Open
University

David Fulton Publishers Ltd
The Chiswick Centre, 414 Chiswick High Road, London W4 5TF

www.fultonpublishers.co.uk

First published 2003
Reprinted 2003 (twice)
10 9 8 7 6 5 4 3

British Library Cataloguing in Publication Data
A catalogue record for this book is available from the British Library.

ISBN 1–85346–975–0

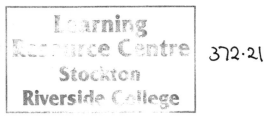
Typeset by FiSH Books, London
Printed and bound by Thanet Press

Contents

Acknowledgements

We would like to thank all those who have contributed chapters to this Reader or who have approved their reprinting from other publications. Grateful acknowledgement is made to the following sources for permission to reproduce material in this book:

Chapter 1: RSA (1994) 'Patterns of provision in the UK', *Start Right: The Importance of Early Learning*, Report by Sir Christopher Ball.

Chapter 2: Moss, P. and Penn, H. (1996) 'A historical perspective on nursery education', *Transforming Nursery Education*, London: Paul Chapman Publishing Ltd, reprinted by permission of Sage Publishers, London.

Chapter 3: Read, M. and Rees, M. (2000) 'Working in teams in early years settings', *Looking at Early Years Education and Care*, ed. R. Drury, L. Miller and R. Campbell, London: David Fulton Publishers.

Chapter 4: Karstadt, L., Lilley, T. and Miller, L. (2000) 'Professional roles in early childhood', *Looking at Early Years Education and Care*, ed. R. Drury, L. Miller and R. Campbell, London: David Fulton Publishers.

Chapter 5: Moylett, H. (1997) ' "It's not nursery but it's not just being at home" — a parent and childminder working together', *Working with the Under-3s: Responding to Children's Needs*, ed. L. Abbott and H. Moylett, Buckingham: Open University Press.

Chapter 6: Mathieson, J., Appendix in Moylett, H. (1997) ' "It's not nursery but it's not just being at home" – a parent and childminder working together', *Working with the Under-3s: Responding to Children's Needs*, ed. L. Abbott and H. Moylett, Buckingham: Open University Press.

Chapter 7: Karran, S. (1997) ' "Auntie - ji, please come and join us, just for an hour." The role of the bilingual education assistant in working with parents with little confidence', *Home–School Work in Multicultural Settings*, ed. J. Bastiani, London: David Fulton Publishers.

Chapter 8: Hurst, V. and Joseph, J. (1998) 'Parents and practitioners: sharing education', *Supporting Early Learning: The Way Forward*, Buckingham: Open University Press.

Chapter 12: Anning, A. and Edwards, A. (1999) 'Language and literacy learning', *Promoting Children's Learning from Birth to Five: Developing the New Early Years Professional*, Buckingham: Open University Press.

Chapter 13: Abbott, L. (1994) ' "Play is fun, but it's hard work, too!" The search for quality play in the early years', *Quality Education in the Early Years*, ed. L. Abbott and R. Rodger, Buckingham: Open University Press.

Chapter 14: Holland, R. (1997) ' "What's it all about?" — how introducing heuristic play has affected provision for the under-threes in one day nursery', *Working with the Under-3s: Responding to Children's Needs*, ed. L. Abbott and H. Moylett, Buckingham: Open University Press.

Chapter 15: Whitehead, M. (1999) 'Great communicators', *Supporting Language and Literacy Development in the Early Years*, Buckingham: Open University Press.

Chapter 16: Duffy, B. (1998) 'Creative and imaginative experiences', *Supporting Creativity and Imagination in the Early Years*, Buckingham: Open University Press.

Chapter 17: Devereux, J. (1996) 'What we see depends on what we look for: observation as a part of teaching and learning in the early years', *Education in Early Childhood: First Things First*, ed. S. Robson and S. Smedley, London: David Fulton Publishers.

Chapter 18: Owens, P. (2000) 'Children growing and changing: the interpersonal world of the growing child', *Looking at Early Years Education and Care*, ed. R. Drury, L. Miller and R. Campbell, London: David Fulton Publishers.

Chapter 20: Macintyre, C. (2001) 'Studying play from a developmental perspective', *Enhancing Learning Through Play: A Developmental Perspective for Early Years Settings*, London: David Fulton Publishers.

Part 1
Provision, practitioners and parents

Jane Devereux

Introduction

'...the lesson of importance of early childhood is surely that we do all in our power to assure that the young get off to a healthy and competent start before they enter school...it should be taken as a given in any national policy that the care of the young should be as thoughtful and as considered as it can be made to be.'

(Bruner 1980: 10)

Working with Children in the Early Years aims to provide an insight into some of the key areas that should be considered if Bruner's ideas above are to reach realisation. It consists of an edited collection of articles that will help practitioners working in early years settings to develop a deeper and broader understanding of their roles and responsibilities in the context of current developments that are taking place in the United Kingdom (UK). The expansion of early years provision, the target to increase the qualifications of those working in early years settings and the drive to improve the quality of provision make for exciting and challenging times ahead. Young children by their very nature are interesting, curious, enthusiastic, motivated and stimulating to work with as they grow and develop and make sense of their world. The rapid increase and interest in early childhood education and care, that has developed over the last 15 years or more, has generated excitement because the value of early childhood education and good quality care are seen as fundamental rights. Early years education and care is gaining status as new funding initiatives are launched to give more children the best start in life. Initiatives such as the National Childcare Strategy, the Foundation Stage curriculum, the framework for under-threes, Sure Start and the National Childcare Standards are all indications of the effort to improve and integrate services for young children.

Through a selection of articles by recognised authorities in their field, this book provides insights into particular areas and ways of working with young children. The book is divided into three sections: Provision, Practitioners and Parents; Curriculum and Practice; Growing and Developing. These sections describe the main areas of work carried out by early years practitioners and air some of their concerns. It is hoped that this reader will help both experienced practitioners and those new to the field, to develop a deeper understanding of the theoretical underpinnings of their everyday practice.

It is important when working with children in the early years to have a sound understanding of both current and past provision in order to understand the diverse nature of early years care and education services in the UK. The two chapters that describe the development of this provision are by Sir Christopher Ball ('Patterns of provision in the UK') and Peter Moss and Helen Penn's 'A historical perspective on nursery education'. We hope that these chapters will enable readers to locate their own setting within the range of provision described. Whilst the diversity of provision can be seen as a strength in meeting different family needs, it also poses problems in terms of ensuring quality and consistency across different sectors. Through an examination of seven types of provision in the mid 1990s the first reading presents a challenge to those responsible, to raise the quality of early years care and education. The second reading explores public attitudes and expectations of nursery education and aims to extend the reader's understanding of how we got to where we are today.

The next two chapters, the first by Mary Read and Mary Rees on 'Working in teams in early years settings' and the second by Lyn Karstadt, Tricia Lilley and Linda Miller on 'Professional roles in early childhood' provide theoretical and practical insights for practitioners into ways of working together and highlight the responsibilities of individuals and teams in providing quality experiences for young children. In discussing and analysing the skills needed to work with others the first reading gives practitioners sound advice on ways forward. The second reading focuses more on the nature of professionalism and the implications for practice and continuing professional development.

The next two readings focus on parents and their concerns in choosing an educational or care setting for their young child. They also explore positive and constructive ways in which parents and practitioners can work in partnership for the benefit of their children. Helen Moylett's, '"It's not nursery but it's not just being at home" – a parent and childminder working together', and Jo Mathieson's 'Information to parents', provide a parent and a practitioner perspective on partnership and on working together and sharing information. The emotional tensions that parents face are sensitively explored by Helen Moylett and provide food for thought. Jo Mathieson shows how, through the information she provides for parents, she is aware of the natural anxieties that parents have of leaving their child in the care of others. Sheila Karran's chapter, 'Auntie-ji, please come and join us, just for an hour' explores partnership with parents in multicultural settings. By looking at the different ways that parents and practitioners can support and help children to learn, this reading also illustrates how parents and practitioners learned different strategies and skills from each other. The reading by Vicky Hurst and Jenefer Joseph. 'Parents and practitioners: sharing education', provides a wider ranging discussion about the nature of sharing and about the holistic way in which children learn. It also provides insight into the different roles and responsibilities of both parent and practitioner's and their different strengths.

The final reading in Part One, 'I can sing a rainbow', by Roger Hancock with Alison Cox, describes a project that took place in 1996 with Tate Britain in which a workshop for parents and children under three helped them to engage with some of the exhibits. The reading explores the nature of the workshops and the ways in which parents worked alongside the children. It reflects on their success in terms of the nature of the partnership established between the parents and carers and provides insight into a wider perspective on partnership that could inform other educational settings.

References

Bruner, J. (1980) *Under Five in Britain.* London: Grant McIntyre Ltd.

Chapter 1

Patterns of provision in the UK

Sir Christopher Ball

[...]

Introduction

Diversity is the hallmark of pre-school provision for the under-fives in the UK. But not choice. Or coherence. There is a wide range of provision, including nursery schools, nursery classes, nursery units in primary schools, day nurseries and, of course, pre-school playgroups. But neither market mechanisms nor planned public provision are enabling parents to find the pre-school education and care they want for their children, or children to make the right start to learning and life. Both the following statements (one defensive, the other critical, of the *status quo*) are true: 'linking all types of provision together, over 90 per cent of three- and four-year-olds now attend some form of education or other group provision'; 'the UK as a whole is near the bottom of the league for publicly-funded pre-school educational places'. How can that be?

In contrast with emerging good practice in Europe, the UK seems to use two strategies as *substitutes* for high-quality nursery education – early entry to primary schools, and playgroups. The importance of these two strategies is clear from statistics for the percentage and numbers of children attending different types of provision in England in 1992 recently quoted by a Minister:

Table 1.1 Children in different types of provision, 1992, England

	Local Authority nursery schools	Nursery classes (at primary schools)	Reception classes (at primary schools)	Pre-School playgroups	Independent schools
%	4	22	23	41	4
'000s	52	278	300	525	46

(The percentages total 94 because some children attend more than one type of provision.)

This is an unsatisfactory, and potentially misleading, statement of the position. There are other ways of presenting the general picture, for example:

- over 45% of places in pre-school provision depend on parental fees, rather than public provision (60%)[+]
- over 40% of children attend playgroups on average for two sessions (less than 10 hours) per week (nearly 60%)[+]
- over 75% of children are being admitted to primary schools before their fifth birthday
- Local Education Authority provision of nursery education caters for a range from 0–80%+ of three- and four-year-olds in different localities.

([+] *The figures in brackets include children under the age of three.*)

Table 1.2 shows the number of places in most types of early childhood provision in 1980 and 1991. It demonstrates the conflicting slow growth of publicly-funded services and rapid expansion of the private sector (childminders and private day nurseries).

Table 1.2 Number of places in early childhood care and education provision, 1980, 1991, England.
Source: Sylva and Moss 1992: 32

Types of provision	1980	1991	% change 1980–1991
Nursery education	130,997	177,863	+36
Reception class	205,673	272,178	+32
Local authority day nurseries	28,437	27,039	–5
Private nurseries	22,017	79,029	+259
Playgroups	367,868	428,420	+16
Childminders	98,495	233,258	+137

Table 1.3 gives a more detailed breakdown of the various *types* of provision. See NCB Table for breakdown on England, Wales and Scotland*. However, it is important to state a general caution against uncritical reliance on the statistics quoted in this and other reports.

Nonetheless, it is clear from these figures that 'early childhood care and education services are unevenly distributed, and receive limited public funding; most provision is in the private market and depends on parents' ability to pay. The UK has one of the lowest levels of publicly-funded pre-school services in Europe', (Sylva and Moss 1992). Furthermore, the available provision fails in a number of ways to satisfy the over-riding requirement for good early childhood services, namely high quality. Nursery education and local authority day nurseries run the risk of creating the ghetto effect because of scarcity and rationing of places. The reception classes in primary schools run the risk of imposing an inappropriate curriculum with insufficient and non-specialist staff. Playgroups run

---

* National Children's Bureau (1991) *Statistics: Under Fives and Pre-School Services*

the risk of providing too brief a period of attendance, with inadequate equipment and inadequately-trained staff. The private sector is unlikely to serve the children from disadvantaged backgrounds, where the potential for benefit is greatest. Others have characterised the pattern of provision in the UK as lacking commitment, co-ordination and cash. In earlier times, it would have been called a public scandal.

Types of provision

There are seven major types of provision (apart from parents at home), and several minor types. The first is **nursery education**, which is designed to further children's emotional, social, physical and cognitive development, complementing the learning that takes place in the home. Nursery schools and nursery classes run by Local Education Authorities provide free education for children between the ages of two-and-a-half and five. They are staffed by specially trained teachers and nursery nurses. (Trained) adult:child ratios stand at about 1:13. Availability of places varies significantly by locality, ranging from 0% to 80%+ of three- and four-year-olds. About four-fifths of enrolled children attend part-time, usually for five half-days a week. Nursery education provides for about a quarter of three- and four-year-old children (about 4% in nursery schools and some 21% in nursery classes).

Reception classes in primary schools admit just over three-quarters of children at age four, although children are not obliged to start school until the term after their fifth birthday. Policies on early admission vary between Local Education Authorities. In the past, it has been usual for children to be admitted at the start of the term in which they will become five: these children are known as 'rising fives'. But the trend towards once-yearly admission has led to some younger four-year-olds being admitted to reception classes. This form of 'pre-school' education is free. Its quality varies widely, depending on a range of factors including the nature of the curriculum, the provision of staffing (which is rarely as favourable as in nursery education), and the training of staff. Primary schools employ trained teachers, few of whom have received specialised nursery training; and some also employ nursery nurses and (untrained) support staff. The children attend full-time.

Local Authority day nurseries provide full-time or part-time care for children who are deemed to need specialist help. They are run by social services departments. Day nurseries are tending to move away from simply providing care for 'problem children' towards an approach involving work with parents and children together. These 'family centres' can offer, not only counselling and classes for the parents, but also in many cases nursery education for the children. Places are allocated according to a system of priorities. The age range catered for is from birth to four (inclusive), but normally day nurseries do not admit children younger than one-and-a-half. The staff are trained nursery nurses, sometimes with additional qualifications in social work. Where there is a nursery class, it is normal for a trained teacher to be employed (or seconded). Day nurseries make only a small contribution to early learning and the care of pre-school children: they cater for less than 1 per cent of under fives.

Private and Voluntary day nurseries are similar to Local Authority nurseries. But they also include a variety of rather different kinds of provision: community nurseries, all-day playgroups, workplace nurseries, partnership nurseries and all-day crèches. They must be registered and inspected by local authority social services departments. They provide full or sessional care for children of parents who can afford the fees. The provision is required to satisfy national standards laid down in the Children Act 1989. Training is variable: no minimum standard is required in this respect. The recent growth in workplace nurseries is particularly important and interesting. It is bound to raise the question whether young children are best served by nurseries close to their home, or close to their parent's place of work. If both patterns continue to develop, it is not clear how systematic provision for all children can be satisfactorily organised or managed. This is a very rapidly growing sector and currently provides for about $2\frac{1}{2}$ per cent of under fives.

Private nursery schools are open for the length of the normal school day. Little information is available, since (if they take only children under the age of five) they are not obliged to register as schools with the Department for Education; but they are required to register with local authority social services departments. There are no figures available on the number of such schools or their staffing or the fees charged. About $3\frac{1}{2}$ per cent of children aged three to four are attending private nursery schools. This is also an expanding sector.

Playgroups cater for children aged three (sometimes two-and-a-half) to four (inclusive), aiming to provide education through play. Parents pay a fee for each session. Groups offer support to parents, and many provide opportunities for learning and involvement. Local availability varies: numbers appear to be highest where Local Education Authority nursery education is most scarce. The playgroup movement gives emphasis to the principle that parents are the prime educators of their children. There are many different kinds of playgroups, but two-thirds are community groups – managed by parent committees and run by playgroup workers with parent helpers. In England group leaders are usually trained through the Pre-School Playgroups Association (PPA), a registered educational charity to which most playgroups belong. Scotland, Wales, and Northern Ireland make different arrangements. Some playgroups are run by local authorities or private individuals. Almost two-thirds are non-profit making groups run by committees of parents; about a third are run by individuals (either on a commercial or non-profit making basis); and some 3 per cent are run by local authority social services departments. Most children attend playgroups for two or three half-day sessions a week. Although most groups remain open for five sessions a week, they have to ration attendance to accommodate more children. An increasing number of groups operate extended hours. Most playgroups include children with special needs, but 'opportunity playgroups' cater specifically for them (alongside other children) and provide links with specialist medical or psychological expertise. Playgroups are required to register with the local authority social services department and are regularly inspected to ensure they conform to national standards. Roughly half of all children aged three and four attend playgroups: estimates vary from 41 per cent (proportion quoted by a Government Minister in the Department for Education) to 60 per cent (estimate published by the National Children's Bureau).

Childminders, who must be registered with local authority social services departments, take children under the age of five into their homes for two or more hours per day, for which the parents pay a fee. The arrangement is usually a private one between parent and minder, though some local authorities sponsor the placement of 'priority' children with 'Day Carers' or 'Day Foster Parents'. Although about half of registered childminders are members of the National Childminding Association, not a lot is known in detail about this sector. Whether it makes a substantial contribution to early learning (as opposed to care) is doubtful. There are wide variations in the hours worked, facilities provided, and the training of childminders. Recommended ratios are 1:3 for children under five; this includes the childminder's own children (if any). These ratios tend to be enforced as a condition of registration. This sector is growing rapidly and currently provides places for about 7 per cent of under fives.

These seven types of provision, do not, however, give the full picture. There are also some minor categories which do not demand detailed discussion here – except for the **Combined Nursery Centres** which offer an excellent model for future provision by fully integrating care and education. Although no two are precisely the same, combined nursery centres offer a flexible combination of daycare and nursery education. In addition to this desirable integration of care and early learning, they often offer support and facilities for parents on a 'drop-in' basis, a centre for toy libraries and help for families with special needs. Some go further and provide adult education and child health advice in addition. Of all existing types of provision, combined nursery centres come closest to the ideal which this report seeks to promote.

Children with special educational needs may be provided for in any of the above settings and will also be amongst the estimated 10 per cent of children at home in the care of parents or nannies (see next paragraph). Some of the young children whose difficulties or disabilities are most pronounced and have been identified at an early stage, receive additional support from a wide range of

Table 1.3 Statistics: Day care and pre-school education 1991. Provisions and costs in Great Britain

Type of Provision	% of children	Hours	Ages	Approximate cost to parents
Day Care	**% of 0–4**			
Childminders	7%	All day	0–4	£1.50 per hour £50 per week
Local Authority day nurseries/family centres	1%	Some all day, some sessional	0–4 (but few under 2)	Means tested
Private day nurseries, partnership and workplace nurseries	2.5%	All day	0–4	Between £45–£150 per week depending on age of child and availability of subsidy
Education and Play	**% of 3–4**			
LEA nursery schools and classes	26%	Termtime: usually 2½ hours a day	3–4	Free
Infant classes	21%	Termtime: 9am–3.30pm	mainly 4	Free
Playgroups	60% (1.8 children per place)	Usually 2½ hours for 2/3 days a week, some all day	2½–4	£1.70 per 2½ hour session
Private nursery and other schools	3.5%	Usually 9am–3.30pm	2½–4	Various fees
Services on which there are no national statistics				
Combined nursery centres	about 50 centres	All day	0–4	Education free, day care means tested
Family centres (May include some LA day nurseries)	about 500 members of Family Centre Network (Dec. 93)	Usually all day	Vary	Vary
Out of school/holiday clubs	700 clubs (Dec. 93)	before and after school, holidays	Vary	Vary

% do not add up to 100 because some children attend two types of provision.

Provided by	Staffing	Training	Ratios	
Private arrangement	Registered childminders	Variable. No national requirements	1:3 1:6	0–5 5–7
Local Authority Social Services	Mainly nursery nurses	NNEB/DPQS/BTec SNNB/SCOTVEC Units	1:3 1:4 1:8	0–2 2–3 3–5
Employers, private organisations and individuals	Nursery nurses, some untrained staff	at least half staff must be trained – as above	1:3 1:4 1:8	0–2 2–3 3–4
Local Authority Education	Nursery teachers	Degree and PGCE/ BEd	1 (teacher):23 1 (all staff):10/13	
	nursery nurses	NNEB		
Local Authority Education	Primary teachers	Degree and PGCE/ BEd	1:30/40 (better if nursery nurse employed)	
	teaching assistant or nursery nurse recommended	NNEB SNNB/SCOTVEC Units		
Parents and voluntary groups	Playgroup leader	Foundation course/ diploma in playgroups practice	1:8	3–5
Private individuals and organisations	Not specified: often teacher or NNEB	Unknown	1:8 1:20/30	3–4 5+
Local authority education and social services, sometime health and voluntary sector input	Nursery teachers, nursery nurses	as for nursery schools/classes and day nurseries	as for nursery schools/classes and day nurseries	
Local Authority social services, health authorities, voluntary sector	nursery nurses, social workers, range of staff	Varied	Depends on nature of centre	
Schools, leisure depts, voluntary sector	playleaders, community workers, volunteers	Unknown	1:8	5–7

Devised by Early Childhood Unit National Children's Bureau, drawing on government statistics and information from voluntary organisations.

Table 1.4 Percentages of young children in major types of provision

| | Centre-based provision | | | | Nursery | No Centre-based provision | |
| | Public | | Private | | | | |
	Education (pre-school)	Social Services	Playgroups	Crèche/ Children's Centres		Child-minders	Homecare
children aged							
0–2	none	nb	na	nb	none	nb	na
3–4	26%	nb	60%	nb	3.5%	nb	na
0–4*	26%	1%	60%	2.5%	3.5%	7%	na

nb – *not broken down*   na – *not available*
* *the percentages add up to 100% (without any figures for those children cared for totally at home) because children may attend more than one type of provision. No statistics are available for children at home.*

medical, educational and social services. Nationally, at least 4,000 children receive support from Portage projects (Kiernan 1993). Portage is a scheme which provides support to the development of the child by working alongside parents. Some children with special educational needs are placed in special daycare provision. This may be attached to a child development centre or other NHS provision where there is ready access to medical, para-medical services and in some centres a range of further support services. Whether or not they have a statement under the 1981 Education Act (or in future under the 1993 Education Act) children with special educational needs may be given priority admission, or early admission to nursery education. However, where there is not widespread provision this may lead to over-concentrations of children with a range of difficulties. The special educational needs of many more children are not identified or may not emerge until they start in educational provision. The importance of good quality early learning provision for these children is obvious: without it they are less likely to be identified and given appropriate help as soon as possible. The Warnock Report advised: 'While recognising the financial constraints, we would like to see a considerable expansion of opportunities for nursery education for young children with special needs on a part-time as well as a full-time basis. We do not, however, believe that it would at present be either practicable or desirable to seek to achieve this through a policy of positive discrimination in the admission of children to nursery schools and classes. Rather, we recommend that the provision for nursery education for all children should be substantially increased as soon as possible, since this would have the consequence that opportunities for nursery education for young children with special needs could be correspondingly extended' (Warnock Report 1978: 5.51).

Finally a considerable group of young children remain at home in the care of parents or nannies – or are placed with unregistered childminders – up to the age of five. This group appears to contain some 10 per cent of children aged three to four. Readers might be forgiven if they feel confused at this point. The complexity of the pattern of provision in the UK, the confusion of the statistics and the absence of principled direction of the early childhood care and education services are obvious. It is a service characterised by diversity: diversity in the types of provision, diversity within each type, and diversity of quality overall. Table 1.4 is designed to simplify the picture – though readers should recall G. K. Chesterton's comment that 'he who simplifies, simply lies'. It seeks to reveal the following critical distinctions: on the vertical dimension, the age of children (0–2, 3–4, and 0–4 combined); on the horizontal dimension, first, the distinction between centre-based provision and (entirely) home-based provision – second, the distinction between private and public provision – and third, the distinction between 'education' (provided by the Local Authority) and 'care' (provided by Social Services). (Of course, it fails to reveal the critical distinction between high and low-quality provision, or the relative amount of time spent in different kinds of provision.)

Commentary

The first thing that needs to be said about the survey presented in the preceding paragraphs is that the statistical base is inadequate and the information incomplete, uncertain and (in places) conflicting. The Rumbold Report found the same difficulty. Its words remain apt today: 'The data we are able to give suffer from a number of defects. The Department (for Education) and the Department of Health collect figures at different times in the year and on different bases, educational figures being for children and childcare figures being for places. The figures are not complete: those for family centres and combined nursery places do not appear, nor those for peripatetic nursery teachers. For these reasons it is not possible to derive a comprehensive statistical base. The national statistics for particular services may conceal wide local variations in what is available. Where they permit meaningful comparisons to be drawn these relate entirely to the quantity of the facilities provided and say nothing of their quality. We believe a more satisfactory statistical base is needed as a basis for policy making and recommend that the two Departments commission a study to establish how this might be done' (DES 1990). This recommendation fell upon stony ground. Nothing has been done. Although all Local Authorities were required to review their services in 1992 (under provisions of the Children Act 1989), the results have not yet been collected, aggregated and published on a national basis.

There might be a variety of reasons for this neglect. One is the lack of real responsibility and the division of (national) responsibility between the two departments of state. This division in part arises from, and in part reinforces, a failure to recognise the principle of the integration of childcare and early learning. But the evidence of research and the lessons from abroad teach the fundamental principle of the 'seamless web' uniting early education and care, 'edu-care'. Those whose primary concern is the health of the child need to understand that good early learning is a critical part of healthy growth; those whose primary concern is education need to understand that 'good teachers should know, but *must care*' (in both senses of 'caring for' and 'caring about'). Education without care doesn't work. This is well understood by most practitioners and many local authorities, but is not reflected in the organisation or behaviour of central government. Successive governments (of different political persuasions) have failed to recognise the need, failed to allocate responsibility, failed to make provision, failed to ensure quality, and failed to collect statistics.

One particularly glaring consequence of the division of responsibility is the different (sometimes conflicting) requirements for the registration, inspection and standards of provision. The Children Act of 1989 has laid down clear (minimum) national standards and requires local authority social services departments to ensure that they are met. While the Children Act urges co-ordination, the Education Reform Act 1988, and succeeding legislation, makes co-ordination more difficult by reducing the role of Local Education Authorities, and failing to make provision for the definition and maintenance of standards and quality in pre-school education. In its evidence to the House of Commons Select Committee (DES 1989), the Association of County Councils stated: 'Educational research has consistently indicated that the most important single step towards the improvement of the quality of education in this country would be to provide a coherent and comprehensive system of pre-school education for all'. This report endorses that statement. And it may be added that, since one of the major requirements for effective early learning is high-quality provision, the Department for Education's lack of interest and (indeed) neglect is little short of disgraceful.

There are no effective national standards, or advisory norms, for the length of time per week (or the age at which) children should experience centre-based early learning, the training of staff, appropriate ratios of (trained) adults to children*, appropriate resources (buildings and equipment) and indicative costs. This has all been said before, and often, and clearly. The Rumbold Report (DES 1990) *Starting with Quality*, stated: 'we believe that the achievement of greater co-ordination could be greatly helped if central government gave a clear lead, setting a national framework within which local developments could take place'. Why doesn't it happen?

Margaret Thatcher's 1972 White Paper accepted the principle of nursery education. It has subsequently been abandoned by governments of both left and right. There can be little doubt that the main reason is cost. Ministers have recently estimated that the recurrent cost of 'forcing the state to provide a place for every three- and four-year-old, irrespective of (parental) income' would be over half-a-billion pounds a year, together with 'substantial capital costs'. They

---

* There are conflicting recommended ratios: the Children Act requires 1:8 for three- to four-year-olds, while the Education Department advises 1:13 for nursery provision – and permits up to 1:40 in reception classes.

challenge those who advocate investment in pre-school education to say where the money would come from, and to state what existing programmes should be cut to provide the necessary resources. While noting that this is a challenge of a kind which others responsible for public provision (the police or the universities, for example) are not required to meet, it is one to which this report offers a response: investment in good pre-school education provides a real economic return to society – indeed, the 'payback' of nursery education is clearer and higher than that so far calculated for any other phase of education. At this point, however, it is important to establish that the debate is more about priorities than resources. Developed nations do not discuss whether they can afford what they value highest – clean water, immunisation, disability benefits, national security or the costs of elections and parliament. The importance of early learning is such that it belongs in this list. The European Council of Ministers has urged member states to improve childcare provision; governments may be encouraged to spend 1 per cent of gross domestic product for this purpose (a sum calculated at about £6 billion for the UK by the year 2000). Ministers should consider the words of one of their supporters and himself a recent Minister in the Department for Education: 'Anyone with the money knows that good nursery schooling is one of the best educational buys available...The fact that nursery education can give a child a lasting advantage...is so self-evident that it scarcely needs proof...How can anyone whose own child has benefited from serious nursery education have the gall to maintain that it is not essential for the children of others?' (George Walden, MP, *Daily Telegraph*, 18 May 1993).

When Ministers say the problem is money, they reveal that their priorities are muddled. The statement that over half-a-billion pounds per annum would be required 'to provide a place for every three- and four-year-old', while no doubt intended to discourage the advocates of early learning, confirms and admits that existing patterns of provision are seriously inadequate. It is difficult to accept both that all is well with what we have got, and that so large a sum would be needed to provide what is recognised as 'good practice' elsewhere in the world. In fact, all is not well. Ministers who believe that the diversity of provision in the UK offers a satisfactory service cannot have seriously considered the evidence. Of course, in moving from an unsatisfactory situation to a better one we should use all the resources available – and in particular build on the strengths of both established nursery education and the voluntary pre-school playgroup movement. Ministers who argue that market forces and private provision will respond to the demand and needs for early learning, have not been able to show how the most disadvantaged parents and children will be helped. (Even those parents who are relatively well off are probably experiencing the most difficult economic stage of their lives, as they face the costs of housing and dependent children while managing for a time on one income.) Ministers who are not persuaded that research has yet proved the advantages of pre-school education should consider whether the nation can any longer afford to take the risk of waiting for further confirmation. Bad management is more often characterised by sins of omission, than of commission. Margaret Thatcher saw what was required in 1972. In the intervening 22 years, research and experience abroad have confirmed the wisdom of her acceptance of the principle of nursery education. It is high time to act.

Conclusions

This brief review of the patterns of provision in the UK suggests the following conclusions:

(a) the diverse pattern of provision lacks coherence, co-ordination or direction;
(b) it fails to meet the needs of either children or parents;
(c) it is unevenly and inequitably distributed;
(d) it falls short in a number of ways of providing an assurance of high quality, without which the benefits of pre-school education are seriously diminished;
(e) many of those most in need, and most likely to benefit, miss out;
(f) the quantitative statistical base and the qualitative knowledge base are inadequate and incomplete;
(g) the division of responsibility between the Health and Education Departments is a major difficulty;
(h) so is the failure to grasp the principle of the integration of childcare and early learning;
(i) the Department for Education has neglected its moral responsibilities for supervising, registering, inspecting and ensuring the quality of pre-school education – and has failed to seek and obtain appropriate statutory authority;
(j) the Government has failed over many years to establish a national framework within which local developments could take place, building on best practice;
(k) while funding appears to be the major impediment to progress, in reality the problem is one of priorities;
(l) pre-school education should be among a nation's first priorities;
(m) ministers have offered an unconvincing and inadequate defence of the *status quo*, by setting a high value on diversity (at the expense of quality, effectiveness and choice), by expressing doubt about the value of pre-school education (in the teeth of the evidence of research and the experience of other countries), and by trusting in the private sector (without ensuring either that those most in need – and most likely to benefit – will thereby be provided for or that the provision will be of satisfactory quality).

Accordingly, it is recommended that:

parliament, political parties, employers, the media, the churches and other voluntary, community and religious organisations should consider whether the provision for pre-school education in the UK is seriously inadequate, and take steps to persuade the Government to undertake an urgent review and act on its recommendations.

References

Department of Education and Science (1978) *Special Educational Needs (Warnock Report)*. London: HMSO.

Department of Education and Science (1989) *Aspects of Primary Education: the education of children under five*. London: HMI Report.

Department of Education and Science (1990) *Starting with Quality*. The Rumbold Report of the Committee of Inquiry into the Quality of the Educational Experience offered to 3- and 4-year-olds. London: HMSO.

Kiernan, C. (1993) *Survey of Portage Provision 1992/1993*. London: National Portage Association.

Sylva, K. and Moss, P. (1992) *Learning Before School*. Briefings, National Commission on Education. London: Heinemann.

Chapter 2

A historical perspective on nursery education

Peter Moss and Helen Penn

If left to their own impulses, (children) fill the air with perpetual questionings. Every new thing being a mystery to them, their demands for information are co-extensive with novelty . . . rational children (should not be) stinted, rebuked or dispirited . . . (but allowed) a continuous elastic spirit, ever inquiring and ever extending to others the fullness of its own aspirations

(Robert Owen 1836)

Man as a child resembles the flower on the plant, the blossom on the tree; as these are in relation to the tree, so is the child in relation to humanity, a young bud, a fresh blossom

(Friedrich Froebel 1897)

As ratepayers and citizens fathers and mothers have a right to send their children to the nursery as to (primary) schools. There are many today who do not begin to realise the meaning of collective buying and collective organisation and who cannot, therefore, imagine that the pleasures and comforts of the well-to-do can ever come within the reach of the poor. Yet it is just this new idea, viz., that all can share the good things of life . . . that is at the root of the open air Nursery School.

(Margaret McMillan 1918)

It is a great mistake to think of the Nursery School idea merely – or even indirectly – in terms of health, or to be satisfied with leaving its practical development to a few enthusiasts or to the most provident local authorities . . . it belongs fundamentally to the question of whether a civilised community is possible or not.

(Education Enquiry Committee 1929)

The nursery school is an excellent bridge between the home and the larger world. It meets certain needs which the home either cannot satisfy or cannot satisfy in full measure, and it prepares the child for his later life in school in a way which nothing else can do . . . experience has shown that it brings the child such a great variety of benefits that it can be looked upon as a normal institution in the social life of any civilised community.

(Susan Isaacs 1954)

Nursery education in Britain, more than any other kind of service to young children, has been the subject of intense discussion, debate and theorising for more than a century. Over this time, the visions and practices of nursery education have been frequently revised and reflective of their wider societal and political contexts. In this chapter, we look at these changing ideas and assumptions about nursery education – about who it is for, how it is delivered, what its content is, who delivers it and how it relates to other educational stages. This history suggests that there is no one immutable concept of nursery education. Indeed, viewed from this historical perspective, our idea that nursery education should be transformed to form an important part of a comprehensive, integrated and coherent early childhood service, reflecting contemporary needs and conditions, is itself repeating history!

Public attitudes to nursery education

Nursery education has had its articulate advocates in the UK for nearly 180 years. However, views about the form it should take have varied according to social and economic conditions, and have reflected the views of the time about the roles of men and women and the nature of childhood. Many, if not all, of the main writers considered their arguments undeniable, and concluded that a breakthrough was imminent.

Compulsory schooling was introduced in 1870. As Britain rapidly changed from an agricultural to a primarily industrial economy, the early infant schools soon took on a secondary role, providing care – of a sort – for the younger children of factory parents who might otherwise have kept their older children from school to look after the younger ones. Deasey (1978: 62) quotes this account of an infant school in 1876.

> My mother and I were somehow led by somebody into a classroom. It seemed an enormous apartment, and was filled with babies arranged in galleries almost to the ceiling, as I thought – all steaming, murmurous and palpitating with suppressed and uneasy life, in an atmosphere thick with dust and smelling acridly of chalk, varnish and dirty clothes...one of the babies at the top of the gallery fell off his seat and rolled right down one of the gangways to the floor at the bottom, raising a dreadful succession of thuds and screams. The teacher went on writing, with just the merest lift of the head. 'It serves you right' she said. 'You're the worst wriggler in class How often have I told you to sit still and keep your arms folded? And now you see you are punished for your disobedience.'

By 1900 more than 50 per cent of 3 and 4 year olds, and many 2 year olds, attended infant schools. This situation was regarded as profoundly unsatisfactory by many professionals, and Katherine Bathurst, an Inspector with the Board of Education, in 1905 issued a famous report criticising the system, calling for 'national nurseries', and arguing that in a male-dominated education system the needs of young children were continually overlooked.

> Surely in this matter I may expect the support and sympathy of the women of this country – little children require nurses rather than teachers, and lady doctors rather

than inspectors. By placing the infant schools entirely in the hands of men inspectors, the whole atmosphere has been made into a forcing-house for the schools for older scholars. Even where kindergarten methods are better understood, the teachers are hampered and hindered by a masculine love of uniformity and order.

(quoted in Van der Eyken 1973: 120)

Bathurst gave voice to the idea that very young children in the public education system should have separate facilities and a different style of teaching from older children. The notion of nursery schools then began to appear in official reports and documents. Provision for nursery education was incorporated into the Education Act 1918, although on an optional basis. This legislation inspired Grace Owen, a well-known protagonist of nursery education, principal of the Mather Training College in Manchester and secretary of the Nursery Schools Association to write that 'the decision to make Nursery School the foundation of England's system of education is one of far reaching importance' (Owen 1928: 11).

In 1919 the embryo Labour Party came out in favour of nursery education, and issued a pamphlet advocating universal nursery education (Van der Eyken 1973). A decade later, in 1929, came a special report, *The Case For Nursery Schools*, from the Education Enquiry Committee. Like the more recent National Commission on Education, the Committee was an august self-constituted body set up to investigate the state of the nation's education, and included such luminaries as Percy Nunn and R. H. Tawney. Its report concluded that 'the Education Act (1921) should be amended in such a way that it would be compulsory for every local authority to provide the number of Nursery Schools required to meet the needs of their district' (Education Enquiry Committee 1929: ix).

In 1931 the Consultative Committee on the Primary School, commissioned by the government, again recommended nursery schooling. The Committee took evidence about how nursery and infant schooling should be organised from Cyril Burt and Susan Isaacs who argued that young children were characterised above all by the intensity of their emotions. Nursery schooling in their view enabled children to become more detached from their mothers, and learn to play with other children. This was particularly important where the home environment was not secure: 'the more orderly environment of the nursery school, with calm dispassionate treatment, may save the child from the permanent ill-effects of an unwholesome environment at home' (quoted in Van der Eyken 1973: 245). The Committee's report called for more research into children's behaviour at nursery school and how this related to their behaviour at home.

The demand for nursery schooling receded in the face of the 1930s recession. But during the Second World War many new day nurseries opened. As Riley (1983) has convincingly argued, they were not good nurseries. They were opened in a hurry and without forethought. There was muddled administration and continual arguments between ministerial departments, employment, education and health, as to who should carry oversight for them and ensure their standards, and who should fund them. Young mothers too did not like working long hours in heavy industry and leaving their children in what were often grimly institutional settings. It was with some relief after the war that many of them were closed. This was partly due to a muddle over who should continue to fund them, partly a matter of deliberate policy in changed conditions.

> The Ministers concerned...are of the opinion that, under normal peacetime conditions, the right policy to pursue would be positively to discourage mothers of children under two from going out to work; to make provision for children **between two and five** by way of nursery schools and nursery classes; and to regard day nurseries and daily guardians as supplements to meet the special needs...of children whose mothers are constrained by individual circumstances to go out to work or whose home conditions are in themselves unsatisfactory from the health point of view or whose mothers are incapable for some good reason of undertaking the full care of the child.
>
> (Ministry of Health 1945, our emphasis)

Although many of the war nurseries were closed down, in the 1940s there were again official recommendations to open more nursery schools. The Education Act 1944 left it open to local authorities to have regard 'to the need for securing that provision is made for pupils who have not attained the age of five years by the provision of nursery schools or, where the authority considers the provision of such schools to be inexpedient, by the provision of nursery classes in other schools' (p. 4).

There were two separate arguments advanced for nursery education. The first was the need for children to learn how to co-operate. The British Medical Journal in 1944, in an editorial, expressed concern that

> in the years from two until five the battle between love and primitive impulse is at its height...Winnicott, Buhler, Isaacs, Bowlby and others all note the turbulent characteristics of the age...Destructive impulses let loose in the war may serve to fan the flame of aggression natural to the nursery age...the Age of Resistance may thus be prolonged to adult life in the form of bitterness, irresponsibility or delinquency.
>
> (quoted in Riley 1983: 1)

The second argument in favour of nursery education related to concern about the low birth rate. There was a huge literature, in 1945 and 1946, which argued 'for nursery schools, after-school play centres, rest homes for tired housewives, family tickets on trains, official neighbourhood babysitters...a revolution in domestic architecture towards streamlined kitchens, and more communal restaurants and laundries' (Riley 1983: 167).

The 1949 Royal Commission on Population took evidence from a wide variety of organisations about the need for nursery schooling. They concluded that a package of measures which included nursery schooling should be provided to encourage mothers to have families: the general aim should be to 'reduce the work and worry of mothers with young children'. The evidence to the Commission included a statement from the Hygiene Committee of the Women's Group on Public Welfare: 'we cannot afford not to have the nursery school: it seems to be the only agency capable of cutting the slum mind off at its root and building the whole child while there is yet time' (quoted in Riley 1983: 171).

The message from the Commission was overlooked. It was nearly 20 years before the case for nursery education was restated in an official report; but again the grounds had changed. The concern of the Central Advisory Council on Education (1967) in their report, *Children and Their Primary Schools*, was social inequality. The Plowden Report (so named after the Council's chairwoman Bridget Plowden) argued that policies should positively intervene against disadvantage, and prioritise resources to those most in need. Nursery schooling was an important part of this strategy, an inoculation against disadvantage. Children in socially deprived neighbourhoods 'need above all verbal stimulus, the opportunities for constructive play, a more richly differentiated environment, and the access to medical care that good nursery schools can provide' (p. 63).

This report was strongly influenced by Bowlby's ideas about mothering (see below). The members of the Council were convinced that children should be at least three before entering nursery, and decried the practice of admitting children at a younger age. They also felt that mothers should not be tempted to leave their children for more than a short time. Before Plowden it was generally assumed that most nursery schooling would be full-time, like ordinary schooling. The Central Advisory Council, however, took the view that nursery education should be part-time, a recommendation which has haunted nursery education ever since.

> It is generally undesirable, except to prevent a greater evil, to separate mother and child for a whole day in the nursery. We do not believe that full-time nursery places should be provided even for children who might tolerate separation without harm, except for exceptionally good reasons... But some mothers who are not obliged to work may work full-time, regardless of their children's welfare. It is no business of the educational service to encourage these mothers to do so. It is true, unfortunately, that the refusal of full-time nursery places for their children may prompt some of them to make unsuitable arrangements for their children's care during working hours. All the same, we consider that mothers who cannot satisfy the authorities that they have exceptionally good reasons for working should have low priority for full-time nursery for their children.
> (Central Advisory Council on Education 1967: 127–8)

It is worth noting that, despite the caveats, the Plowden Report estimated that 15 per cent of 3 and 4 year olds would require full-time nursery education, a figure which has still not been reached!

The conclusions of this report have profoundly shaped the delivery of nursery education in the UK. While many other European countries continued to view nursery education as a full-time service largely separate from primary schooling, in the UK part-time nursery classes attached to primary schools became the norm. Since Plowden recommended that the primary schools should utilise 'discovery' methods of teaching and a 'free curriculum', as nursery schooling had long since done, and that most access to nursery schooling should be limited to children aged 3–4 on a part-time basis, it made sense to see nursery education as part of primary schooling, and to emphasise the continuity between them – a reversal of the position espoused by Katherine Bathurst at the turn of the century and by subsequent reformers.

The recommendations of the Council were sanctioned by Margaret Thatcher, then Minister for Education, in the 1972 White Paper, *Framework for Expansion*, followed in 1973 by a Circular on Nursery Education (Department of Education and Science 1973). The White Paper and the Circular referred to Plowden, and accepted its arguments for nursery education unquestioningly. The Circular stressed that 'nursery education is particularly valuable as a means of reducing the educational and social disadvantages suffered by children from homes which are culturally and economically deprived' (p. 3).

While Plowden had been relatively open-minded about where nursery education was to be sited, the Circular took a clear position. It stressed the desirability of nursery classes as opposed to nursery schools.

> There are educational advantages in enabling most children attending school below the age of five to do so at the school they will attend after five. This avoids a change of school and enables educational development to be planned as a whole from three or four to the beginning of the junior- or middle-school course. This avoids a change of school and enables educational development to be planned as a whole...Nursery provision within primary schools is also more economical to provide and maintain than separate nursery schools. For these reasons, although nursery schools already in existence or at an advanced stage of planning should continue, it is recommended that most additional places should be provided in units attached to primary schools in so far as their sites allow.
>
> (p. 5)

The White Paper and the Circular predicted a steady increase in nursery education over a 10-year period in order to make two years' nursery education available for children whose parents wanted it, from the beginning of the term after their third birthday until the term after their fifth birthday.

Although the objective of part-time nursery class provision has been implemented, the 10-year expansion target was not and has never been. Within four years, the English Departments of Health and Education (1976) were convening a Conference on the theme of 'low cost day provision for the under-fives'. In 1977, the National Union of Teachers, drawing attention to the failure to implement the White Paper policy, argued in a pamphlet *The Needs of the Under Fives* that 'now more than ever there is a need to improve the level of nursery education' and defined the aims of nursery education as 'firstly the satisfaction of the needs of the child and the development of full potential and, secondly, by early intervention, ensuring that every child obtains the best possible start in his educational life' (National Union of Teachers 1977: 7–8).

Three years later, in the report of an influential research study commissioned by the Department of Education, Jerome Bruner questioned

> whether the pre-school out-of-home care for the child has kept pace with our knowledge of early human development...the lesson of importance of early childhood is surely that we do all in our power to assure that the young get off to a healthy and competent start before they enter school...it must be taken as a given in any national policy that the care of the young should be as thoughtful and as considered as it can be made to be.
>
> (Bruner 1980: 10)

The 1980s brought a further shift in views about nursery education, this time in response to a growing emphasis on the process of schooling and the development of the National Curriculum. The Education Select Committee of the House of Commons asserted that 'education for the under fives can not only enrich the child's life at the time but can also prepare the child for the whole process of schooling...there should be steady expansion until all 3 and 4 year olds whose parents desire it have access to places' (Education, Science and Arts Committee, 1988, para 9.5). Instead of being seen as an aspect of social policy, nursery education was viewed more narrowly as an opportunity for individual children to improve their learning competencies in line with the National Curriculum. In 1989, HMI issued a booklet, *The Education of Children Under Five*, which attempted to define the underlying principles of the education of young children, and illustrate these principles with good practice, concluding that 'the nine areas of learning and experience discussed in *The Curriculum from 5–16: Curriculum Matters* are widely recognised as essential for all children including under fives' (Department of Education and Science 1989: 9).

A year later, the Rumbold Committee of Inquiry, set up to consider the quality of educational experience offered to 3 and 4 year olds, issued its report, *Starting with Quality* (Department of Education and Science 1990). The report stressed the need for a quality nursery curriculum which promoted early learning. This was defined as 'aesthetic and creative; human and social; language and literacy; mathematics; physical; science; spiritual and moral; technology' (p. 14). Around this time, also, a group of early years educators further defined and encoded what they saw as the relevant areas of the early years curriculum, and published a widely distributed booklet giving details of how this curriculum might be applied (Early Years Curriculum Group 1992).

Most recently, the National Commission on Education in their report *Learning to Succeed* yet again stressed that nursery education was being unwisely ignored. Like other commentators in the 1980s and 1990s, they remarked on the adverse effects of admitting children early to school, instead of offering nursery schooling. They argued for expansion of nursery education and revived the notion of nursery education for priority areas first, arguing that the cost of expansion would be mitigated by avoidance of remedial costs in adolescence while stressing the hidden cost of taking no action.

> We are persuaded that the gains made by children who receive high quality pre-school education will reduce the need for remedial education at a later stage, help to ensure that we do not waste talent, and perhaps also reduce the social costs which arise from youth unemployment and juvenile crime.
>
> (National Commission on Education 1993: 137)

This ambitious claim that nursery education not only prevented school failure, but might circumvent life failure, was taken further in the report of the Royal Society of Arts, *Start Right: the Importance of Early Learning*, published soon after. The author, Christopher Ball, argued for part-time nursery education for 3 and 4 year olds, which could be part-funded by offering part-time nursery education, rather than full-time schooling, to 5 year olds and raising the compulsory school age to 6.

This report presents a challenge to the nation – to parents, educators, employers, parliament – indeed to our society as a whole. It demonstrates the importance of early learning as a preparation for effective education to promote social welfare and social order, and to develop a world-class workforce.

(Ball 1994: 6)

These are just a few selections from the plethora of public and published statements over this century about the importance of providing nursery education. Although all the documents quoted support the expansion of nursery provision (and there is another literature altogether which explores concepts of need, demand for and practices of 'day care'), the ideas about what nursery education is for, the format it should take, and what it can accomplish differ considerably.

References

Ball, C. (1994) *Start Right: the Importance of Early Learning*, London: Royal Society of Arts.

Bruner, J. (1980) *Under Fives in Britain*, London: Grant McIntyre.

Central Advisory Council on Education (1967) Children and Their Primary Schools (the Plowden Report), London: HMSO.

Deasey, D. (1978) *Education Under Six*, London: Croom Helm.

Department of Education and Science (1972) *Education: A Framework for Expansion*. London: HMSO.

Department of Education and Science (1973) *Circular 2/73*, London: HMSO.

Department of Education and Science (1989) *Aspects of Primary Education: The Education of Children Under Five*, London: HMSO.

Department of Education and Science (1990) *Starting with Quality: The Rumbold Report of the Committee of Inquiry into the Quality of the Educational Experience offered to 3- and 4-year-olds*, London: HMSO.

Department of Health and Social Security/Department of Education and Science (1976) *Low Cost Day Provision for the Under-Fives*. Papers from a Conference held 9–10 January 1976.

Early Years Curriculum Group (1992) *The Early Years Curriculum*, Stoke on Trent: Trentham Books.

Education Enquiry Committee (1929) *The Case For Nursery Schools*, London: George Philip & Son.

Education, Science and Arts (House of Commons) (1988) *Educational Provision for the Under Fives, Vol 1*, London: HMSO.

Froebel, F. (1897) *Pedagogics of the Kindergarten*, London: Edward Arnold.

Isaacs, S. (1954) *The Educational Value of the Nursery School*, London: Nursery School Association of Great Britain and Northern Ireland.

McMillan, M. (1918) *The Nursery School*, 1930 edn, London: Dent.

Ministry of Health (1945) *Circular 221/45*, London: HMSO.

National Commission on Education (1993) *Learning to Succeed. Report of the Paul Hamlyn Foundation*, London: Heinemann.

National Union of Teachers (1977) *The Needs of the Under Fives*, London: National Union of Teachers.

Owen, G. (1928) *Nursery School Education*, London: Dutton.

Owen, R. (1836) *A New View of Society and other Writings*, 1927 edn, London: Everyman's Library.

Riley, D. (1983) *War in the Nursery*, London: Virago.

Van der Eyken, W. (ed.) (1973) *Education, The Child and Society: A Documentary History*, Harmondsworth: Penguin Books.

Chapter 3

Working in teams in early years settings

Mary Read and Mary Rees

In all the many and varied early years settings there is perhaps one common characteristic: a number of adults work together to meet the needs of children. The likelihood of excellent early childhood provision is enhanced by the team's ability to work collaboratively, and being a member of an effective team is a source of satisfaction and support for many early years workers. The variable nature of settings and the range of people involved mean there is no guaranteed recipe for team success. An effective group of early years practitioners emerges as the result of an investment of time and energy by all concerned. If an effective team is valued as an essential part of quality early years provision, it is necessary to identify how this can be achieved. In many instances too little attention or status is given to either the skills of teamwork or to the process of working collaboratively. This chapter addresses these important areas. It encourages consideration of the role and skills of the early years practitioner and questions how these contribute to the efficiency of the whole team. It places the skills of teamwork in a management context, seeking to elevate the status of teamwork beyond a 'muddling through together' to a planned, professional activity.

In any early years setting there is probably a core team of adults who work together on an ongoing daily basis consisting of staff and volunteers, all with different roles and expertise. In a large organisation early years practitioners may work in a small core team which is only part of the whole. In either case the core team may form part of a wider team encompassing, for example, speech and language therapists, physiotherapists or professionals from social services. In reading this chapter it may be helpful to identify specific teams in individual contexts and reflect on current practice and professional development.

So how can effective teamwork be developed? A number of features characterise successful teams.

Finding time for professional dialogue

Finding time

Young children make continuous, challenging demands on the adults who work with them. Finding time to focus on adult needs can be difficult as there is a real danger of responding to children's immediate needs to the exclusion of all else. Looking at the daily or weekly programme to identify potential time availability for staff to meet is a vital step in team development. Finding an appropriate time which includes part time and hourly paid staff can be problematic, therefore solutions have to be found through open discussion and negotiation. Perhaps a monthly rota of short meetings is more viable than a weekly set time.

The Cherry Tree case study (Figure 3.1) shows how one large nursery faced the important issue of planning for children with special needs. The willingness to confront these problems and seek a workable situation provides a starting point for team commitment. Whalley (in Pugh 1996) documents an interesting approach to finding quality meeting time at Pen Green Centre for Under Fives and Families by freeing up Wednesday afternoons. Failure to secure an appropriate meeting programme involving everyone, may lead to individuals feeling marginalised and devalued. The potential contribution of some team members is lost and the cohesion of the team is damaged as a result.

Cherry Tree is a large nursery including several children with special educational needs. The specific needs of the children mean that the team felt it was important that all staff were familiar with the different programmes and targets necessary for their development. Many of the staff were paid on an hourly basis so meeting time was precious. This is how planning was coordinated.

- Monthly one-hour meeting for all staff defining main activities. All staff to attend, either paid or time off in lieu.
- Booklet for each session where all significant events are noted.
- Children's records open to all staff.
- Assessment meetings to discuss individual children weekly on a rota basis. Minutes written up and available for staff who cannot attend.

Planning recorded (see below) so that all staff are familiar with learning focus of activities.

wk beg 3rd Oct			
activity	focus	specific children	comments
wet sand	tracing numbers for week	Kirsty – K Alan – say name as he traces	
water	vocab: full empty	Gary – talk to other children	
story	remember and repeat sequence	all	

Figure 3.1 Case study

Using time effectively

Valuable staff time needs to be used effectively. This is easy to say but rather more difficult to establish and maintain. A possible starting point is to keep a brief log of meetings taking place over a week or two (Figure 3.2). The resulting information can then be shared within the team or raised with the manager. A log of this type can show whether the meeting time is well used or that there are areas for significant improvement. Meeting B could be probed further – was the manager meeting with staff when the decision had in fact already been taken? If so, why? Could the relevant information have been provided as a written proposal? How was the original decision to purchase outdoor play equipment reached?

meeting and purpose	no. of people	contribution	achievement	comments
A. weekly planning to establish outline of week's activities 1 hour	total 8 4 teachers and 4CAs (classroom assistants)	teachers 85% CAs 15% Miss X and Mrs Y (both CAs) no contribution	plan agreed mainly repeat of previous week 2 new activities	lacked focus; some useful evaluation; dominated by teachers
B. purchasing decision meeting – order for outdoor play equipment 1 hour	10 nursery manager + full-time and part-time staff	manager – majority others – questions	order not agreed	staff insufficient info. to reach decision. Lots of disagreement, staff raising alternatives – soft play, books etc.

Figure 3.2 Meeting log

The use of logs to investigate the efficiency of meetings has potential to be extended by two or more people comparing perspectives. Figure 3.3 shows the manager's view of meeting B. Manager and staff were at cross purposes, everyone was dissatisfied and the opportunity for agreement was lost. In this case the simple log would enable the team to focus on the real issues standing in the way of a team decision making approach, and make sensible changes rather than continue to set up frustrating experiences.

The log format can be adapted in a number of ways to access the desired information: the length of meetings; the cost (number of people x number of hours x hourly rate of pay) and the contribution of individual or particular categories of staff. The decision to investigate meeting efficiency through logs

meeting and purpose	no. of people	contribution	achievement	comments
purchasing decision meeting – order for outdoor play equipment identified by OFSTED as priority for upgrading 1 hour	10 nursery manager + full time and part time staff	little contribution from staff	order not agreed	staff reluctant to use outdoor play area – especially through winter. Suggesting alternatives based on personal preference.

Figure 3.3 Meeting log – manager's perspective

or other methods needs to be openly shared with all team members and the outcomes discussed. This ensures real use of the material and pre-empts any sense of seeking someone to blame.

Setting the agenda

A clear agenda is a key tool in ensuring that meeting time is well used. The list of items commonly provided has limited value. It gives only the area of discussion and provides no clue about key questions or issues, parameters for the discussion or desired outcomes. Meetings, particularly those where crucial decisions are necessary, have greater potential for success if everyone attending has the opportunity to consider the critical issues beforehand. Figure 3.4 illustrates an agenda which has this purpose. It allows participants to think about the items and be ready to offer a view. A meeting which is structured in this way helps to avoid the pitfalls of participants changing their mind afterwards or feeling that they have been pressured into a course of action without time for thought. Ideally all team members should leave a meeting feeling satisfied with the decision making process, even if they have had to make some personal compromises.

The agenda should also give the timing for the meeting, perhaps for the individual items, but essentially for the start and finish. The quality of contributions deteriorates rapidly if staff are worrying about collecting children from the child minder or wondering how much longer they will have to sit there.

Minutes of meetings can be very useful in recording decisions made and action agreed, although it should not be assumed that they are always necessary. It is very rarely useful to record the detail of discussion, particularly as this is a time consuming and tedious task. A rotating responsibility with a standard proforma provided can be a simple solution. The proforma need be nothing more than a version of the agenda with a column for decisions, dates and responsibilities.

Staff meeting agenda
3.30   tea available
3.45 – 5.00   meeting in large staffroom
Minutes   Susan's turn

1. Update on calendar
2. Use of equipment fund
£500 available. Various possibilities
               a) outdoor equipment (catalogue marked with possibilities on staffroom
                   noticeboard – please look) Storage is an issue
               b) replacement sand/water equipment for Red Room
               c) new book stock
               d) other suggestions
NB: money has to be spent by end of this month so decision required at meeting
3. Open Day
Date? Needs to be Tuesday or Thursday in February. Please come with suggestions.
Particular idea/events to be included? Foyer display – suggestions?
4. AOB
Unless just brief announcement please notify to manager in advance.

Figure 3.4 Agenda

Forging and maintaining professional relationships

Building the team

Successful teamwork requires a group of individuals to share the daily working experience in a positive and proactive manner. Over time the members of a team develop ways of working with each other, responding to the needs and idiosyncrasies of colleagues, recognising strengths and weaknesses, and valuing the complementary contributions that each makes to the team effort. Handy (1990) summarises teams as a:

> collection of individuals gathered together because their talents are needed to perform a task or to solve a problem. If the team wins, all those in it win. If the team loses they all lose. There is a common purpose, and the sense of camaraderie that should go with a common purpose. (p. 128)

The challenge for the team is to have a shared understanding of the common purpose so that team members can act confidently and with a clear understanding of their individual role. Handy (1990) also puts forward an analysis of the stages of team growth, using the headings 'forming, storming, norming and performing'. He suggests that all teams have a period in which they are finding their own identity – the forming stage. Then comes a period of challenge (storming) when individuals begin to assert themselves, moving into the norming phase as they settle to new ways of working. The final phase comes when the team is mature and able to perform at high levels of efficiency. Part of this process in Handy's view is about the establishing of the trust which has to build over time to allow a team to work efficiently.

Trust and shared understanding cannot be merely agreed upon in a meeting or laid down in a set of policies. They grow through the daily occurrences in the work place, the discussion between individuals and the decisions that are made. Teams that have been working together over time develop their own forms of verbal short-hand to share ideas and suggestions, and are able to ground their discussion in an understanding formed through day-to-day communication and awareness of each other's views. This can be an unnerving experience for a new team member who may feel shut out or de-skilled by exchanges which he or she cannot follow. For example in planning an event an established team draws upon the knowledge and experience of all the previous events of this type; making tacit assumptions and using abbreviated references to occasions, incidents, successes and disasters. Individuals who have collaborated with one another in an ongoing situation are able to rely upon each other's skills, making allowance for personal preference or dislike for particular tasks.

Positive communication

As the days and weeks pass the early years team members will communicate with each other on a myriad of subjects and with thousands of interactions. The key feature for success is the quality of this communication, rather than the quantity. The notion of positive communication is a helpful one in that it contains several strands. Being positive, in the sense of ensuring our communication includes plenty of praise and affirmation, is an important aspect of working successfully with others. It is important to reflect honestly and ask questions such as ... how often do I communicate praise to my colleagues? ... to a volunteer or part time worker? ... to a parent? ... to my boss? The expectation that the manager will praise the subordinates sometimes leads to disappointment and frustration if workers feel their manager does not give sufficient recognition to their efforts. The successful team member looks for opportunities to communicate positively with support, praise and even delight throughout the daily interaction with colleagues. Honest and sincere positive feedback oils the wheels of the daily task and enables all team members to benefit from both giving and receiving affirmation. The valuing of the contribution is key to team success.

Another strand of positive communication is that of the locking together of team thinking. To operate effectively the various individuals needs to mesh ideas and actions. Where two or more colleagues are working together there should be clear communication with specific instructions as necessary. This requires time for individuals to check their understanding with one another and perhaps even to have written clarification. The key issue is that team members need to understand the importance of appropriate communication and the need for others to question and seek clarification. A team which is able to communicate openly and clearly avoids wasting time on frustration and misunderstanding. Look at this example and see whether it could happen in your setting.

'The other day the class teacher said "I want them to paint rainbows. Paint rainbows using as few colours as possible." So we mixed colours and talked about it and painted rainbows. And then she said "Oh, you could have done it this way". And I thought "Oh knickers, she didn't say that, she wasn't that specific." That's happened a few times and I feel I haven't just got the wrong end of the stick, I've got the wrong stick!'

(Classroom assistant talking about her experiences.)

Managing conflict

It is important not to have an over-optimistic picture of the effective team. An established ability to work together does not deny the possibility of conflict or disagreement. A good team will also develop strategies for dealing with those occasions on which agreement is not easily reached. In fact some teams may thrive and operate extremely efficiently with an element of argument or challenge which pushes the team forward. Continual agreement may indicate a team that is complacent or bored. Teams tend to have a productive period and then need to be challenged or changed (Handy 1990) to reinvigorate and remotivate them.

One of the vital aspects in managing conflict is the separation of the disagreement and the person. It is possible to disagree completely with a colleague's view of how to manage a child's difficult behaviour and yet continue to work with them in a professional and appropriate manner. Goleman (1998) summarises the paradox: 'On one hand, the wisdom holds that the more freewheeling and intense the debate, the better the final decision; on the other hand, open conflict can corrode the ability of a team to work together' (p. 220). The ability to listen to colleagues is a key feature in avoiding conflict. There is a significant difference between merely listening to the words used and trying to actively understand meaning and feelings. The team that values listening to one another and devotes precious time to exploring feelings and concerns is likely to avoid the potential descent into disagreement and acrimony. Pedler and Boydell (1994) put forward the useful notion of 'supportive listening' and give some strategies for practising this skill with a 'speaking partner' in order to help your development. If this is an area which is relevant some of these ideas could be tried by the early years team.

A clear understanding of roles and responsibilities

We have established that there is a great diversity of expertise within the early years team. This is a strength of the team, as children need to mix with a variety of adults who relate to them in different ways. The different skills of individuals all add to the strength of the team if recognised and deployed sensitively. It is also important to take careful account of the current employment legislation, legal requirements and best practice in the appointment and management of staff; these are dealt with comprehensively by Reason (1998) elsewhere.

Establishing roles

In order to operate effectively within a team, each member needs to know where they fit in, how their own role relates to that of others, their particular responsibilities and, equally important, what tasks should be referred to others in the team. Each team member needs the confidence of understanding where the pieces of the jigsaw fit in. However in any setting which is flexible and responsive enough to meet the changing needs of children, there are bound to be grey areas where responsibilities are not always clear or there is a degree of overlap.

Roles and responsibilities are often implicit in an established team. Staff seem to instinctively work with each other. However, when there is a new member, it becomes more difficult to explicitly describe current working practice. There are occasions when a team can become too stagnant, when the different roles become too rigid to allow for personal and professional growth. Thus it would seem to be part of an effective team's responsibility to make roles and responsibilities more explicit, understood by everyone and regularly reviewed, perhaps as part of the staff development or appraisal process.

Role definitions

Roles and responsibilities often operate on two levels, the formal and the informal. For example, it may be a particular team member's responsibility to organise the mid morning drink for children. This is a routine task which is understood by all. However, there may be different aspects of the role which are less explicit but none the less important to the efficiency of the team, for example who takes responsibility for dealing with lost property. The shared understanding of the parameters of individual responsibility is crucial; we all need to know that our individual contributions are important and valued.

Job descriptions provide a formal definition of roles and responsibilities and need to be as clear and precise as possible. In Figure 3.5 the working relationships section describes how the member of staff relates to others in the team, for example who works with whom at different times. The duties and responsibilities clarify in as much detail as possible the boundaries of the post and provide a clear starting point for the formal role and responsibility of staff. However, the remit of the early years setting is so wide that such descriptions cannot entirely capture the reality. Job descriptions are sometimes couched in very general terms and try to encompass every eventuality. They do not always relate directly to the day to day pattern of work. Informal allocation of duties is an important function and needs to recognise the different strengths of individuals. Members of the team may have particular strengths in the following areas:

- relating to parents
- dealing with children's tantrums
- diffusing potentially problematical situations
- having new ideas for craft activities
- displaying children's work

Job description

Post title

Department   Post grade

Location   Post hours

Purposes and objectives of post

Accountable to

Immediate responsibility

Working relationships

Duties and responsibilities

Support for children

Support for staff

Support for unit/setting

Other duties

Agreed by the post holder

Agreed by the supervisor   Date

Adapted from Lorenz (1998)

Figure 3.5 Job description

- observing children
- settling new children in
- remembering key dates
- working together.

It is important to consider how these skills may be exploited within the team. Members tend to grow into these roles rather than be allocated to them. In deploying staff, individual strengths should be recognised and valued.

Opportunities for change

There are of course occasions when acquired roles, formal or informal, seem impossible to amend or to shed. For example, does a particular member always clear up, look after the sick children or tend to work with those children who need extra help? The more roles are reinforced by continuing to perform duties that fit with it, expectations to adhere to those roles will be placed upon particular members of the team. This may be perfectly acceptable or it may limit the skills of individuals who are unable to extend and develop their practice beyond certain parameters. A skilled manager will give the team opportunities to develop by varying the tasks that they perform. Confident team members will be flexible enough to extend their practice through new challenges. The balance between using individual strengths and extending personal and professional development is important.

Team skills: personal and professional development

How does this relate to individual team members in a specific context? How can everyone in the team be encouraged to take responsibility for the development of their personal skills? Is there shared ownership of team building and working together to achieve goals? The questions below may be used to analyse current practice and identify ways forward.

- Are all staff active team members? Do they accept and act upon their own responsibilities when working with others? How often do they put forward ideas or actively respond to other people's suggestions? Small improvements can be equally as important as major innovations. Are staff at all levels encouraged to put forward good ideas, and are there positive opportunities for these to be shared and acted upon?
- Does everyone in the team take an active part in meetings? Are there main contributors? A meeting log is a useful way to find out. Can everyone contribute to the agenda for meetings? Is it possible for staff to suggest items that they consider to be important?
- Are all contributions (including your own) valued? How is this demonstrated? Do all staff take responsibility for praising and supporting others? Put

yourself in another team member's position and think about whether they feel valued.

- Do all staff communicate directly and sensitively with others in the early years team? Do they actively listen to everyone's contribution? Is communication always clear and unambiguous? Often people think they are clear but give quite another signal to the listener. One way of checking communication skills is for colleagues to pair up and give each other feedback.

Our final message is that working with other adults should be an enjoyable aspect of being in an early years team. Using some of the strategies suggested in the chapter may enhance team skills and foster real professional benefits from interaction with colleagues.

References

Goleman, D. (1998) *Working with Emotional Intelligence.* London: Bloomsbury.

Handy, C. (1990) *Inside Organisations.* London: BBC Books.

Lorenz, S. (1998) *Effective In-class Support: the management of support staff in mainstream and special schools.* London: David Fulton Publishers.

Pedler, M. and Boydell, T. (1994) *Managing Yourself.* Aldershot: Gower.

Reason, J. (1998) *Good to work for.* London: National Early Years Network.

Whalley, M. 'Working as a team', in Pugh, G. (ed.) (1996) *Contemporary Issues in the Early Years Working Collaboratively for Children.* London Paul Chapman/National Children's Bureau.

Chapter 4

Professional roles in early childhood

Lyn Karstadt, Tricia Lilley and Linda Miller

Introduction

Professionalism can be difficult to define. Some people might claim to know it when they see it, but ideas vary about what it is. Dictionary definitions suggest that it involves belonging to or being connected with a particular profession or demonstrating the skills relating to a profession. It is likely that in the field of early childhood education and care, early years practitioners will be at various points along a continuum of professionalism depending upon their age, stage in their career and level of training and qualifications. As Penn (1998) notes, work involving caring has traditionally been done by women; 99 per cent of those working in early childhood services are women. She cites a worrying survey by Penn and McQuail (1999) which revealed that women thought they brought a 'natural' talent to the job and felt that this aptitude was at least as important, if not more important, than training. Penn goes on to argue that such attitudes are problematic. Firstly, because they devalue the theory underlying professionalism. Secondly, they do a disservice to men wishing to enter the profession, as they suggest that men do not possess such aptitudes. Such attitudes create barriers to raising the status of the professional roles associated with early childhood practitioners.

Traditionally, training to work in the field of early years education and care has been practically based. However, the onset of early childhood studies degrees and the new training framework (QCA 1999a) should lead early years practitioners towards a new professionalism. The importance of training for practitioners is recognised in recent curriculum guidance from the Qualifications and Curriculum Authority (1999b). In this chapter we address some of the issues which have been a barrier to professionalism in the past. We also look to the future and consider the broadening role of the early childhood professional in early childhood settings. We do this through a consideration of training, the role of the early childhood educator, the health dimension, the important role of all adults who work with young children and finally, the importance of all early years professionals working together.

The national picture of training for working with young children

Traditionally, in the United Kingdom, we have a philosophical and structural divide between care and education provision. This has evolved as a result of administration by two different government departments – the Department of Education and Science (DES) (now the Department for Education and Employment (DfEE)) and the Department of Health and Social Security (DHSS) (David 1990). This has resulted in damaging differences in training routes, status, pay and conditions for those who care for and educate young children in early years settings. In a review of early years training Hevey and Curtis (1996) found that the majority of day care and pre-school services are staffed by 200,000 unqualified child care and education practitioners. Another survey showed that 65.7 per cent of qualified teachers working with children under eight had received no specific training for working with children under five (Blenkin and Yue 1994). As the numbers of young children in early years settings have increased, the question of who their carers and educators should be and what they need to know needs to be addressed.

In 1996 a group of early years trainers and advisers who met regularly at the National Children's Bureau published a report on Education and Training for Work in the Early Years (Pugh 1996). This presented a snapshot of training developments in the areas of teacher training, early childhood studies degrees and vocational training in childcare and education and outlined a value base and the underpinning principles for this training. This debate is further developed in Abbott and Pugh (1998) which includes a discussion of the issues relating to different training routes, diverse professional roles, the quality of provision and their impact on young children. In May 1999, the Qualifications and Curriculum Authority (QCA 1999a) published the response to a consultation paper on qualifications and training in the early years education, childcare and playwork sector. The consultation document set out a training framework for this sector and the underlying principles on which it would be based. It proposed that national occupational standards would form the basis of all qualifications in the framework and for all recognised training provision leading to those qualifications. A follow up document (QCA 1999b) describes the first phase of the framework. Although not yet part of a national plan, early childhood studies degrees are recognised as an important part of this training route alongside teacher training and vocational training. As Abbott and Pugh (1998: 156) acknowledge 'The ways in which early years workers become competent, knowledgeable and skilful will continue to be many and varied'.

The early childhood educator

In a critique of recent curriculum developments in England, Peter Moss (1998) referred to what he described as a factory model of learning, which has a centrally controlled curriculum and which emphasises learning goals, targets and outcomes. He considered the implications of this model for early years practitioners. He questioned whether the early childhood worker was, 'A technician, a neutral transmitter or reproducer of knowledge to young children' or 'a pedagogue, researcher and producer or co-constructor of knowledge with children'. Nutbrown (1994) argues for the latter definition. She describes all those who work with young children in a professional capacity as 'professional educators' and defines such people as 'adults who have some relevant training and qualifications and understand something of how young children learn, and who are active in their thinking and interaction with children in group settings'.

Later in this chapter we argue strongly that a key role of the adult in young children's development and learning, is to build upon the child's early experiences and so promote greater understanding. In order to do this, the adult needs to be skilled and knowledgeable and have a willingness to reflect upon his or her practice and to learn from this. Tiziana Filippini (1997), the pedagogue who accompanied The Hundred Languages of Children exhibition, which features the work of nurseries in the Reggio Emilia region of Italy, has said 'a nice lady is not enough' to ensure that this happens. Lilian Katz (1995) has also argued that children need to be around thinking adults. She has spoken about nurseries where 'all the adults are nice and kind . . . and lovely, but inside (i.e. the head), there is nobody at home' [our parentheses]. This may seem harsh and unkind, but we believe this statement underlines the need for professional training for early years practitioners as discussed below.

What does the early childhood educator need to know?

The debate about the content of and the knowledge base for training and qualifications for early years practitioners is ongoing (see Thompson and Calder 1998). What seems to be agreed, is that practitioners working with young children need to take a critical stance in relation to both theory and practice. The challenge for early years practitioners, who undertake further professional development after years of valuable practical experience, is to acknowledge that experience, and more importantly to analyse it. It is necessary for them to step back and to develop a critical perspective in relation to their practice, in order to see the familiar with a new, professional eye. One student on an early childhood studies degree course, who had worked for many years in early years settings, queried why the group needed to participate in a paint mixing exercise. The tutor's response was to ask, 'Why have you been mixing the paint with the children? How do you move children on from this? How do you know what they are ready to learn next?' Lally (1995) has said that practitioners who cannot give confident answers to 'why' questions about their practice will be weak on rationale and therefore vulnerable to outside pressures. Gibbs (1988) argues that to have an experience is not sufficient for learning to take place; there also has to be reflection on the experience or the learning potential may be lost and cannot then be used to inform new situations. The learner must make the link between theory and practice as illustrated by Tracey below.

Tracey is a mature student on an early childhood studies degree course. She is the parent of two children and is a very experienced practitioner. The following is an extract from her address to incoming students at the Open Day for her course, in which she reflects upon her experience of the previous year.

> As the course progressed, I began to look at myself in a different light. I looked much more closely at the way I worked, putting into practice a lot of the learning, but with the realisation that I needed to question myself a great deal more about the 'why' of doing things. I also began to come to the conclusion that much of what I learned came from what I was prepared to put in. Maybe the most poignant moment for me, were some words said to us by one of the tutors during a teaching session on creative expression. She said that we needed to look deeper at our own learning, under the surface of what was being taught. From that day these words stayed with me and I looked at the teaching and learning assignments in a different light, not just taking the modules for what they were, but questioning, thinking, reading and researching more abut the subject concerned.

The health dimension

What early years practitioners need to be authoritative and knowledgeable about extends beyond the way children learn and how to structure that learning. As mentioned in both previous and subsequent chapters, it is difficult to study children in isolation from the families in which they grow and develop. Holistic ideology values the whole child and views each individual in the context of its family community and culture. Taylor (1998) reminds us that it is impossible to study discrete areas of early childhood without gaining at least some knowledge of other important and related areas.

When considering the development of the early years practitioner, relationships with small children are an important part of that development. In addition, however, one must also consider the relationships that such a practitioner builds with the significant adults in the child's life. Within many early years settings practitioners not only guide children in the way that they learn but also their parents with regard to their role in the day to day life of these children. Advice proffered is extremely important and must be professionally credible and not merely anecdotal. The example of Tracey is a powerful one and her attitude toward her learning fairly typical of such students. This changed attitude, enabling analytical consideration of her charges would surely have extended to their well-being, their health needs and the advice that she was offering to parents in her context as an early years professional.

The Department of Health publication *Health of the Young Nation* (DoH 1995) charges all those professionals who work with young children with the responsibility of enabling each child to reach and maintain optimum health. This may be done by working with the child in a guiding capacity or by working with the parent(s) who in turn, may then exert positive influences on the child's environment and experiences. Eisenstadt (1999) analyses the potential contribution of the 'Sure Start' initiative with its better co-ordinated services aimed at improving the life chances of young children in disadvantaged areas. Good quality play and learning as well as support for families are introduced as strategies to enable these desired improvements. Community ownership and parent participation are valued by this initiative which certainly views the child and family holistically.

Eisenstadt (1999) aims her analysis and subsequent discussion at Health Visitors, although much of what she says is applicable to all who work with children in the early years. Sure Start initiatives can be led by any appropriate professional and partnerships between voluntary agencies and health bodies are encouraged. Potential for the involvement of early childhood practitioners in association with health, social services, education and community or parent organisations is therefore great (QCA 1999c).

Our Healthier Nation (DoH 1998) cites good health as what everyone wants for themselves, their family and friends and as the supreme gift that parents can give to their children. Knowledge and expertise in this field can enable the early childhood practitioner to have a positive influence within the environment of the children in their care. As Drummond (1997: 7) has said 'The key to quality in early years provision is sustained, rigorous and disciplined training in early years practices and principles'.

The role of the adult in young children's learning

'Adults have the power to make a major difference to children's lives and their development by what they offer children and by how they behave towards them' (Lindon 1993: 75). Consider the power of the early childhood practitioner, to make that difference, not only in their direct contact with young children but in their support for other adults who know them, usually their primary carers. The importance of the adult in the development of children's learning and their well-being has been well documented in research on children's development (Bruner 1963, Vygotsky 1978) and the ways in which adults can use this potential power positively are discussed in this section.

Gura (1996) draws attention to the changing relationship between adults and children which has emerged in recent years following research on the importance of the social context in which children learn. She describes a shift towards a 'flexible repertoire of roles and relationships' (p. 32), acknowledging that learning is not always individual and internal but can also be influenced by a child's interactions with others. As the young child strives to become independent perhaps in feeding herself, in reading a favourite and often repeated story, or in taking her first few steps, the adult offers support, sometimes described as 'scaffolding', for the child's learning. Bruner (1963) regards scaffolding as one of the key roles of the adult who provides a kind of structure or series of steps for the child to explore a new experience successfully and add to her initial learning. The key for the adult is to know how to provide steps which are small enough for the child to gain success but challenging enough to motivate her and take her learning forward.

Bruner identified several ways in which an adult can provide this level of support or scaffolding by gaining the child's interest, ensuring that the required responses are achievable, giving plenty of feedback and encouragement to keep the child focused and by modelling the task for the child. The adult will need to be observant and know what the child can do already, building on this existing learning to support development in a structured way. The relationship between the adult and the child should be flexible. For example, sometimes the child might be seen as an apprentice working alongside the more experienced adult as they read a book together. At other times the relationship can become a loan arrangement, with the adult supporting or 'loaning' expertise to the child, for example by helping to cut food into manageable pieces or by providing a suitable plate to make the task easier for the child as she moves towards independence in using a knife and fork herself. Alternatively the adult and child can be partners playing alongside each other in a mutually supportive way (Gura 1996). Whatever the format of the relationship, scaffolding learning is one of the ways early childhood practitioners can make a powerful difference for the young child.

Vygotsky (1978) was particularly interested in the ways in which knowledge is passed from one human to another and much of his research on child development and communication focused on the effects of our social interactions on learning. He suggested that although we can all learn new skills and knowledge as individuals, it is through our interaction with others that our early experiences are extended. Vygotsky believed that it was very important for adults to identify what a child could do and knew already and then build on this existing knowledge to help the child to make sense of the world. He believed that if a child was left to explore something new on his or her own, such as some bricks, the ways in which he or she played and used the bricks could be described as the child's 'actual level of development'. However, if an adult interacted with the child, he or she may build a more complex structure with the bricks, perhaps finding different ways to position bricks and so build a taller tower. This extension of learning arising from skilful adult intervention was described by Vygotsky as the child working within a 'zone of proximal development' or, more simply, as a next stage of learning which could only be achieved with adult support. So by scaffolding or supporting learning, skilfully interacting with a child at appropriate moments in his or her learning, the adult could help the child to move into the next zone or stage of his or her development.

More recent research by Rogoff *et al.* (1998) extends the notion of a zone of proximal development to take account of guided participation where young children and adults are interacting in non-academic activities. They point to the limitations of Vygotsky's work which appeared to focus predominantly on language development and work within contexts of learning which were largely academic in nature. Rogoff *et al.* draw attention to wide cultural variations in the range of household activities that young children participate in and observe adults undertaking. Although many activities are common to children from different cultural communities, the range of role models, the types of activities, the extent of any scaffolding for learning provided by the adult and the accepted level of independence for the child is varied. As early childhood practitioners it is important to be aware of the differences that may exist in children's early experiences of guided participation.

Woods (1998) asserts that in the best early years provision education and care are not separated but are combined to produce the concept of 'educare'. This enables young children to be cared for sensitively and competently while their early educational needs are addressed by those responsible for that care. Healthy practices are promoted primarily when the adults act as role models to the children in their care. Good habits relating to personal hygiene, social skills and healthy lifestyle are all examples of desirable behaviours transmitted in this way. As with all other learning children often work in partnership with adults or more knowledgeable peers who guide their participation until they feel able to manage the task alone.

Bruner also placed particular emphasis on the adult modelling behaviour for a young child. The importance of adults modelling literacy for young children, reading stories or perhaps writing a shopping list is crucial. The power of example cannot be over-emphasised. Holt (1989) argued that it is through watching and listening and joining in with others, often adults, that a young child begins to make connections between experiences. He calls for adults to make their skills visible to young children, for example by modelling the ways in which they read, write, play, cook, shop, learn new things. Consider the powerful impact that watching someone at work has perhaps had on your life, your attitudes, your self-image. Adults have a responsibility to recognise the power of their influence as role models and use this opportunity to enhance learning. Other contributors to this book have made various references to the importance of the adult's role in a wide range of contexts across curriculum and developmental areas which will give you further insights into the significant contribution that skilful adult interactions make to a young child's development.

Working together

Wherever early years practitioners are on the continuum of professionalism and whether they are working in an education or a care context, with other early years professionals, or the multi-disciplinary team, they must embrace a philosophy that recognises that each child is an individual with rights, that have recently been discussed and made explicit (DoH 1999). The development and well-being of children is influenced by the relationship they have with their family, their environment and their individual health status. The interests of all parties within any given situation should be considered, remembering that the rights of the child are paramount (DoH 1990).

The authors would like to thank Tracey Alexander for her contribution to this chapter.

References

Abbott, L. and Pugh, G. (eds) (1998) *Training to Work in the Early Years*. Buckingham: Open University Press.

Blenkin, G. M. and Yue, Y. L. (1994) 'Profiling Early Years practitioners some first impressions from a national survey', *Early Years* **15**(1), 13–23.

Bruner, J. (1963) *The Process of Education*. New York: Vintage.

David, T. (1990) *Under Five – Under Educated?* Buckingham: Open University Press.

Department of Health (1990) *An Introduction to the Children Act 1989*. London: HMSO.

Department of Health (1995) *Health of the Young Nation*. London: HMSO.

Department of Health (1998) *Our Healthier Nation: A Contract for Health*. London: The Stationery Office.

Department of Health (1999) *Convention on the Rights of the Child: Second Report to the UN Committee on the Rights of the Child by the United Kingdom 1999*. London: The Stationery Office.

Drummond, M. J. (1997) 'An undesirable document', *Coordinate* **57**, 7–8.

Eisenstadt, N. (1999) 'Sure Start: a new approach for children under 4', *Primary Health Care* **9**(6), 26–27.

Filippini, T. (1997) *The Reggio Approach*. Paper delivered at The Hundred Languages of Children Exhibition Conference, The Picture Gallery, Thomas Coram Foundation for Children, London, 11 July.

Gibbs, G. (1988) *Learning by Doing: A Guide to Teaching and Learning Methods*. London: Further Education Unit.

Gura, P. (1996) 'Roles and Relationships', in Robson, S. *et al.* (eds) *Education in Early Childhood: First Things First*. London: David Fulton Publishers.

Hevey, D. and Curtis, A. (1996) 'Training to Work in the Early Years', in Pugh, G. (ed.) *Contemporary Issues in the Early Years: Working Collaboratively for Children*, 211–231. London: National Children's Bureau/Paul Chapman.

Holt, J. (1989) *Learning all the Time*. Ticknall: Education Now Publishing Co-operative.

Katz, L. (1995) 'Multiple perspectives on the right start'. Paper delivered at the *Start Right Conference* Barbican, London, 20–22 September.

Lally, M. (1995) 'Principles to practice in early years education', in Campbell, R. *et al.* (eds) *Supporting Children in the Early Years*, 9–27. Stoke-on-Trent: Trentham Books.

Lindon, J. (1993) *Child Development from Birth to Eight*. London: National Children's Bureau.

Moss, P. (1998) 'Young children and early childhood institutions: who and what do we think they are?' Paper delivered at the *Child at the Centre Conference*.

NES Arnold/National Children's Bureau Conference, East Midlands Conference Centre, 16–17 July.

Nutbrown, C. (1994) *Threads of Thinking*. London: Paul Chapman.

Penn, H. (1998) 'Facing some difficulties', in Abbott, L. *et al.* (eds) *Training to Work in the Early Years*, 26–38. Buckingham: Open University Press.

Penn, H. and McQuail, S. (1999) Childcare as a Gendered Occupation: Research Report. RR23. London: DfEE.

Pugh, G. (ed.) (1996) *Education and Training for Work in the Early Years*. London: National Children's Bureau.

Qualifications and Curriculum Authority (1999a) *A Draft Framework for Training and Qualifications in Early Years Education, Childcare and Playwork Sector*. Suffolk: Qualifications and Curriculum Authority Publications.

Qualifications and Curriculum Authority (1999b) *Early Years Education, Childcare and Playwork: a framework of nationally accredited qualifications*. Suffolk: Qualifications and Curriculum Authority Publications.

Qualifications and Curriculum Authority (1999c) *Early Learning Goals*. London: Qualifications and Curriculum Authority.

Rogoff, B. *et al.* (1998) 'Toddlers' guided participation with their caregivers in cultural activity' in Woodhead, M. *et al.* (eds) (1998) *Cultural Worlds of Early Childhood*. London: Routledge/Open University Press.

Taylor, J. (1998) 'Working with young children and their families', in Taylor, J. *et al.* (eds) *Early Childhood Studies*. London: Arnold.

Thompson, B. and Calder, P. (1998) 'Early years educators: skills, knowledge and understanding', in Abbott, L. *et al.* (eds) *Training to Work in the Early Years*, 38–55. Buckingham: Open University Press.

Vygotsky, L. S. (1978) *Mind in Society*. Edited by Cole, M. *et al.* Cambridge, MA: Harvard University Press.

Woods, M. (1998) 'Introduction', in Taylor, J. *et al.* (eds) *Early Childhood Studies*. London: Arnold.

Chapter 5

'It's not nursery but it's not just being at home' – a parent and childminder working together

Helen Moylett

I returned to work when my son was 7 months old. On my first day back I left him playing happily with someone he had got to know gradually over the previous few weeks. From birth he had been used to relating to, and being left with, different adults and children. I did not expect him to be distressed when I left him. I made a good show of being happy and confident, and indeed parts of me were feeling happy and confident, but much more of me seemed to be feeling bereaved. That day, and on many others, I wept in the car on the way to work.

I suspect that this paragraph could have been written by almost any working mother. Wherever we live; however rich or poor; however supportive our partners, families and friends; whatever our beliefs about childrearing; however strong our self-esteem – we all had to make a choice about work and then had to look for day care for our children. Then we had to cope with the practical and emotional consequences.

This chapter explores some of the issues associated with the choice of one particular form of day care – childminding. It draws on my own experiences as a parent and uses my relationship with one childminder to look at concerns which are relevant to many other parents and childminders. An important theme running through it, and discussed in more detail towards the end, is the development of the child's sense of self.

Firstly, some personal details will help contextualise the choices I was making. I had Connor, my first child, at the relatively advanced age of 38. Maternity leave was my first break from full-time work since I was 22. I have always enjoyed the job of teaching, whether in primary school or university and, for me, the personal and professional are very close: much of my self-esteem derives from success at work. Despite this I had very mixed feelings about returning to work. I was really enjoying full-time motherhood. I had met several new friends with young babies, and, in some ways, I envied those who were planning to stay at home full-time; in other ways they made me feel guilty about wanting to work. But want to work I did. Financially it would have been very difficult for me not to work, I also knew that I needed to have an identity outside the home and family, to be part of my profession. At the same time I knew I loved Connor very deeply and did not want to leave him. This ambivalent mix of feelings and needs informed my choices about Connor's day care.

[...]

Choosing a childminder means normally choosing another mother for one's child. This may seem an exaggerated view to those who see childminders more as paid educare workers than as mother figures. However, it is interesting to note that there appears to be little chance of choosing a male childminder. The world of early years education is predominantly female, male educarers are rare.

I recognise how lucky I was to have several educare options available. Although, like many other people these days, neither my partner nor I have parents or other relatives living nearby; we live in an area which is relatively well provided with day care and we could afford to pay for it. As Moss (1996: 19) emphasises, 'most young children in the UK depend on an unsubsidised private market for the supply of services'. Surveys have revealed that most children under 3 with working parents are cared for by relatives, followed by childminders. The National Childminding Association figures show that over 300,000 under-fives spend part or all of every weekday with a registered childminder. There has been little recent research which has looked in any depth at the reasons for parents' choices and their attitudes and expectations about their children's day care. As Warner (1994) points out, it is difficult to ascertain why so many parents choose childminders in preference to other services such as nurseries or nannies – their reasons may be more pragmatic than ideological. My own reasons for choosing childminding, in preference to other forms of educare, were certainly ideological and will be explored presently.

As a prelude it might be useful to consider some research carried out by Long *et al.* (1996). This was a response to the general lack of reported studies which explore parents' attitudes and expectations about their choice of day care. The researchers analysed the responses of 275 parents – 273 mothers and two fathers (another indication that in the early years field, 'parent' usually means 'mother'!) – to an open-ended survey. Although one must be cautious about their conclusions based on such an opportunity sample (might reported parental ideas about the importance of educational – in preference to social activities for instance – have been influenced by parental perceptions of the researchers as educationists?), one is left with some interesting questions about parental motivation.

The majority of parents were happy with their day care choice. Reasons for their choice were often pragmatic: affordability and flexibility of hours, for instance. The survey also attempted to investigate parents' knowledge of activities carried out during day care and where they obtained this knowledge.

The researchers expressed concern about the relative importance parents attached to the activities they were aware of. Social interaction was not seen as particularly valuable although we (the experts) know it is fundamental to cognitive and emotional development. There seemed to be little awareness that social values were an important part of childcare – in combating sexism and racism, for example. There was also little mention of the children's reactions to the care received. Parents were generally confident that they had enough information to make a choice about childcare, although the majority said they would have liked more beforehand. They had usually obtained information from friends rather than experts.

Although there were limitations to this study, it raises some interesting issues about the pressures on parents and the way in which they are seen by the 'experts'. It might be appropriate at this point to ponder what Penelope Leach says about the sort of expert colonisation of parenting that is a consequence of the separation of parents' work from children's care:

> . . . children have lost their taken-for-granted presence in, and apprenticeship to, what adults see as the most important aspect of their lives. Instead of spending much of childhood watching, 'helping' and emulating a range of adult people doing adult things, Western children spend it in special environments designed to keep them out of harm's and adults' way: children's worlds, staffed by people – usually women – for whom childcare or education is paid work and therefore valued more highly than the personal care of parents.
>
> (Leach 1994: 20)

Long *et al.*'s research would seem to indicate that parents do indeed have a tendency to undervalue ordinary social interaction as educational.

As I said earlier, my reasons for choosing a childminder for Connor were ideological; in fact, because I felt so strongly that childminding was what both he and I needed, I did not even visit available nurseries or consider nannies. That might seem an intolerant or unfair attitude to many readers, and possibly a little surprising coming from one of the editors of a book full of examples of good practice in a range of educare settings. It might also seem strange that somebody who might be seen as some sort of expert in early education should choose educare in a setting that requires no formal qualifications from practitioners and no special premises. However, although I recognize the vast amount of wonderful work that goes on in all sorts of educare establishments and the importance of our youngest children having access to committed and well-qualified staff, I did not want my son to attend an institution.

'Institution' might seem an unkind word to use about some of the informal educare establishments which feature elsewhere in this book, but I believe the best childcare is loving, responsive and individualised; the sort of care that is very hard to give in a routinised group setting – which even the best nurseries must necessarily be. My son was a baby who had so much learning to do; I believed that his learning could be best facilitated in a loving home environment. There is some research which has shown that children cared for in home settings tend to have more vocal communication directed at them and that this may lead to faster rates of language development (see for example

Melhuish 1991). However, it seems likely that the quality of interaction between educarer and child is the crucial factor. I felt that this quality would be easier to assess in one individual childminder than in a nursery where there are several educarers. As Goldschmied and Jackson (1994: 74) say, 'Good care by one person is almost certain to be more loving and sensitive than care by a number of different people, however competent. The key person system is only a partial attempt to compensate for this inherent disadvantage of group care.'

Connor's immediate family consists of his parents and his two much older half-sisters and half-brother. I was therefore keen that he got used to relating to other very young children in a family setting. This effectively ruled out a nanny.

I have a great deal of sympathy with Leach's view of the separation of parents' work from children's care. I felt I wanted Connor to be engaged in 'real' life for as long as possible: to be with an adult doing her job, running her house, visiting her friends, going shopping, as well as engaging in specifically child-centred activities.

I started searching for a registered childminder who had young children of her own, who had loving and respectful attitudes to children and who would provide a stimulating environment matched to my child's needs. There is not space here to talk about the variety of childminders Connor and I met during that search, and the things that put me off or drew me to certain minders. However, it did help me to understand some of the reasons some parents might find it easier to place their child in a nursery!

Although social services registration means that the childminder's premises and resources have been inspected and found to be appropriate for up to three full-time children under 5, and that she has received some basic training, it has to be a baseline from which to start, rather than an assurance of excellence. Childminders rarely have glossy brochures and useful jargon-laden phrases for reassuring (or intimidating?) anxious parents; they rarely have strings of impressive-sounding qualifications or large super-hygienic houses with different areas for different activities. It is no easy task to go to somebody else's home and chat with them about their job and the way they see it; or to remember to ask the questions one feels one needs to ask and then, using the data gained, to make a decision about one's beloved child. I suppose I found it easier than some, because over the years I have gained a fair amount of experience in home visiting and interviewing. Nevertheless, the emotional investment I had in this decision making process made it very stressful.

In the end I found a good childminder, relationships seemed to be developing well and then, after a couple of months, she told us that she would be unexpectedly leaving Manchester. (Institutions, of course, do not tend to do this!) Luckily one of her friends had a vacancy for a full-time child. This friend already knew Connor and had expressed interest in minding him; she had also been previously recommended to me by two other mothers. Desperately worried about continuity of care, I went to see her and was reassured. She talked about my 9-month-old baby as a person she was fond of, and she and I liked each other immediately. So began a relationship with Mags and her family which has been, and continues to be, a source of support, education and care for both Connor and myself.

I am now going to explore some of the aspects of that relationship which seem to make it work for Connor, Mags and myself. Although this exploration is based on our particular childminding relationship the issues raised are relevant to many educare situations.

I claimed earlier that choosing a childminder was choosing another mother for one's child. On one level that can be taken as an unambiguous statement of fact – the overwhelming majority of childminders are mothers who have young children of their own.

However, I would like to explore some of the implications of wanting to have one's child 'mothered' by someone else.

Mothering is about loving and, for me, being a mother has certainly been a love story. However I have never believed in the soft focus, roses round the door, happy ever after sort of love stories (however powerful such fantasies may be!). Relationships may begin with hearts and flowers, but to survive they usually need compromise and commitment. Babies are neither sugarcoated bundles of joy; nor screeching sleep deprivers – two of the most common stereotypes on the birth congratulations cards! They are people with rights and feelings and the capability to do much and become more. They, like all humans, need to be loved when they are in very sharp focus behaving angrily for example, 'having an off day', or not being very obviously loving themselves. They also need to be loved when they are quietly sleeping, 'being a good girl' or saying their first words. In other words they need people who can offer unconditional love; who are consistently loyal; whose own self-esteem is well anchored. Through this loving behaviour they learn how to be loving themselves – to love both themselves and others. Years of being a teacher has led me to believe very strongly that children need loving role models who treat them as individuals worthy of respect, if they are to learn and grow up to become loving adults themselves.

All this may sound obvious to the point of banality, but we are all powerfully influenced by traditional constructions of childhood – some of which are antithetical to the position advanced above. Take the concept of original sin (with its attendant notion of the inherent wickedness of children) and the idea of children as adult property as examples. How many times have you heard a new mother being asked 'Is he good?' as if a new-born baby *could* be good or bad. What the questioner usually wants to know is how much inconvenience this new arrival is causing its owner. It may only be a year or so before this same child is hearing himself described as a naughty boy and is being regularly smacked by his parents; parents who would regard smacking another adult as completely out of order. How often have you heard two adults talking negatively about children over their heads as if they were not present? These smackers and chatterers have one thing in common – a disregard for the rights of the child. They would not smack another adult or talk about them in that way, either because they would not dare – an adult could hurt them back – or because they would think it abusive or socially inappropriate.

Earlier I wrote that I was looking for a childminder who had loving and respectful attitudes to children – who was definitely not a smacker or chatterer. I wanted this second mother to have ideas like mine about loving and learning, and to love my child in similar ways to myself. I wanted Connor to be getting consistent messages about his worth in the world. Some mothers I know told me that they did not really want this for their children; they worried about their children loving the childminder 'too much', resulting in less love for them. My belief is that we all have an infinite capacity for love and being loved, and the more loving we are exposed to the better. Goldschmied and Jackson (1994: 39) refer to some parents needing help 'to understand that sharing love and affection with another caregiver is not like sharing an apple or a sandwich where the more people the less there is for each'.

During the first conversation I had with Mags she was careful to tell me that she treated the children she minded as her own and 'loved' them, and that this meant kissing and cuddling. When I reacted positively to this statement she explained that some parents did not like this and she felt she had to make it clear that she could not mind children if she was 'not allowed to love them'. Mags has one daughter (Anna May), the same age as Connor, and another who is five years older. She and her husband are very openly affectionate with each other and their children, and the words 'I love you' are often heard. However, before any cynical reader begins to feel a trifle nauseated by all this sweetness and light, let me emphasise that Mags is no superhuman paragon of virtue who never gets cross or tired. One of the first sentences Connor uttered was 'Me a bit cross and I mean it!' which was more or less a direct quote from Mags. Mags and I both feel that part of loving is being real!

It must be apparent that one of the reasons that I felt happy to leave my child with Mags was because she had similar ideas about the practice of mothering to my own. However, what about the huge difference between us encapsulated by Mags when she said 'it must be so hard for you. I'm doing this job because I just can't leave my child'? As Ferri (1992: 68) indicates:

> The employed mother who places her child in the care of a childminder is doing something which the minder would never do herself. The childminder, on the other hand, by remaining at home with her own children, is pursuing a course, which the mother, either from choice or necessity, has decided against. This distinction is of fundamental importance to the way in which minders and mothers perceive each other's role, and is likely to be a key factor in the way in which relationships develop.

Ferri's research involving the compilation of detailed case studies of 30 childminding relationships led her to make that statement, which gets to the emotional core at the heart of the parent-childminder relationship.

Mags and I were lucky in that we liked each other as soon as we met. We share some important commitments to young children and their educare; we both refuse to take life too seriously and are tolerant of each other's occasional disorganisations. We are both extrovert, upfront types of people who like to get any concerns out in the open. I believe that these similarities must have made our relationship easier, while still not wishing to minimise the potential conflicts embedded within it.

Earlier in this chapter I mentioned the ways in which parenting of young children is still seen to be mothers' responsibility. Mags and I, like all mothers (and fathers) are influenced by current political and social constructions of mothers and working women. To summarise some of these crudely: on the one hand we hear statements about children's needs for their mothers that have their origins in the work of people like Bowlby (1953), who talked about the importance for emotional and social development of natural attachment; and on the other, we are exhorted to contribute to the economy and become 'have it all' superwomen. One could read implied criticism into Mags's remark about how hard I must find it to leave my child: I can somehow abandon my child and endure the pain of that separation whereas she (being a more loving mother) cannot. Alternatively one could see it as an empathic statement which lets me know that she understands what I must be feeling. Yet again one might be able to read some envy into what she says. All these readings are no more nor less 'true' than each other, but they do point to some of the possible ambiguities involved in the childminder-parent relationship. Roles are not always clear-cut; people may feel conflicting emotions. Neither of the mothers (childminder or parent) may feel that she is always 'doing the best' for her child.

At the beginning of the chapter I mentioned the guilt I experienced about wanting to work and my feeling of bereavement on leaving my son. Mags has helped me to cope with these feelings in various ways. Apart from empathy and a generally non-judgemental attitude she sets things up so that there is always time made for transitions – first thing in the morning and in the evening. During this time we talk and she tells me about what she and the children are going to be doing during the day, or about what has happened. It is during these times that I have got to know Mags and her family better. Sharing activities with the children and a cup of tea or a glass of wine with the childminder is a good way to find out about what my son experiences every day.

When, after a few months, I was able to negotiate part-time work, Mags did not in any way imply that I should have done this sooner; she merely said she understood why I needed to do it and observed that she loved Connor so much that she would miss him. I had been worried by the loss of income that this change would mean for Mags. Would she be able to find another part-time child for those two days? Would she really prefer not to have Connor part-time and replace him with another full-time child? Mags was adamant that she loved all of us – not just Connor, but me and his dad as well – and did not want to lose us. This situation brought home to me just how complicated the relationships involved in childminding can become. We have an emotional relationship based on our love for one child and we are friends – we think highly of each other. Nevertheless, we employ Mags, in the sense that we pay her – although we do not determine to any great extent what she does, and she draws up the contract between us. Penelope Leach (1994: 95) describes the parent-childminder relationship as 'an equal partnership based on what really matters – the child's well-being and happiness'. I think I would describe it somewhat differently. If it is really soundly based on the child's well-being and happiness it has more chance of being an effective partnership, but it can never be truly equal because various inequalities and tensions are structured into it.

To illustrate this let us look again at the economic basis of the relationship. In our case, and in many others, the parents are professional people with qualifications which enable them to earn sufficient salaries to make paying a childminder a realistic prospect. A National Childminding Association briefing (1996a) points out that nearly three-quarters of women with high educational qualifications are at work when their children are under 5, and quotes an OPCS survey which showed that childminding was the first choice for households where the occupation of the main wage earner was 'professional, employer/manager or white collar'. The picture seems to be different as regards the childminders – a smaller percentage of them and their partners have professional qualifications and/or jobs. Ferri (1992: 64) noted that day care arrangements may thus bring together two families from different socio-economic groups. Also the childminder is being paid a derisory wage for being totally responsible for the parents' beloved children, even though that wage usually represents a substantial part of the parents' income. This illustrates the kind of inequality perpetuated where the political climate encourages the 'unsubsidized private market' approach to childcare to flourish.

Warner (1994: 30) sums up both the political and the practical nature of this situation when she says:

> Childminding has been seen mainly as 'women's work' and often equated with parenting, so it has traditionally been poorly paid. Childminders have sometimes felt exploited when parents are late paying or refuse to pay for holidays, or when their child does not attend because of sickness, or when Social Services are late sending money for a sponsored child.

Mags and other childminders have told me some stories about parents' non-payment that make my toes curl. Why is it that some apparently caring, solvent parents do not always see paying for their child's day care as a priority? It would be too easy to brand them as 'nasty' people who do not care about their childminder's financial well-being. It seems likely that their actions stem more from their difficulty in recognising childminding as a job, than from any personality defect. The chapter in Ferri (1992) entitled 'The Business of Childminding' includes some interesting anecdotes which illustrate childminders' and parents' differing views about payment and contracts. My own view as a parent is that the contract we have with Mags is very useful. Her rates of pay are clearly set out and have been helpful when trying to remember what happens during holidays or sickness for example. A contract is also an encouragement to treat the childminder as another professional person. Mags feels very strongly that the work she does is both important and of good quality; parents should appreciate that and treat her, both personally and financially, with respect. Consequently, however, they need to rate her job as highly as their own. I feel that I certainly do that, but – given the beliefs I have and the job I do – I would be likely to.

Childminders generally are in a difficult position as regards status. On the one hand, they want recognition, but on the other there are no formal entry qualifications required and only basic training is needed for registration. Jo, a Manchester childminder says:

> I did have the opportunity of registering my childcare practice as a private nursery but was told that all 'household' furniture had to be replaced with equipment as in the play room. I chose not to continue this route because I felt it was very important for very young children to be in a home environment.
>
> (Mathieson 1996)

Looking back to my early interviews with childminders, this sort of documentation would certainly have made my life easier. It paints a picture of Jo's priorities, values and beliefs, and gives a strong impression that this is a childminder who takes her job very seriously. It also has the potential to educate parents who may be unaware of the importance of providing a range of experiences for their young children. (This seems to be what Long *et al.*'s research, mentioned earlier in this chapter, indicated.) However, my feeling is that there are dangers involved in advocating a status for childminding based on similarity to nursery. There has long been a tendency to look to the next stage in a child's life for a rationale and validation for current practice. One has to look no further than the effect of the National Curriculum on nursery practice.

Most recent writings about quality in early childhood provision have referred to the way values and beliefs influence relationships and interactions – and, therefore, the quality of the educare – more significantly than any other factor (see, for example Abbott and Rodger 1994; Moss and Pence 1994; Moss 1996). Moss (1996) talks about the importance of valuing diversity within an inclusive model of childcare services. He points to the dangers inherent in regarding these services as either businesses or vehicles for delivering national programmes.

Of course no amount of brochures with appropriate-sounding phrases will actually ensure quality of provision. So how do I judge the quality of the educare Connor is receiving when he is with Mags? How do I know that the values she talked about when I first met her are translated into some sort of daily reality for my son? On a simple level I know that he is loved. I can see that in the way he and Mags interact and the ways in which he talks about her. Although he is always pleased to see me or his father, he is often reluctant to leave Mags's house, particularly if he is involved in something interesting. 'I love Magsy', he often says. She and the rest of her family are always included in his lists of people he loves. (He is now 2 and very keen on listing things.) Recently, when helping me get ready to go to Sainsbury's, he wrote a shopping list which included presents for Mags and her daughter.

On another simple level I know he is playing with all sorts of appropriate and stimulating resources and toys, both at Mags's house and at the various toddler groups she both organises and attends. I know resources are chosen with equal opportunities in mind – there are no 'boys" and 'girls" toys and there are positive images of people from a variety of cultures. I know they read lots of stories and go to the library for story sessions. But what about the more complex values underlying interaction with people and resources, the hidden curriculum? Presumably at this stage it is less hidden than it will be when we come into contact with the institutions that he will eventually attend. It's hard to hide your real values from someone who enters your home several times a week in an informal way.

I want Connor to be confident in himself and to grow up respecting other people. The first step to respect for others is respect for oneself, and Mags works hard to allow the children she cares for to develop their sense of individuality and autonomy. This can be seen in all sorts of small ways. She believes in the value of exploratory play and allows the children to explore materials in their own way – they can set the agenda, everything is not structured by her. Connor feels quite comfortable experimenting with face painting and telling everyone, 'When I a bit older I going to have perfume, lipstick and mascara for my own'; nobody has implied that this is an inappropriate choice for a boy. Of course one could say that Connor is inhabiting an unusually female world at Mags's (and probably an unusually liberal one at home) and that sooner or later he is going to be confronted with the reality of the ways in which mainstream maleness is constructed in the world. Phillips (1993) has some powerful things to say about the ways in which boys become men and the implications for their parents. In a chapter entitled 'Mother Power' she warns of the potential problems looming for mothers and sons when the son encounters 'other children and adults, who may have a more developed sense of gender and need to enforce those divisions to prop up their own identity'. All I can hope is that when Connor does begin to realise that others have expectations of him based on his sex, that his early years will have built some solid rock beneath the shifting sand of experience.

Mags gives the children choices as often as possible about small things, like which biscuit they want; which car seat they will sit in; which story they would like; which colour felt pen to use. When their wants conflict, ways of sharing fairly are discussed and the rationale explained. Mags answers all questions as honestly and fairly as she can and she is tolerant of the children's feelings – they are allowed to be angry or upset, for instance. She has few rules, but she applies them consistently and, when conflict occurs, uses various strategies such as distraction, negotiation, firmness and occasionally, shouting. Connor does a good imitation of her warning the children that this might happen: 'Now do I have to shout?' He tells me he does not like it when this happens. He still occasionally recalls an incident when he, Anna May and another child pulled a lot of flower heads off. 'Mags did shout and we cried 'cos we was very naughty and them lovely flowers they was all gone aahh!' He often says to me 'Don't look at me like that, I don't like it!', but he is quick to say 'Sorry' and amend his behaviour. My belief is that this is partly because he has not been treated aggressively either at Mags's or at home; adults being cross or shouting means that he has overstepped a serious boundary. I hope he will grow up to be appropriately assertive – the way in which he is asked to make decisions already and the way in which his choices are respected should help that process.

Already he believes that he can influence adult behaviour in quite subtle ways, not just by crying or shouting. He has learned to say 'excuse me' when he interrupts conversation. When this is repeated very forcefully and with rising volume if ignored, it is usually a successful opening gambit. On one recent occasion he had been told that his dad and I were having a serious conversation which he must not interrupt. His response to this was to go away and make some marks on a piece of A4 paper which he then brought into the room and held up. When we inevitably stopped talking to look at it, he announced 'This says please be quiet.' He also uses 'adult' behaviour to regulate adult actions. The other day, for example, I asked him if he wanted me to read his Fireman Sam comic with him and he said 'This is not a comic, this is my newspaper and I am reading about that train on fire [a reference to an article in that day's *Guardian*], you be quiet now.' Another time he was making marks on paper and I asked him what he was doing and he said 'This is very important. I am going to school with this picture, I am Emily [Mags's elder daughter].' He also often says he is 'doing work' when he is writing or reading. Mags is a qualified hairdresser, and he makes her sit still while he 'does' her hair. These are more than amusing anecdotes; they show that Connor is a child who believes he has some control over his world and some access to that adult world of work that Leach regrets is so often denied to children these days.

Obviously at the age of 2 he is fairly egocentric but he knows and meets a range of adults and young people via his family; Mags has friends from all sorts of backgrounds and is always very positive about the diversity of society and different ways of life. I know from the way in which she speaks, the friends she has, the resources she provides, that she recognises the harm that discrimination based on prejudice does. Mags also minds children for social services and sometimes undertakes emergency short-term caring. This has meant Connor meeting people who are much more distressed than others he is used to, but Mags has always talked about all the children's behaviour in a positive way and he appears to take everything in his stride. The messages he is getting are all about valuing himself and others; he is beginning to develop empathy. Recently Mags's elder daughter was off school and Connor told me that she 'had a poorly tummy and she was in bed and me and Anna May we did give her cuddles to feel her better...I been sick once...it was horrid'. The other day he came and stood in the doorway of the room where I was working. A tape of Chopin nocturnes was playing in the background. The next minute he was leaning his head against me asking, 'Oh mummy, are you sad?' I responded by saying 'No, why do you ask that?' to which he replied, in a very sad small voice, 'This music very sad, I don't like it, turn it off.'

So far I have painted a very positive picture of this educare relationship – but what about the inevitable differences between home and childminders? As a parent, I came to the conclusion long ago that we can all live quite happily with all sorts of differences between what happens at home and at the childminder's as long as they are not differences in values and beliefs. My view is that small differences remain small if one keeps that perspective.

Of course any child being part of two different households will notice differences. For instance, very soon after he could walk and climb he was told that he was not allowed to climb on the kitchen table at home. However, at Mags's he and Anna May were allowed to climb up and walk around on the table. He went through a period of climbing onto Mags's table as soon as I arrived to collect him and standing smiling at me. Mags and I dealt with this by just acknowledging what he was doing and saying that we knew that he was not allowed to do this at home. I assume that seeing us discussing it calmly and the fact that he was receiving a consistent (if different) message from both of us, helped him come to terms with this and other differences between home and his childminder's.

He certainly understands that there are appropriate behaviours linked to different places. When we were returning from the library recently he said 'I was a bit noisy in there and running around – you didn't mind [remind] me first and I forgotten.' When I asked what I didn't remind him about he replied, 'About being quiet.' When talking about a trip to work with his father he said, 'I played with my toys and done some work on daddy's pooter [computer] and I be very quiet when daddy talking with those people . . . you not allowed to do shouting at work.'

Of course as a proud parent I am biased, but it seems to me that Connor is developing respectful and loving attitudes and an appreciation of others' feelings. He also feels that he is important and that his opinions matter. I am sure that because he has been so well loved, educated and cared for by his childminder, it has contributed enormously to this development. Mags sees childminding as a balancing act: 'It's not nursery but it's not just being at home – you've got to think about what the children need as well, that's my job.' Ferri (1992: 160) points to the importance of this balance when thinking about childminder training and talks about the need 'to address the underlying issue of how far the childminder's role should be, in the broadest sense, explicitly educative, or – as so widely seen by its practitioners – one of recreating the ethos of the home environment'.

It seems to me that Mags manages to achieve an appropriate balance, not just because she is aware of the importance of providing learning experiences, but because she sees everyday life in the home environment as a learning experience. I recently watched her making rhubarb crumble with Connor, Anna May and another toddler. All three were standing on chairs at the work surface in the kitchen with Mags in the middle using a sharp knife to chop the rhubarb. While the children watched her chop, while they were exploring the pieces of rhubarb and then, when they were all engaged in transferring the rhubarb to the pan, Mags encouraged them to talk about how the rhubarb grew, where it had come from, grandad's allotment, why they had to remove the leaves, why they cannot yet use sharp knives, what was going to happen to the rhubarb in the pan, how they could tell how much sugar to use, when they would make the crumble mixture and lots more relevant issues. Connor and Anna May joined in enthusiastically, contributing their ideas and listening to the others. Connor felt confident to contribute details about the rhubarb in our garden and what he could remember about crumble making. Mags was careful to create space for the other younger, less confident child to speak and also checked that she understood what had been said. This short anecdote seems to me to illustrate an approach to childminding which sees the educational potential in everyday life; which is responsive to individual children's needs and which depends both on a belief in children's ability to get involved in adult life, and on a respect for the contribution they make to it.

Mags and I both feel that our shared views of the world in general, and the development of young children in particular, have helped us to build and maintain a relationship based on mutual trust and understanding. Although our jobs are different, we respect each other on a personal and professional level and have avoided some of the potential areas of conflict explored earlier. In various ways we have supported each other in a relationship which is loving and friendly but also formal and contractual. At the moment the plan is that this will probably come to an end when both our children are $3^{1}/_{2}$ and we will, somewhat reluctantly, send them to nursery. For both of us and our children this will mark the end of an era in our lives and the beginning of whole new sets of relationships. I hope they will be as happy.

References

Abbott, L. and Rodger, R. (eds) (1994) *Quality Education in the Early Years.* Buckingham: Open University Press.

'Bowlby, J. (1953) *Child Care and the Growth of Love.* Harmondsworth: Penguin.

Ferri, E. (1992) *What Makes Childminding Work?* London: National Children's Bureau.

Goldschmied, E. and Jackson, S. (1994) *People Under Three.* London: Routledge.

Leach, P. (1994) *Children First.* London: Penguin.

Long, P., Wilson, P., Kutnick, P. and Telford, L. (1996) Choice and childcare: a survey of parental perceptions and views, *Early Child Development and Care* **119**: 51–63.

Mathieson, J. (1996) Assignment contributing to assessment for BA (Honours) Early Childhood Studies. Manchester Metropolitan University.

Melhuish, E. C. (1991) Research on day care for young children in the United Kingdom, in E. C. Melhuish and P. Moss (eds) *Day Care for Young Children: International Perspectives.* London: Routledge.

Moss, P. (1996) Defining objectives in early childhood services, *European Early Childhood Research Journal* **4**(1): 17–31.

Moss, P. and Pence, A. (1994) *Valuing Quality in Early Childhood Services.* London: Paul Chapman Publishing.

National Childminding Association (1996a) *Briefing re. Daycare Services in England*. London: NCMA.

National Childminding Association (1996b) *Briefing on Nursery Education and Grant Maintained Schools Bill*. London: NCMA.

Phillips, A. (1993) *The Trouble with Boys, Parenting the Men of the Future*. London: Pandora.

Warner, J. (1994) Childminders and children, in T. David (ed.) *Working Together for Young Children*. London: Routledge.

Chapter 6

Information to parents

Jo Mathieson

Jo Mathieson
NNEB
Registered childminder

Dear parents

What will your child be doing, while in my care? What will they learn? What will be provided for them? Will your child's individual needs be met? What experience and knowledge does your childminder have?

These are very common questions, asked by the majority of parents: those who come to me for a placement, those who come to me for information and advice (I run a vacancy scheme in the area), and sometimes those who are unsure about their child's childminder.

I have, therefore, written these notes for your information – regarding my child care practice. They will explain my approach to child care, health and development. They give you information about each area/activity your child will be involved in and the developmental values and benefits.

Hopefully, this will generate more questions and ideas from yourself – read it, think about it and let me know your views.

My experience and knowledge

I am a qualified Nursery Nurse and have been working with young children for over 14 years. During this time, I have learnt and come to understand a great deal about children: the various stages of development, how they behave, how they acquire knowledge and skills, how they build an under standing of the world around them – the basic ingredients needed to meet the challenges that face them as they grow.

I am aware of what is required, by me the educator, to assist their development at each stage in their early years.

I have seen and experienced the many difficulties, problems, concerns and worries that arise in the first years of life – for parents and children – and work closely with parents to help overcome these challenges in a positive way.

Qualifications

NNEB in nursery nursing
Valid first aid till 1999
Special educational needs training
Various short courses – related to early years

Currently undertaking a BA in early childhood studies

Are you reassured?

Why am I a childminder?

When I was expecting my daughter, I visited many childminders but could not find one that provided the kinds of things I wanted for my daughter. I was, as you would imagine, quite concerned, amazed, worried…I didn't feel that my expectations were any different to any other parents. I had my son, 13 months later, and had already decided to leave my job (in a nursery) and become a childminder myself – providing what I felt was the right environment and setting for young children of working parents.

My aim

Each child is an individual and will grow and develop at their own pace. My aim is to provide them with all the experiences and opportunities I can, in order for them to grow to their full potential. I feel it is important for young children to be in an environment where they can interact well with the adults and children, build their communication skills with confidence, express their individuality confidently and build a good attachment with their childminder. Children learn through play. What is 'play' and what is 'learning'?

PLAY is the method by which children gain all the knowledge, skills and understanding they need to fulfil their potential. Play is fun, exciting, productive.

LEARNING is the process of absorbing information, experiences, opportunities and concepts to develop emotionally, physically, intellectually, linguistically, socially and creatively.

My aim is to assist this by providing a variety of activities and experiences to allow each child to: have fun, learn new skills, experiment, use their senses to understand and gain knowledge, explore a variety of concepts and ideas and collect information about their world and the people around them, in a safe, warm and stimulating home environment.

What I do

You are your child's first educator – I am their second

I believe in working in partnership with parents to provide the best for each child in my care.

I operate a 'open door' policy – parents are always welcome to join in with activities and stay for as long as they wish. I respect the parents I work with – after all, you know your child better than anyone else. Your views, ideas, comments, etc. are valuable and I feel that it is very important for me to be able to work with you in partnership.

I am always available and like to spend as much time as possible with parents. It is very important for your child to be able to see that Mum/Dad and childminder can communicate well, make time to talk, respect each other and can work as a team to provide continuity of care. This builds your child's confidence, sense of security and promotes a happy child. Having gone through this situation myself, I am fully aware of the worries, anxieties and concerns parents feel when leaving their child with a childminder.

I encourage equal opportunities – each child should have the opportunity to develop to his or her full potential regardless of race, origin, sex, disability, cultural or social background. Each child is an individual, and his or her needs, wishes and ideas should be met. We live in a multi-cultural, multiracial society and the children of today will be the adults of tomorrow – promoting equality of opportunity and opposing discrimination of any kind will help them to combat these injustices in later life. Children pick up ideas and values from the adults around them. My aim is to promote positive views and ideas. Amongst my equipment you will see: positive images, through books, posters, activities. Artefacts in the home corner. Black and male dolls. Asian and other dressing-up items.

I use language that does not discriminate or influence stereotypes.

Discipline

I do not smack or use any form of physical punishment. Instead, I use the 'time out' method to encourage positive behaviour. What is time out? Removing the child from the conflicting situation, diverting their attention, reassuring and comforting them, teaching right from wrong in a positive way. I feel it is important for myself and the parents to work together to encourage positive behaviour, so the child does not face conflicting ideas and values.

Outings

I take the children to three drop-in sessions each week – I am key holder and organiser for these sessions. Attending the drop-in enables the children to build their social skills and develop new relationships with other children who are also minded. It gives them an opportunity to use different equipment and materials, experience other surroundings and become familiar with facilities in the local environment. The children, all ages, enjoy these sessions very much.

I take the children on local 'discovery trips' – perhaps to reinforce a theme or activity we are doing or sometimes to follow a child's individual request or idea. This extends the child's learning process, familiarises them with the local environment and gives them first-hand experience.

Routine

I feel it is important for children to have a routine – this helps children understand the concept of time. They become familiar with the events of each day. A good routine provides a sense of security, comfort and stability. When working with young children, flexibility is a must. Although the basic needs are always there – sleep time, meal time, snack times, free play time, structured activities – the children exercise freedom of choice about the activities they do, thus encouraging independence.

Individual needs

Children's needs vary according to a variety of factors, situations and circumstances. I make sure that each child in my care has my attention and understanding when needed, for as long as it is needed. The children build a strong relationship with me in a warm, comfortable, safe and stimulating environment. They also build a strong relationship with my assistant. Between us we can give each child all the love, warmth and attention they need, in a home environment with plenty of stimulating and enjoyable activities.

Under one

Babies require a lot of one-to-one attention. This is no problem as there are always two adults present. I feel it is also important for them to be part of the group and be involved in what is going on – not to be left in a chair, at a distance or separated from the other children. The baby is often with me experiencing, watching and listening. Babies learn very quickly and, given the right kind of care and attention, they will thrive and develop quickly.

They build relationships with the other children and the older children learn to be considerate, caring, loving and become aware of the babies' needs. This is a valuable experience for both.

My voluntary roles

I am an active member of the Manchester City Childminding Association, taking the role of voluntary Fund-raising and Social Officer. Within this role, I organise local fund-raising events, assist other childminding groups around Manchester to hold events and write short articles for the MCCMA news letter.

I am also a voluntary Link Visiting Officer for my area – I provide support and help to new childminders in my area, give them ideas and advice, encourage them to attend the drop-in sessions, reinforce issues discussed on the registration course – child safety, importance of play, equal opportunities, Manchester's no smacking policy – how to provide the best for the children in their care.

The children in my care come first and these voluntary roles do not take up my working time with the children.

For your information

Activities and their values

Physical play

The garden is large and outdoor equipment is plentiful. I take children to the local park and outdoor play is also available during a drop-in session.

Values – enjoyment, release of surplus energy, offers new freedom from possible tension. Stimulates an appetite, digestion, circulation, sleep, mental alertness, skin health. Promotes muscle tone, coordination, manipulative skills, balance, control, body awareness, resistance to infection. Develops skills such as: running, stopping, climbing, jumping, etc. Offers elements of challenge and adventure. Builds concepts of height, width, spatial awareness, distance, speed. Develops social skills, sharing, collaborating, working together. Builds self-confidence. Stimulates intellectual curiosity, observation, aesthetic awareness and a sense of wonder about animals and nature. Encourages imaginative play. Given a variety of equipment all these skills will be met.

Sand and water play

These activities are provided every day when the weather is fine. They are also provided at each drop-in session.

Values – enjoyment, sensory experience, release of tension, outlet for aggression and frustration, therapeutic values, language opportunities. Encourages manipulative skills, builds imaginative development. Mathematical and scientific discoveries concerning: volume, capacity, floating, sinking, material properties. Links with home life: holidays, other family events.

Clay and playdough

Playdough is used almost every day, as asked for by the children. Clay is used once or twice a fortnight.

Values – lots of enjoyment, endless possibilities – there is no right or wrong way to use these materials. Emotionally an outlet for aggression, tension, therapeutic values. Links with their own home environment – cooking. Scientific discoveries, properties of each material, effects when wet, dry. Satisfies curiosity, promotes questions, ideas. Opportunity for imaginative play. Language development.

A variety of objects are introduced at each play session – to promote new ideas and uses.

Imaginative play

A wide variety of materials and situations are set up to encourage imaginative play – house corner, shop, hospital, cafe, post office, etc. Each is well stocked with accessories. There is an outdoor play house with kitchen area, bedroom, living room. Other materials and equipment are provided – dressing-up items, 'the real macoy' – and as a group we make large play items such as cars, boats, buses, etc. Children develop their imaginative skills in all the other areas/activities provided.

Values – enjoyment, develops social skills, helps child to understand people and relationships. Encourages role play – what they see the adults around them doing. Encourages manipulative skills, coordination, thinking skills, problem solving. Provides an opportunity to release frustrations, anger, other emotions. Helps children to come to terms with areas of concern, fear, difficulty. Provides an insight into adult behaviour. Mathematical experiences, sensory experiences, stimulates language development. Helps children learn about themselves – their abilities, their feelings, their likes and dislikes – and lots, lots more!

Cooking activities

I bake with the children at least once a week. We make a variety of things for tea times, snack times and tea parties. If we make biscuits, small cakes, etc. the children take one home.

Values – enjoyment, linked with home, sensory experiences – feel, smell, taste. Provides an emotional release – beating, whisking, kneading. Mathematical experiences – shape, size, weight, capacity, counting, changes in texture, shape, effects of heat, cold. Provides an opportunity for language development. Early reading skills – labels, recipe books, etc. Social skills are developed. Understanding of food, nutritional information, hygiene, home safety, diet. Encourages concentration, thinking skills, observation skills. Produces an end product and encourages self praise, self-ability.

Wonderful to watch them learn and absorb information through a cooking activity.

Creative activities

I keep a good stock of paints, glue, collage materials, a variety of papers and card. I collect items such as wool, fabric pieces, shells, cones, string, empty containers, feathers, bottle tops, lolly sticks, newspaper computer paper, pastas, rice, beans, etc., old cards, paper plates, ribbon – in fact, anything I can use for creative activities.

Values – self-expression, freedom to discover, experiment, explore the properties of each medium. Enjoyment, release of tension, aggression. Opportunities to experience a variety of materials – some out of context. Encourages imagination, stimulates language development. Develops creative expression. Promotes self-awareness, self-appraisal, achievement. End product to show parents. Fosters tastes and personal preferences. No right or wrong way to use the materials. Perception of shape, texture, spatial relationships. Scientific learning – consistencies, colour mixing, effects of other materials. Stimulates language development. Avenue of expression. Sensory experiences. Promotes decision making, choice, independence, self-appraisal. It also introduces them to equipment such as brushes, glue spreaders, scissors, etc.

Creativity arises in many areas, not just by using paints, glue, etc.

Construction toys

Mobilo, Duplo, Lego, bricks, magnetic bricks, stickle bricks, linking cubes, Superstrato, etc.

Values – enjoyment, feeds imagination, language development, encourages social development. Gives first-hand experience in spatial relationships – next to, on top of, underneath. Introduction to three dimensions. Self-expression, self-awareness. Pleasure at own creations.

Construction occurs in many areas, not just with specific equipment.

Jigsaws, sorting, matching toys

Lots of different items used.

Values – improves hand and eye coordination, fine manipulative skills, language development, social development, thinking skills, intellectual development and lots more!

Games

Structured games outdoors, board games, lotto, matching games, recognition games, number games, etc. all stimulate intellectual development, social skills, thinking skills, imagination, language development, patience, consideration to others, listening skills, mathematical awareness, etc.

Children learn from everything they are involved with. If the adult is dedicated, enthusiastic, interested and gives children the attention, time and respect they require, the child will develop skills and understanding in each of the important areas.

Other activities

Planting seeds, nature hunts, washing dolls and equipment, exploring nature, drawing, writing skills – using a variety of mediums – chalk, crayons, pastels, felt pens, charcoal sticks, fabric pens, to name just a handful!

Remember – babies come into the world with none of these skills – everything comes from experience and opportunities.

You may feel that your baby is too young for most of these activities – may I just add that babies from 5–6 months can engage in a number of these activities and develop their senses, early knowledge and understanding. Babies are not babies for long – so it is important for you to know what lies ahead for them.

Settling-in procedure

I feel it is very important for parent and child to spend as much time as possible with me before a childminding arrangement begins. I advise a staggered settling-in procedure, over a minimum of two weeks.

Book list for your information

The Growth and Development of Children – Catherine Lee, published by Longman

Child Care and Health – J. Brain and M. Martin, published by Hulton Educational Publications

Child Development – A First Course – K. Sylva and 1. Lunt, published by Basil Blackwell

Day Care – Alison Clarke-Stewart, published by Fontana Paperbacks

Discipline Without Shouting or Spanking – J. Wyckoff and B. Unell, published by Meadowbrook Books

People Under 3 – Young Children in Day Care – E. Goldschmied and S. Jackson, published by Routledge

The First Years of Life – Open University, published by Ward Lock

The Pre-school Child – Open University, published by Ward Lock

There are plenty of books on the subject of child care, under fives, child development, play, etc.

The above are part of my personal collection and are available should you wish to borrow them.

Chapter 7

'Auntie-ji, please come and join us, just for an hour.' The role of the bilingual education assistant in working with parents with little confidence

Sheila Karran

Introduction

This chapter considers strategies which aim to inform parents about their child's learning, particularly in those situations where that learning is accredited by means of the completion of parent courses. The chapter focuses upon the question of how we involve those parents who are reluctant to take part in the courses offered for linguistic and cultural aspects. It will make reference to the importance of having access to staff or personnel with whom parents can identify and communicate comfortably.

It is generally agreed that an individual's attitudes about education are founded on that person's own experiences of 'formal learning'. These experiences vary greatly when considering differences within class and culture. However, it is dangerous to make general assumptions from surveys of individual groups and this chapter carries such a health warning.

The definition here of 'courses' for parents includes any information exchange within the range of a structured dialogue taking place between teachers and parents on a regular basis and that where parents gain some national accreditation for their learning.

Courses for parents in Coventry since the 1970s

In some cultures the role of the educators is seen as distinct and separate from the role of parenting, and educators may need to take some time explaining and illustrating how the child can benefit from partnership and continuity of educational experience across early years settings and home (Siraj-Blatchford 1994).

For the past two decades home–school work in Coventry has been committed to parental involvement and parental empowerment. This has been demonstrated by reading workshops; the family curriculum; the 'Put Yourself in Their Place' series of participatory activities to extend parents' understanding of children's learning; the home early learning programme; home school link worker parent courses which enable parents to encourage other parents to be involved in school activities. In 1980 the 'Eburne – Further Education College Outreach Programme' enabled hundreds of inner-city parents to take up, each year, 'free' GCSE and A level classes. A course about working with young children and their families was accredited with the RSA in 1984. The consequence of this has been that dozens of mothers have since become employed as valued education assistants by Coventry schools. Several have gone on to higher education and are now in teaching or social work. Today Coventry has over ten courses accredited with the Open College Network that specifically focus on the involvement of parents in their child's education.

Throughout the 1970s and 1980s Coventry was renowned for its vast production of home-grown community education certificates which acknowledged completion of a course. Successful parents were able to present these at interviews. In 1996 these have been mostly replaced by Open College Network and the NVQ Child Care and Education Level 11 portfolios.

Support for bilingual pupils and their families

Coventry LEA has also been committed for almost two decades to English language support for its bilingual pupils. About 6000 such children are supported each year by a team of 150 full-time and part-time teachers and 60 full-time and part-time bilingual education assistants. The latter are almost all placed in the early years settings in schools where the need for language support is identified, using here a bilingual approach to enhance the child's learning opportunities.

> Language makes accessible culture, culture includes the bilingual pupils' experience, and experience shapes knowledge...If teaching strategies encourage, value and support the use of bilingual pupils' home language, the children are more likely to share their language and culture freely without feeling that they are the centre of attention.
>
> (Blackledge 1994)

This applies equally to their bilingual parents.

The role of bilingual assistants in courses for parents

Part of the bilingual education assistant's role is to take opportunities to share the child's learning progress with the parent. To gather parents together in a group for this purpose is cost-effective in respect of staff and it is mutually supportive for the parents.

Many of the bilingual education assistants have completed an OCN course about how to facilitate learning opportunities within parent groups. They usually begin by co-tutoring on parent courses with a home-school links teacher. After which they go on to work with an experienced parent working with new parent groups.

Why do parents embark upon accredited courses which so often demand vast amounts of their time and energy? Generally, the intention is to gain qualifications and experience that may lead them to paid work with children. Also more and more committed parents, particularly mothers, have been encouraged to take the first step into the realm of further education. Parents who have attended courses often say they have developed a greater insight in their own child's learning; they are better equipped to support this learning; and above all they have achieved greater confidence in their own ability.

Mirpuri- and Sylheti-speaking families

As this new-found confidence is a positive factor for so many parents we need to focus on some who are least likely to benefit by courses for parents. This chapter focuses on the experiences of Mirpuri and Bangladeshi families for the reason that these two groups share certain social and educational concerns. The greatest concern is that Coventry children from these two communities make up the largest number of pupils, proportionally, requiring additional English language support. Teachers fear that these children are failing to gain access to the whole curriculum. This is a particular worry when the children are still at this basic level of English in Year One and in some cases, subsequent years. The Sylheti dialect, being similar to the Bangla language, is used by most of the Bangladeshi families in Coventry. The Mirpuri dialect although similar to Panjabi (Urdu) is used by a small minority of Asian families in Coventry. Both of these dialects are spoken and not written. When information is translated for the Mirpuri and Sylheti community it is written in Urdu script and Bangla respectively. A similar example in Britain might be in the northeast of England where the Geordie dialect speaking families would get standard English written letters sent from school. This doesn't present much of a difficulty for such parents where they are used to seeing written standard English and hearing it spoken on the radio and television. However, this is not generally the case for the Mirpuri- and Sylheti-speaking families who, brought up in Mirpur and Bangladesh, will probably not have had as much exposure to the media.

Within the Asian community, when both parents of preschool children are out at work the children are often cared for by grandparents. Many of these children are starting school with a limited range or vocabulary in their first language and almost no experience of hearing and speaking English. For Mirpuri and Bangladeshi children from relatively small Asian communities in Coventry their linguistic isolation is accentuated.

The faith shared by the majority of Mirpuri and Bangladeshi families is that of Islam. According to Sitara Khan (1985), many Moslem families share a similar attitude towards British education and racism in Britain. She states:

Muslim parents feel that the British educational system has failed them and their children. In general Muslim children have consistently failed to fulfil themselves academically within the system and have often emerged at the end of it feeling estranged from their parents and their culture. (p.33)

Mirpuri- and Sylheti-speaking pupils are sometimes overlooked because they are the smallest minority ethnic group within the school. Unless there is someone available who speaks the Sylheti language and Mirpuri dialect, the language and dialect used by these pupils can remain unidentified for some considerable time by the school.

During the autumn term 1995 four Mirpuri and Sylheti bilingual assistants and two case work officers from the home–school links team talked to some of the mothers about their own personal experiences of education in Kashmir and Bangladesh. They were particularly interested in talking with the mothers as they found that it was the mothers who generally underestimated their role in their child's education. Some of the comments are given in Table 7.1.

Table 7.1 Mothers' comments

My memories of school in Bangladesh/Mirpur	What I think is most different about schools in Britain
'If we didn't do well enough we were made to do that year over again.'	'In the primary school the children just seem to play.'
'My father refused to pay for my education after my ninth birthday as the teacher said I was a slow learner.'	'They are not given enough homework.' 'The British teachers' life must be easy because they are just child minding, they are not teaching.'
'I learnt the ABC and the numbers 1–100 at five years old. I didn't understand what it meant though.'	'I think they learn things more slowly in Britain but they do understand what they are learning.'
'We were taught that it was impolite to have eye contact with our elders or those in authority.'	'The children here are encouraged to question the teachers. We could never do that.'
'The quick learners at school were given responsibility to teach the slow learners. Those who had difficulty learning were punished with the stick, with a detention or writing lines.'	'Here children aren't afraid when they are learning in school. They seem to enjoy it. I think it's better.'

A few weeks later the same home-school links staff conducted a small survey by listening to 30 Sylheti and 20 Mirpuri-speaking mothers talking about their involvement in their own child's school – see Table 7.2.

Table 7.2 Home–school links survey

Are there any reasons which prevent you from coming into your children's school? (Please tick)

	SYLHETI-SPEAKING MOTHERS %	MIRPURI-SPEAKING MOTHERS %
a) I work during the day	3	18
b) I have too much work to do in the home	53	55
c) I have a younger child/ren not yet at school	20	36
d) I speak very little English	27	73
e) Other members of my family speak English and talk to the teachers instead of me	3	91

Involvement of Sylheti- and Mirpuri-speaking parents in courses in three primary schools

The first school

The first school is an urban primary school with over 500 children on role of which 5 per cent of children are from Sylheti-speaking families. Over the years the school had been successful in running several Open College Network courses for parents. Some of the courses were open to all parents. Other courses were geared to attract parents from specific ethnic groups so that in one instance the Gujerati bilingual education assistant was made available to recruit and support Gujerati mothers who were anxious about their competency in the use of English. The African-Caribbean education assistant and the deputy headteacher together offered a course for the African-Caribbean parents and parents of dual-heritage children. Usually the recruitment for courses about the curriculum would focus on parents whose children attended a particular year group.

In October 1994 the school offered a course for Sylheti-speaking parents with children in the nursery and reception class. The course was delivered by an English teacher and a Sylheti-speaking bilingual education assistant.

That is to say that the initial content was delivered in English and translated with further explanations in Sylheti. Discussion took place in Sylheti and translated back into English. The course was called 'Parents and Learning' and aimed at explaining the components of a successful school. Of the seven mothers who began the course, one had a rudimentary understanding of English, the others spoke and understood very little English. None of them had any formal education. Their children's illnesses prevented three of them from attending every session. There were ten sessions in all. The final session focused on evaluating the course. The headteacher joined in for this and presented course attendance certificates.

The general consensus from the mothers was that they had enjoyed the course and were genuinely sorry that they had missed certain sessions. The mothers had completed most of the science, language and maths activities with their children at home. They were asked what their greatest fear had been when they embarked on the course. They said it was the fear of making a fool of themselves and being shown up by not being able to read and write Bangla as well as the English language. They said that they felt safer with a group of Sylheti speakers only. They were asked how the course could have been improved. The one who understood a little English said that she would have liked more practice writing English. The others said they would like to have started to learn English at the same time as learning about the school. They asked for the next course to be about disciplining children. One said and others agreed with her: 'My greatest fear is that my child will no longer respect me when my child's English becomes much better than mine'.

Summary of the school's strategy

The positive outcomes were that:
• the parents felt more confident learning alongside others with whom they closely identified;
• they were able to discuss complex issues in Sylheti that wouldn't have been possible in English.

On the negative side:
• there was pressure from their families for the women to concentrate their energies on learning English.

It is therefore recommended that courses should:
• combine learning English with learning about children;
• attempt to enable different Asian language groups to learn together so that the most isolated groups build confidence in mixing with others;
• encourage discussions to go on within separate language groups and English to be the main language used for delivery and recording key words and phrases.

As a result, materials have been prepared for the next course on 'Handling Children's Behaviour' within the context of learning to read and write English. In fact the next course was later delivered as one of the twice weekly English classes and included other Asian parents learning English. The Asian languages represented within the group of fifteen mothers were Malay, Gujerati, Urdu, Panjabi as well as Sylheti. All the mothers completed the course achieving OCN accreditation at Entry Level.

The second school

This school is another large urban primary school and has almost equal numbers of families who are English, Gujerati, Panjabi and fewer Mirpuri speakers. The staff were concerned that, although the majority of Mirpuri-speaking mothers would come to school to bring their children and some would attend their children's medical examinations, they were reluctant to discuss with the teacher their children's educational progress. The staff had always known that this was probably caused by the mothers' lack of confidence in their spoken English. The staff also found that the Mirpuri-speaking mothers were reticent to join the English class for adults and were also reticent to come into the nursery family sessions. The appointment of a Mirpuri-speaking bilingual education assistant certainly improved the communication between the staff and the parents. However, the early years staff particularly wanted to explain just how much parents can support their children's learning. A parental involvement programme was planned to operate from the second half of the spring term and to start with the nursery. By this stage in the academic year the nursery children had settled in to the routine and were less likely to be upset by any changes, however slight.

The school is now fortunate to have bilingual staff, or access to staff who can communicate with parents from each of the four main language groups. The Mirpuri-speaking mothers understandably tended to cluster together when bringing and collecting their children and they were by now comfortable conversing with the Mirpuri bilingual education assistant on a daily basis. An invitation to come into the nursery one afternoon a week for three successive weeks was offered to the Mirpuri-speaking mothers. During the afternoon sessions different activities were taking place where parents and children were encouraged to interact. The staff explained the educational value of the activities and how similar learning experiences could be tried out at home. The bilingual education assistant explained how she sold the idea to the parents. The dialogue tended to go as follows: 'Auntie-ji, please come in to the nursery next Wednesday afternoon, just for an hour. We're doing some cooking with the children and could do with your help. You can bring a friend'.

Initially, she said that there were protests from the mothers about too much work to do at home or having younger children who could not be left. However, after it was explained that the mothers would get a chance to see how their nursery children were progressing, they agreed. Most parents attended the three sessions. The nursery staff were pleased to answer their questions, such as, 'Is – mixing with the other children?', 'Does she talk in English or our language when she's here?', 'Does he do what he's told?'

The mothers were encouraged to take part in the activities. Where they preferred just to observe, this preference was respected. Although the school particularly targeted the mothers of the nursery children, fathers and grandparents and other relatives were also welcomed. The nursery staff invited parents from the English, Gujerati and Panjabi families in turn to attend similar nursery sessions.

Summary of the school's strategy

The positive outcomes were:
- the daily exchanges with the parents were now shared by all the staff and not only the bilingual assistant;
- the children's attitude towards their work changed. They took a more serious, interested approach, as though they were thinking, 'It's OK now that my mum approves of this';
- the mothers began to talk about the educational activities that they had been doing with their children at home.

On the negative side:
- the Mirpuri mothers didn't progress to becoming part of the parent and toddler group as did the other more confident groups.

Recommendations:
- take into consideration the timing of Ramadan in the year as this inevitably curtails the involvement of Muslim parents;
- greater explanation and encouragement needs to be given to the Mirpuri mothers regarding the benefits for pre-nursery children by attending the parent and toddler session.

The third school

Here the nursery class has a family session every Wednesday morning. Eighty per cent of their children are from families of Bangladeshi, Pakistani or Gujerati heritage. The majority faith is Islam. This urban primary school nursery class is particularly successful in its family session attendance. The Sylheti-speaking mothers, who had previously been reticent in attending, were encouraged by the presence of the newly appointed Sylheti-speaking bilingual education assistant in 1992. The family session is truly a family session. Some times as many as 30 parents, aunts, uncles, grandparents plus their preschool children come into the nursery. The nursery children are only allowed to attend if they are accompanied by an adult carer. Other younger siblings are also welcomed. Every week an activity for the adults is offered. The activities alternate from being adult centred to being child centred. For example, one Wednesday family session offers jewellery making. The next session might be about the educational value of children using paint to express their ideas, followed by sharing and cooking different traditional recipes.

The secret of the success in this family session is that no visiting adult is put under pressure. The monolingual staff concentrate upon engaging the children in stimulating activities; the bilingual staff focus on the parents/ carers. The latter may be in the activity corner or move between the other adults who may wish to sit and observe or chat in small groups with others who share the same home language. Some adults stay for as little as half an hour; some stay all morning. No one is ever made to feel that they must become involved in any activity which makes them feel uncomfortable. However, increasingly parents/carers do become more involved. Some parents have offered to share their own particular skills with others. At present the 'activity' corner is embarking upon an Open College Network ten-session craft course. The Sylheti parents are assured of moral support from the Sylheti bilingual education assistant should they feel they would like to take part.

Summary of school's strategy

The positive outcomes are that:
- the parents/carers feel confident to attend on their own terms. Within this non-threatening atmosphere adults are more likely to try out initiatives new to them;
- the more confident parents began to take the initiative to provide or suggest a tutor for the week's activity.

This cross-cultural skill-exchange continues to thrive.
On the negative side:
- the morning session is labour-intensive i.e. staff to look after the children (mostly pre-nursery age), bi-lingual staff to communicate with the parents/carers;
- the minority European white parents now rarely attend the morning family session as they feel marginalised.

Recommendations:
- to ensure staff make maximum effort to encourage families from all ethnic groups to attend;
- to capitalise on offers of extra staff such as work experience students to attend the family session to share some of the responsibility.

Conclusion

For parents to participate in the daily life of an early years' setting there must be real and obvious commitment from staff. It is not enough to use the rhetoric of parents as 'partners' in the education of their children. Some educators do use such phrases, and through using these words feel committed to them. In reality this is not always the case, and it is all too easy to neglect the most vulnerable and needy parents (Siraj-Blatchford 1994).

This chapter has emphasised the crucial role of a bilingual member of staff. Without doubt, this is one of the most effective factors in the involvement of minority ethnic families who are not confident in their use of English and their acceptance in an unfamiliar environment. The ideal is, of course, to employ appropriate qualified teachers who are themselves from minority ethnic families.

School budgets rarely enable immediate employment of bilingual staff to accommodate all the languages that the school requires. In this situation a helpful suggestion might be to cultivate and enlist the support of the most confident of the minority ethnic parents as volunteer home school link workers to encourage other parents (Karran 1985).

As well as employing bilingual staff, the school and nursery staff need to ensure that they consider the hidden messages that their classroom environment and practices transmit to the community that they serve.

> An atmosphere should be created where ethnic minority parents feel comfortable to come and interact with children and their educators. Home–school links are vital to this endeavour and can be promoted in a number of ways. Parents should have access to information about their child. Letters should be translated and efforts made to use interpreters with parents who are still learning English. Bilingual signs should be displayed around the classroom and outside it. Dual-language books and tapes should be displayed where they are easily accessible. Use can be made of a variety of multicultural resources offering positive images through such things as poster, play utensils, dolls, games, puzzles and music tapes. The curriculum on offer should also incorporate a variety of festivals, family life and art and craft materials. If the classroom resources and curriculum reflect the children's lives, the children are more likely to want to engage in and learn from the activities we provide.
>
> (Siraj-Blatchford 1994)

I would add that as this affects the learning process of minority ethnic children it also affects that of their parents.

If the Bangladeshi and Mirpuri communities are feeling isolated within Coventry's inner city, where there is a relatively high 19 per cent of Asian pupils in school, then account must be taken of the effect of isolation of the geographically scattered Asian families in the Coventry suburban schools. All the recommendations mentioned here have relevance for home–school liaison with minority ethnic groups generally.

Finally, courses which involve parents in the process of their children's learning have proved to be an ideal opportunity to create a teacher, parent and child partnership. Courses offer the school, and its parent groups of mixed ethnicity, the benefits of a rich intercultural and educational exchange. Parents and teachers are able to discuss issues, consider each others' concerns and bring about appropriately supportive changes both at school and in the home.

Summary of strategies which encourage the involvement of isolated groups of Asian parents in their child's learning

- Consider resources which acknowledge cultural heritage and language;
- outwardly value parents' skills as well as the skills of being a parent;
- provide access to an adult worker or volunteer who can share the same cultural identity and home language;
- offer activities, discussions and courses which address the important issue of children's education;

- offer opportunities to parents for improving their English literacy and oracy skills;
- offer parents practical activities to use at home with their child which complement the child's learning in class. (e.g. IMPACT maths). Check first on the cultural acceptability of the activity from an informed source;
- listen to concerns parents may have;
- be prepared to act upon suggestions made by parents.

References

Blackledge, A. (1994) *Teaching Bilingual Children.* Stoke-on-Trent: Trentham Books, p.58.

Karran, S. (1985) Volunteer Parent Home School Link Workers', *Outlines* **2**, CEDC, p.41.

Khan, S. (1985) *The Education of Muslim Girls.* Leeds: Leeds Community Education Council, p.33.

Siraj-Blatchford, I. (1994) *The Early Years: laying the foundations for the racial equality.* Stoke-on-Trent: Trentham Books, pp.51, 94, 95.

Chapter 8

Parents and practitioners: sharing education

Vicky Hurst and Jenefer Joseph

When we consider the relationship between parents and practitioners, the need for a developmental view of the curriculum is clear. In all but a very small proportion of families, parents (and carers who fulfil that role) are the agents who provide the context of each child's first learning. Writers such as Trevarthen (1993) and wide-ranging analyses of many research studies (e.g. the Carnegie Corporation of New York 1994) show the formative role of the parent's engagement with the child. This offers both the stimulus that presents the child with something new to deal with, and also the response which shapes the child's learning from the encounter. To give an example:

> Two babies, Eleanor and Mark, are cousins. Mark is 18 months old and Eleanor is three months. They live quite close to each other and to their grandmother, whose daughter is Eleanor's mother; and whose son is Mark's father. The grandmother is delighted to help the young families by caring for the children when she is free. She finds the babies fascinating in their differences and similarities. One thing that particularly interests her is that she can always calm and reassure Eleanor by singing to her the songs that she sang to her own children when they were little, but she has noticed that, at the same age and now, Mark's response is not the same. He responds to the songs and comfort strategies that his own mother and her mother use, which she herself, his paternal grandmother, has now learned. The babies have learned to be comforted in different ways.

Recent research such as that of the Carnegie Corporation (1994) shows that it is not only the particular kinds of initiative and response that parents use with their babies that are important, but rather the levels and suitability of the interaction. The closer the relationship between parent and child, the more likely it is that there is a good match between the communications of each side, and that the child's growing understanding, knowledge and skills are rooted in experience shared with the parents. Emotional well-being, which as we have shown affects learning, is also founded on the relationship between child and parent.

When it comes to educational and care settings outside the home, a new stage begins. There has to be an opening up of this parent and child world to other influences, and the practitioner has to learn something of what has gone on so far in order to help the child make a transition into the world beyond the familiar one.

We have to think what it means for the practitioner that parents are the first in the field with their influence on children's development and learning. We have to ask ourselves what it means for parents that they know the child best but that the practitioner has a responsibility for decisions about the child's learning. We need to reflect on what can happen when to this basic difference of responsibility is added a contrast of culture and experience of life. Working in partnership is not just about the two very different spheres of home and educational setting. It is also about people from different cultures learning to work together for the good of the child.

Human beings live in divided societies. People who appear to be different from the so-called mainstream are often looked down upon by members of the dominant group. Judgements by practitioners about parents as members of particular social groups or about parents as partners in their children's education, are sometimes based on beliefs about particular groups. If parents as individuals belong to groups that are not part of the dominant group in society, stereotyped views of such ethnic minority groups can affect how the parents are perceived and what the expectations are for their children. Decisions have to be made fairly, but also with sympathy.

> An African-Caribbean mother and father obtained a part-time place for their daughter Sarah in a nursery school, but they really wanted one of the full-time places that they knew were available. The head explained to them that only in real emergencies, such as illness at home or concern for the child's safety, were children allowed to go straight into a full-time place. These places, which were valued highly because they made it easier for parents to work, were usually offered after the child had spent one or two terms in a part-time place. Sarah's parents were upset because they needed both incomes to support the family, and another child was expected. The interview was rather an uncomfortable one.
>
> Later, Sarah's mother asked if she could leave Sarah until mid-afternoon on the days when she had to go to the clinic at the hospital, as she found it a strain looking after Sarah while she waited and during the examination. The head refused, explaining that while she could do this for one family, she could not do it for the many who would ask if they thought it was a possibility. Towards the end of the pregnancy the mother asked again, hesitantly. The head and another member of staff felt that the mother was tired and low in spirits, so it was agreed.
>
> On another occasion, a white mother living in bed and breakfast accommodation had her daughter in a part-time place (there were no full-time places) when her baby boy was born. The baby was suspected of having a genetic disorder and had to be taken to various hospital appointments. The mother explained she might not be able to bring her daughter every day because she could not collect her at the end of the morning. The head offered to keep her daughter with her between the part-time sessions and have lunch with her. Every day that the baby went to hospital, and every day for the following three months that it took the family to adjust to the care their son needed, the head and Stacey lunched together.

We often expect children and parents to be able to make do with what is offered to the main group, whatever their circumstances. It sometimes appears that the degree of conformity can determine whether family or individual shall have access to the rewards available. The same can be true on a much wider scale. Patterns of speech and pronunciation, private/local authority schooling, income, where one lives, skin colour, religion, family history, marital status and sexual orientation – all give signals to others about whether people are in a favoured group or not. We all need to guard against our prejudices and misconceptions.

This is the problem with having one stated version of what the curriculum should contain; it is not flexible enough to incorporate the perspectives of different groups. An example of this is the insistence in the National Curriculum Key Stage 1 history syllabus on retaining the story of Guy Fawkes as part of our heritage. It is a heritage, but it is a debatable one. For instance, it is a different heritage depending on whether families are bringing up their children in the Catholic faith or as Protestants. Furthermore, for those with other faiths and those with none it must be hard to tell what message is intended to be taken from this story of religious conflict, political unrest, conspiracy, betrayal and judicial torture followed by a hideous death.

There are also individuals in society who are not able to build a viable life for all sorts of reasons including illness, domestic disasters, unemployment and so on. People in these situations need and deserve as much help as possible, and their children's rights to an appropriate education must be upheld with particular care. High standards are vital; it has been shown that children are by no means destined for a life of failure, even when their early lives are full of difficulties and deprivations. What they need was clearly identified by a study based at the National Children's Bureau (Pilling 1990). She showed that, of a group of children from the most disadvantaged backgrounds of all, some children succeeded to a marked extent in later life in spite of their early disadvantages. The parents of the successful ones retained high ambitions for them and spent time with them, playing with them, reading to them, taking them to the park. Practitioners can help if they can find ways to show their appreciation and support for the relationship between parent and child, and if they can contribute their own understanding of what the parent is trying to do. However, as it is quality of relationships that is the crucial factor, practitioner intervention needs to be very sensitive to family relationships and situations, and to cultural differences.

Parental confidence is the key to much of their children's success (Pugh *et al.* 1994). What helps children to make a success of their lives is the value of good child-rearing at every level of society, and practitioners should show awareness of this at every stage of education. This can happen as long as we recognise the importance of not having one rigid picture of good child-rearing practices; we have to be culturally adaptable and respectful, with criteria for effectiveness based on children's progress.

Practitioners and parents sharing intentions

A young father, Chris, is pleased that his daughter Christina has made a smooth transition into the infant school from the nursery class. He and his wife have been teaching her to recognise her letters. The teacher has asked them not to use upper case only, but to show her lower case when it is appropriate. This is quite a surprise for the parents; they had assumed that they would start with all one kind of letter because it was easier, and that capitals were best because of the way that shop signs and names on packets of food are so often in capitals.

Chris is willing to follow the teacher's request, however. He appreciates that she has been trained in how to teach and that there will be differences between the way he and she see things. While his daughter was settling into the nursery class he noticed that there was little direct teaching going on, and a lot of learning through play. He says 'It wasn't the way I thought, at first, but now my wife has explained that the children are supposed to learn through doing, I can see the way the school is thinking.'

But there are also things that happen at home that would change the way the teacher sees this little girl if she knew about them. For instance, Chris is bilingual; he was born in Greece and speaks Greek with his parents and family friends. He would very much like to pass this inheritance on to his daughter, but he worries about her having to learn a language she cannot use in her daily life. 'There's a Saturday school attached to the church where my father goes...My mates try to teach their kids, but when I try and talk to them they don't seem to want to answer. One of them told me it was dead boring and she didn't see the point of it.'

Even if there was no other way to give support, the teacher could show her interest in Christina having a bilingual parent and be sure to include Greek in the languages and scripts available in the classroom. There might be other things she could do to help, like telling Greek stories among the folk tales and fairy-tales, and asking Christina to teach the other children Greek words for familiar people and objects.

Some might wonder how much difference it would make if the teacher knew about Chris's wish to teach Christina Greek. With all the other things she has to do, is it a good use of her time? Two significant aspects are:

1. Understanding of this part of the relationship between Christina and her father and grandfather is helpful at times when the teacher, Mrs S., wants to make a particular effort to help Christina feel at home in the classroom. It can also help with Christina's understanding of others who are or are not able to speak more than one language.
2. Sharing this part of their home life will help Chris and his wife feel more 'in tune' with Mrs S., and will make them feel that their perspectives on Christina are valued.

But the sharing of intentions and perspectives between parents and practitioners is not easy in a busy classroom. There has to be a rationale for it, and it needs links with a curriculum model which sets a value on children's experiences at home with family and friends. It requires just as much commitment as sharing intentions with children does.

Contacts with the home should be seen as a part of the curriculum, and a part of the practitioner's responsibility to provide for children's learning in ways that suit them. The first step is to consider what kind of contact with parents is most valuable, and to find out what kind of contact with the setting is needed by parents.

We have begun with practitioners' wishes for contact because there is a lot of work that may have to be done on their side before contacts, however much wished for, can be successful. Practitioners need to establish in themselves what they believe about home-setting partnership and how important they think contacts with parents are for their work. They also need to think about how to overcome barriers that may be causing some parents to hold back. Comments such as 'these parents wouldn't really understand' show that sometimes practitioners feel completely out of their depth in relating to parents; this can happen for all sorts of reasons and is a definite sign that something is going very wrong. Similarly, 'You only see the parents of the good children – you never see the ones you really want to see' is a warning that the children who most need help are getting the least. Somehow barriers must be overcome, and differences made into a source of strength.

In the early years, home and community culture are extremely influential on learning and children do not leave their culture behind them as they come in through the doors of the setting. This gives practitioners the challenge of planning a curriculum that embraces children's culture and draws on its strengths. Perhaps the most demanding task practitioners face is to make links for children between their current understanding and knowledge and the more advanced learning that the practitioner wishes them to progress to. We have described already the difficulties presented by a curriculum which seeks to be standardised and is therefore not able to reflect the experiences and cultures of minority groups. A curriculum with its aims set out in broader and more flexible terms would make it easier for early years practitioners to draw in all their children. However, it is also the task of the practitioner to be flexible and creative in interpreting the requirements of the existing curriculum and adapting it to children's circumstances. Nothing makes the case for well-educated practitioners more obvious. In the end, it is the quality of practitioners' understanding of the nature of the different subject disciplines that determines how well they do this, just as it is the quality of their understanding of child development and of the children as individuals that determines how they construct and implement the curriculum as a whole so as to give all children the opportunities for learning that they need.

Practitioners need to know the children and to understand enough of their cultures to be able to construct an appropriate curriculum. This is where they gain one great benefit from contacts with parents and where the parents also have much to gain since, while practitioners are learning what they need to know, they are also sharing information about how they work, which is invaluable to parents when they help their children at home. However, for these contacts to take place, time is needed, whether for home visits or for conferences in the setting. Parents and practitioners need time to talk together because the educational value of these contacts is clear. The setting will gain from sharing such concerns as:

I worry about underestimating children when they are so young and come from a great range of different backgrounds and experiences.

I need their help with monitoring progress.

I can learn a great deal from the parents, who have known the child from birth.

The closer the partnership the more consistency of handling for the child – we can share our intentions for children's behaviour.

The child needs to feel secure, that parents and practitioners are working together.

Parents need to know what goes on in the setting in order not to be panicked by political or media manipulation.

It helps parents to make judgements about the quality of what is provided by the setting if they have real experience of what happens in their child's class or group.

Parents have a lot to offer to the setting; not just any special talent, but just as ordinary supportive adults who will tell or read a story, chat to children, help with puzzles, share games and work with children generally.

Practitioners may not be the victims of society's prejudices against particular groups, yet they may be resistant to sharing their professional domain with parents. Practitioners may be understandably concerned about encroachments on their area of responsibility. The meaning of professionalism is that you have an area of expertise which is acknowledged as being highly specialized, and rightly so. Lawyers, doctors and architects are in the same position. All professionals have to ask themselves two questions:

1. To what extent is it right for me to share my specialised knowledge, for which I received many years of training by experts? Would it weaken or dangerously undermine the real value and meaning of this knowledge if I shared a small area of it with those who did not have access to an informed starting point?
2. If it *is* right, to what extent can I convey this knowledge to others in such a way that they can use it to make informed decisions for themselves or their children?

In the case of practitioners, it is appropriate to explain and share as much as possible because it is best for the child, who is their professional responsibility. Unlike a lawyer, they depend on the parents of their 'client' to support their professional intentions. But it is not easy to explain all the professional issues, and we have to help practitioners to become better able to articulate their work to parents and others.

But these are not the only issues at stake. There is a question which is even more important and which should come before the others. The care and education of young children is personally sensitive. As in many other professions, early years practitioners need to have good ongoing relationships with the families (parents and children) and a constant flow of communication between themselves and parents. How is this to be fostered and shaped to include what both sides need to share and to know? There is much information that practitioners can only have access to through parents, and they need practical ways in which to learn it – occasions for easy exchanges of view. It is important also that parents share just as much as they feel able to; practitioners must be careful not to exercise pressure or push people in directions that are not suitable or even possible for them. Conversely, practitioners need to be able to hear and understand parents' communications when they do happen, and it may be personally quite challenging to respond appropriately.

The following example illustrates both the nature of the partnership between practitioners and parents, and how a structure based on respect for the parent–child relationship can support it.

The nature of partnership in education in the early years

Life is one long transition for the under-6s; if parents do not offer constant well-informed support, who else can do this job? Sometimes parents are in serious trouble and need support themselves. The setting can help them and be a kind of buffer area for parent and child without turning the relationship into a social-work one. Sensitivity and self-awareness are essential for this (Whalley 1994: 28–33).

> Adam was 5 when his parents parted, after some very painful months. Soon his mother was dealing with his sense of rejection, his anger and his grief. His outbursts were hard to contain, and his behaviour deteriorated in other ways too, becoming very distractible and aimless. His mother asked his teacher whether he showed any signs of disturbance at school, but apparently there were none. She felt that the teacher and headteacher did not understand how serious the problem was; the head told her that a firm hand was all he needed. After a few days with no improvement she sought help through her doctor and was referred to a local hospital's child guidance clinic. Gradually, Adam's behaviour at home improved. It therefore came as a bombshell to learn a few weeks later that the school was now experiencing the same behaviour that had so concerned her, and that if it did not improve they felt that they would have to exclude the child. His level of achievement had dropped, and he was falling behind the other children in his work. His mother did her best to get Adam to behave at school, and somehow he came through the behaviour difficulties in the end, but she felt very let down by the way the problem had been handled. She felt strongly that if the school had taken Adam's difficulties seriously when she first reported them there could have been a joint approach instead of a fragmented one which seemed to give him little sense of consistency and prolonged his unhappiness. It had also caused him to miss several months of his schooling and to have a sense of himself as a failure. Over a year later she was oppressed by a sense that Adam had been failed when he most needed help.

Ways and means

Children and parents can go through very difficult times together in the early years, and practitioners can do much to help or hinder them. How can we help practitioners to help parents? We have to recognise that practitioners need proper training, and they need a pedagogy that accepts the importance of understanding children's development. At present, the model of the curriculum that practitioners have to work with does not do this, and the training of intending teachers marginalises child development and assigns the role of customer to parents. It is to be hoped that before long, a new understanding of the care and education of such young and emotionally vulnerable children will permit practitioners to work with the support of a curriculum that is founded on child development theory as well as on subject knowledge.

Then, perhaps, intending teachers will have time in their courses for developmental approaches to learning, and for sessions and practical experience devoted to how to work side by side with parents. Perhaps this will help them to understand the experiences that all parents share, whatever their culture, and to find ways to assign equal importance to the developmental concerns of each child and family in spite of the great differences that there are between them.

References

Carnegie Corporation of New York (1994) *Starting Points: Meeting the Needs of our Youngest Children*. New York: Carnegie Corporation.

Pilling, D. (1990) *Escape from Disadvantage*. Lewes: Falmer.

Pugh, G., De'Ath, E. and Smith, C. (1994) *Confident Parents, Confident Children*. London: National Children's Bureau.

Trevarthen, C. (1993) *Playing into Reality: Conversations with the Infant Communicator*. Winnicott Studies, No. 7, Spring 1993: 67–84. London: Karnak Books Ltd.

Whalley, M. (1994) *Learning to be Strong: Setting up a Neighbourhood Service for Under-Fives and their Families*. London: Hodder and Stoughton.

Chapter 9

'I can sing a rainbow': parents and children under three at Tate Britain, London

Roger Hancock with Alison Cox

Museums and their visitors

In recent years many museums and galleries have endeavoured to become more inviting to a wider group of visitors, including families (West 1998; Hooper-Greenhill 1999; Cox *et al.* 2000). A cluster of factors has contributed to this change.

For instance, along with other publicly funded institutions, museums now need to demonstrate 'value for money'. Equal opportunities legislation has led to an increased awareness of the need to promote access for people with disabilities, but also those who feel that museums are not for them. There are now many more education posts in museums and those who interpret these posts are tending to work across audiences, rather than focus mainly on school groups. Museums are also being asked to support the policy objective of 'life-long' learning (Jones 1999; Anderson 1999; Aspin 2000). A report on the role of museums 'in the learning age' states:

> If museums are to be effective as educational institutions, they must provide opportunities for all who might use them to learn at every stage of their educational development from early childhood to old age.
>
> (Anderson 1999: 69)

With regard to teaching and learning, the methods for helping people to engage with art works are much more varied. Formal lectures are less common and interactive approaches are more in evidence. There is encouragement too for visitors to express their own thoughts and ideas and to develop personalised ways of looking and understanding (see Baldwin 1997).

Tate Britain and families

Tate Britain has, for many years, been very active in the area of educational projects for schools and community groups. Recently, Tate's Interpretation and Education Department has promoted family activities and events and developed ways of helping very young children to engage with what the gallery has to offer. Accommodating to the needs of this specific group of users in a gallery environment has been a challenging brief.

It was in 1996 that Tate Britain first explored the idea of running workshops for parents and children under three – sessions that would enable both children and adults to enjoy and learn from being in a gallery. These were run in conjunction with Pimlico Family Workshop, a local community project with experience of promoting family learning and working with very young children. Following the success the 1996 pilot session, further parent and child workshops were run during 1997 and 1998. It was in 1999 that 'Big and Small; Short and Tall', a series of eight Friday morning workshops, was conceived and well received by the 46 parents and children who attended (Hancock and Cox 2001).

These eight workshops drew upon a format that had been evolving over time. Each of the 'Big and Small' workshops had a two-part structure whereby music and movement activities in an art room would precede a group visit to the gallery. This served to help parents and children feel welcomed and relaxed, and also enabled the workshop leaders to introduce a theme that would relate to the selected gallery exhibits. Once in the gallery, parents and children would look at the art works and, sitting on the gallery floor, work on a practical activity linked to an exhibit. The distinctive nature of the workshops lay with the fact that they involved parents and children learning together but also aimed to promote parent interest in art and artists.

Parent feedback suggested that this dual intention was, to a considerable extent, achieved. Although parents were asked to stay close to their children and work collaboratively with them, many felt they were also able to engage with the gallery as adult learners.

The set of workshops that comprised Big and Small was evaluated through end-of-session parent questionnaires and telephone interviews with a number of parents. Further details on the evaluation and, particularly, parents' experiences and views about the workshops, are to be found in Hancock and Cox (2002).

Much arises from the workshops that is of interest to early education practice. For instance, there are issues related to:

- the structures, interactions and experiences that enable children to learn;
- children's engagement with art works, ways of looking and 'meaning-making' in a gallery;
- the nature and purposes of children's artistic achievements;
- the most effective ways of helping children and parents to 'learn in tandem';
- the inclusion of very young children in public places;
- the selection and presentation of art materials for children.

The main focus of this chapter, however, is the nature of the partnership that was established between the workshop leaders and the parents and carers who attended with their children. This is revealed in the following portrayal of the first of the eight Big and Small workshops. The portrayal invites the reader into the 'inner life' of 'I can sing a rainbow', so named because it focused on the themes of colour, line, and shape.

'I can sing a rainbow'

It's Friday morning. The art room has been prepared to receive parents and children. There are paints, coloured papers, pencils and scissors. In one corner there's tea, coffee and lemonade. A mother and her son are the first to come. She looks relaxed. She knows roughly what will happen during the morning. She and Mirak attended a previous programme. He walks around on his own, looking, touching and exploring.

Annie Smuts, a workshop leader from Pimlico Family Workshop, passes Mirak's mother a clear plastic bag that comes from the gallery shop. The mother works with her son to cut out armholes so that it can be used as a protective smock when he does some painting. Kate Bagnall, another workshop leader, also from Pimlico Family Workshop, stands nearby talking to Mirak.

Four other parents have just arrived. One carries a baby, two walk in with toddlers and one pushes a buggy with her sleeping daughter. They are welcomed by Kate and Annie who offer white stickers and felt pens for names. Kate talks to the newcomers whilst Annie works with Alison Cox, Education Curator, to lay out materials and make finishing touches to the resource trays that will be needed later in the gallery itself.

It's now ten o'clock, the time when the workshop is scheduled to start, but parents and children are still arriving. The session has already begun for a number of parents and children. There's a lot of excited talk, questions, movement and greetings. All the children are under three years old, the oldest, Mirak, is 2 years and 10 months.

Emma, undisturbed, continues sleeping in her buggy. Other children stay close to their parents. Two children walk around the room with confidence – they have their own ideas about what they want to do. Many of the parents don't know each other. Mainly they stay close to their children attending to their needs. They help them remove their coats, answer their questions, provide drinks from bags and rucksacks, point to things in the room, write out names and stick the labels on their chests – which some children immediately peel off!

After ten minutes or so Annie and Kate ask everyone to sit on the floor in a circle. Most children are with their parents. The sleeping child, Emma, has woken up and joins her mother. The two 'independent' children, Mirak and Susie, continue with their own activities, occasionally looking to see what the larger group is doing.

Annie welcomes everyone to the first of a series of eight Friday workshops for parents and children under three. Today's workshop is called, 'I can sing a rainbow'. Kate asks the parents to introduce the adult and child to their left. It's a good way of interacting and learning some names. Kate introduces the morning's theme and talks briefly about the many different sorts of shapes and colours. She then leads the group into an action song that gets everyone thinking about shapes as they sit on the floor. Some children are a little taken aback, somewhat surprised at the way in which most of the group is singing in unison. The youngest, Timothy, who is just a few months old, is a member of this audience. His gaze reveals an engagement and his attention is held for the complete duration of the song.

This is followed by an activity involving movement around the room and then some music and movement with everyone dancing and trailing coloured chiffon scarves in the air. By this time, most of the children are participating with the adults. There's much fun and laughter.

Jane Elliott, a workshop leader and artist, talks about the next stage of the morning. She briefly mentions how the selected works of art will relate to the workshop 'rainbow' theme. She also talks to parents about safety in the gallery and their responsibility for their own children. She explains that if a child becomes unsettled or unhappy parents are free to take them for a walk or return to the art room for a while.

Kate and Annie lead everyone out of the room through a number of gallery areas and then to the first chosen exhibit, Eileen Agar's 'The Autobiography of an Embryo'. The group sits on the floor facing the painting. Jane quickly captures parent and child interest by talking with them about circles and making links to Agar's painting. By asking questions, and encouraging the group to notice, select and point at various elements, she focuses their attention and encourages participation. To reinforce what has been discovered in the painting, she invites the group to produce circle pictures from brightly coloured paper. Within minutes the parents and children are busily talking, cutting, tearing and sticking circles onto pastel coloured sheets of paper.

Figure 9.1 Parents were essential to the success of the workshop

Sometimes it's the parents who are cutting and children who are placing and sticking the circles – a division of labour. Sometimes there's an overlap of involvement with, for instance, parents holding the paper while children use the scissors to begin to cut the shape which is completed by the parent. Whatever the arrangement, there's clearly value in all forms of collaboration. In particular, there's much discussion about what is being done.

The buzz of activity, the chattering children, and the novel nature of the group, attract the interest of other gallery visitors who pass by. Their faces show delight at seeing such young visitors engaged in an activity that is related to a celebrated exhibit. Secondary pupils file past. They too are surprised to see the busy young visitors.

Jane announces that it's time to move on. Parents and children gather up their pictures and materials, put them into the red trays that have been provided and make their way further into the gallery.

They arrive in a room with a high ceiling where larger art works are displayed. Jane encourages the group to stand close together in a semi-circle so that they can hear her voice. She is in front of 'The Snail' by Henri Matisse. The children stand by their parents. Jane suggests that they point to the black rectangular shape at the top of the picture. 'Move your finger anti-clockwise to the next colour, then to the next, and the next,' she says. Most of the parents follow her suggestion. Some children are doing it too; others prefer to watch the actions of others, made curious by some unexpected adult behaviour. Susie prefers to explore a corner of the room. Most of the group is now making a circular 'shell-like' movement in the air with their fingers.

The activity reveals the way Matisse has unusually chosen to evoke a snail – through the arrangement of a small number of angular, coloured shapes which don't, at first sight, appear to suggest a snail at all. Some of the parents are intrigued by Jane's demonstration. They enjoy the element of adult education that has just been introduced.

Once it becomes clear that there is a pattern to being in the gallery, i.e. finding an art work, looking at it, sitting down and talking about it together, the children find it easier to respond and settle.

Following Jane, the group moves to another room. She asks everyone to sit in front of 'Pompeii' by Hans Hofmann. 'Pompeii' encourages exploration of square and rectangular shapes. This work has been chosen to contrast with 'The Snail'. Here the shapes are brick-like, vertical and horizontal, the paint heavily textured. In the second activity, parents and children quickly get down to work – selecting colours, cutting and sticking. Annie and Kate take it in turns to hold baby Timothy. This enables his mother to spend time looking at 'Pompeii' and work on a picture herself.

One or two children decide they want to do other things. Susie paces along a ventilation floor grille that spans most of the room – she likes the feeling of the metal on her feet. Gerry is rolling on his back looking at the small halogen spotlights on the ceiling. Suresh is sucking his thumb as he sits beneath a sculpture plinth displaying Picasso's 'Head of a Woman (Fernande)'. Jemma is weepy – perhaps she needs the refreshments that await her in the art room.

Jane indicates that it's time to return to the art room. The group makes its way back through the gallery rooms looking at art works as they go. It's just after 11.00 and Tate is beginning to get busy. The crocodile of parents, children and workshop leaders attracts glances and smiles from others in the gallery.

Figure 9.2 A moment of 'spontaneous looking' when moving through the gallery

Gradually, the group arrives at the art room and Annie and Kate offer drinks and biscuits. Alison has laid out tables and paints for a final picture-making activity which is linked to the shapes and colours that have been explored in the gallery. Parents and children sit at the tables together and soon enjoy using the thick, deeply coloured mixes for their final creation. This activity lasts some twenty minutes. Most of the children are very engaged and many are wearing their makeshift 'Tate Shop bag' aprons.

It's approaching 12.00 noon. The parents and children begin to finish off their paintings and respond to the workshop leaders' invitation to form a circle on the carpet. It's time for a closing activity. Annie and Kate lead them through two action songs. The last one is the tried and tested 'Ring a Ring o' Roses' and it's a resounding success with everyone.

Some children are ready to go home; some would like to stay longer. As they leave a number of parents call out 'see you next week'.

Discussion and conclusion

On the face of it, the nature of the practitioner–parent partnership between the workshop leaders and the parents and carers who accompanied the children, could be seen as fairly straightforward. Parents brought their children to the eight workshops and joined in with them. However, at another level, it was apparent that something significant took place in terms of the way in which parents participated.

The workshop leaders had a range of experience and professional skills to bring to their work. One was an artist-educator. Another was an education curator responsible for setting up family and school programmes at Tate Britain. And two were used to running Pimlico Family Workshop activities for pre-school children and parents. However, despite this, it was clear that the success of 'I can sing a rainbow' (and the other seven workshops that were provided) depended, to a considerable extent, on parental willingness to work closely with the leaders and their own children.

Parents were thus essential 'workshop assistants' who took on the responsibility of drawing children into the collective activities of the larger group. Parents sang, danced, painted, sat on the gallery floor, and made things in collaboration with their children. In many ways, they acted as though they were older children taking the lead – 'interpreting' the workshop leaders' suggestions where necessary, and fostering children's participation when this was needed.

Although the leaders encouraged this parental support through the inclusive way in which they ran the workshops, this partnership role was not made explicit. Most parents found they could enter intuitively into it because the situation required it, and there was a strong sense that children would benefit much more if they did this.

With such a young group of children – the oldest were not yet three and the youngest were only a few months old – it would not have been possible for the leaders to run the workshops, in the way they did, without establishing this form of partnership. Parents were therefore vital 'intermediaries' in terms of enabling young children to be in a public gallery, and in terms of increasing the likelihood that children would enjoy it and learn from it.

The structure of the workshops, and particularly the parental involvement dimension, thus provided a supportive and productive milieu for the children. The workshops enabled an unusual group of gallery visitors to be in a place where many would not normally have been – 'a temple built for the worship of art' (Newhouse 1998). Big and Small; Short and Tall therefore serves to give salient messages about what can be achieved when practitioners and parents work in interdependent ways to promote children's early education.

Acknowledgements

The authors wish to thank Jane Elliott, artist-educator, and Kate Bagnall and Annie Smuts from Pimlico Family Workshop, for providing the practice that forms the basis of this chapter.

Both photographs are the copyright of Tate Photography Department.

References

Anderson, D. (1999) *A Common Wealth: Museums in the Learning Age, A Report to the Department for Culture, Media and Sport.* London: The Stationery Office.

Aspin, D. (2000) Lifelong learning: the mission of arts education in the learning community of the 21st century, *Music Education Research* **2** (1), 75–85.

Baldwin, B. (1997) *Looking into the Tate: exciting ways to explore the Tate Gallery's collection.* London: Tate Gallery Publishing.

Cox, A., Lamb, S., Orbach, C. and Wilson, G. (2000) *A shared experience: a qualitative evaluation of family activities at three Tate sites.* London: Tate Modern.

Hancock, R. and Cox, A. (2002) 'I would have worried about her being a nuisance': workshops for children under three and their parents at Tate Britain, *Early Years* **22** (2), 97–110.

Hancock, R. and Cox, A. (2001) *Big and Small; Short and Tall:* an evaluation of workshops for parents and pre-school children at Tate Britain. London: Tate Britain Interpretation and Education Department.

Hooper-Greenhill, E. (ed.) (1999) *The Educational Role of the Museum.* London: Routledge.

Jones, T. (1999) Art and lifelong learning, *Journal of Art and Design Education* **18** (1), 135–42.

Newhouse, V. (1998) *Towards a New Museum.* New York: Monacelli Press.

West, L. (1998) *Micro Gallery; Macro Discovery,* unpublished MA dissertation. London: Institute of Education.

Part 2
Curriculum and practice

Jane Devereux

Introduction

The introduction of the National Curriculum for primary and secondary schools in England and Wales in 1988 brought about changes in the control and regulation of educational settings in these countries. Centrally imposed directives such as Standard Attainment Tests (SATs) for children age 7 and the publication of leagues tables, brought about significant changes in primary schools which gradually impacted on early years settings. In 1996 in England the curriculum became more closely linked to the curriculum in primary schools; consequently many early years practitioners experienced the 'downward pressure' of these changes as they felt the need to 'prepare' children for the next stage of education. This had a uniting and motivating effect on the early childhood community to protect the fundamental principles of early years educational practice. The resulting Foundation Stage curriculum introduced in 2000, for children aged three to the end of reception year and the new framework for working with under-threes, provided a response to the concerns generated by the developments described above.

The second part of this book begins by exploring, from the perspective of authorities in all four countries of the United Kingdom (UK), the similarities and differences between the early years curriculum guidance provided. The chapter by Linda Miller, Joyce Hughes, Ann Roberts, Liz Paterson and Lesley Staggs endorses the importance of early years education, of play and of the shared principles which underpin the published curriculum documents in the four countries. The next chapter explores five examples of different approaches to early years curricula – Steiner, Montessori, Schema, Te Whaariki in New Zealand and Reggio Emilia in Italy. The authors, Linda Miller, Jane Devereux, Alice Paige-Smith and Janet Soler suggest that looking at other approaches provides practitioners with different ways of positively looking at their own practice (Moss 1999).

Angela Anning and Anne Edwards's chapter, 'Language and literacy learning', considers the benefits of a holistic approach to young children's development.

Through their research with practitioners, they describe their concerns about the emphasise being placed on academic development at an increasingly early age, influenced by government initiatives. They stress the need to emphasis children's social, emotional and physical development alongside their academic achievements. The next two chapters explore aspects of play. The first by Lesley Abbott, 'Play is fun, but it's hard work too!' uses a case study in a reception class to examine the crucial elements and key features of quality play. She identifies factors such as the role of the practitioner, the nature of provision, support given to children, space and time and the opportunity to explore and investigate ideas and materials. Ruth Holland's chapter 'What's it all about?' describes the nature of heuristic play, through observations of very young children playing with and exploring objects and materials. She raises some fundamental concerns about the nature of play and the importance of providing time for children to explore.

The last two chapters in this section continue the theme of curriculum and practice by looking at two different aspects of provision in different settings. The first considers how children develop as 'Great communicators' and the second explores how their creativity can be developed and supported as they grow. Marian Whitehead's chapter describes the roles of parents, practitioners and provision in supporting children's developing communication and language skills. She also describes the stages that children pass through as these skills develop. The chapter provides a sound introduction to early communication and language that is steeped in practice. Bernadette Duffy's chapter on creativity gives a brief introduction to the nature of creativity before exploring in some breadth and depth, ways of developing and supporting creativity across the curriculum in early years settings. It encourages practitioners to reflect on and develop their own role in supporting creativity in individual children.

References

Moss, P. (1999) *Difference, Dissensus and Debate: some possibilities of learning from Reggio.* Stockholm: Reggio Emilia Institutet.

Chapter 10

Curricular guidance and frameworks for the early years: UK perspectives

Linda Miller, Joyce Hughes, Ann Roberts, Liz Paterson and Lesley Staggs

Introduction

The curriculum is something that early years practitioners work with every day; both the formal curriculum and the informal curriculum that operates throughout early years settings. In this chapter we are concerned with curriculum as outlined in published documents, which are designed to lead towards particular educational aims and goals. For many years, early years practitioners in the four countries of Scotland, Northern Ireland, Wales and England, had their own approach to curricula, although Local Education Authorities (LEAs) often produced guidance for nursery settings maintained by them. In many settings such as playgroups, child minders or day care settings, the curriculum was not written down, which meant that these settings were not formally accountable to outside agencies and stakeholders such as the inspectorate or parents and carers. The lack of a shared curriculum framework also led to children in different settings encountering diverse approaches to their learning and teaching. This raised issues about curricular entitlement and equality of opportunity for all children and made settings vulnerable and open to criticism.

Bennett (2001) argues that a written curriculum helps practitioners to clarify their teaching aims, keep progression in mind, provide a structure to the child's day and helps to focus on the more important aspects of child development. A curriculum can also be an indicator of belonging to a professional group with recognised responsibilities. The Organisation for Economic Cooperation and Development (OECD) review of early childhood education and care in twelve countries noted that there is a growing acceptance of goals and curriculum in the early childhood field. All countries featured in the review set national objectives which included subject areas and learning and developmental goals for young children, although curricula varied in relation to the degree of explicitness and directivity (Bennett 2001).

The debate about early years curricula

During the 1990s all four countries of the United Kingdom (UK) introduced published curriculum frameworks or guidance documents for children aged 3 to 5. Each of these documents covered broad areas of learning that showed links to the curriculum in primary schools. This development extended the debate about what kinds of learning are appropriate for young children. In England the publication of centralised curricular guidance for four year olds (DfEE/SCAA 1996) highlighted tensions between practitioners' perspectives on young children's needs and the 'top down' pressures that a centralised approach to meeting government agendas may bring to bear on early years settings. The demands of the primary school curriculum and concerns about national standards of literacy and numeracy led to more formalised practices in some early childhood settings and fuelled the debate about the pre-school period as 'preparation for school' (David and Nurse 1999, Miller 2000, Anning and Edwards 1999). These concerns have been addressed through the development of the Foundation Stage curriculum guidance (QCA/DfES 2000) as discussed later in this chapter.

In Wales the introduction of a Foundation Stage for children aged 3 to 7 is part of a move to ensure that the early years curriculum does not lead to formal approaches to learning. The Northern Ireland pre-school guidance stresses that there is no place at this stage of education for the introduction of formal education (CCEA 1997). In Scotland the early years curriculum is not seen as preparation for school and formalised practices are considered to be inappropriate (Paterson 2001, personal communication). In all four countries, while recognising the need for guidance to take account of the transition to primary school, concerns about formal learning too soon have been strongly acknowledged.

The early years curriculum in the four countries of the UK

In the following sections an authority from each of the four UK countries offers their perspective on the early years curriculum in that country. In Northern Ireland, Joyce Hughes, Principal Officer in the Northern Ireland Council for the Curriculum, Examinations and Assessment (CCEA) describes 'Curricular Guidance for Pre-School Education' (CCEA 1997; Hughes 2000). Ann Roberts, former Development Officer for Wales for the British Association for Early Childhood Education writes about the 'Desirable Outcomes for Children's Learning Before Compulsory School Age' (QCAAW 2000; Roberts 2000). Liz Paterson, Principal Curriculum Officer in Learning and Teaching, Scotland reports on 'Curriculum Framework for Children 3 to 5' (SCCC 1999). In England, Lesley Staggs, Senior Adviser at the Department for Education and Skills outlines the development of the 'Curriculum guidance for the foundation stage' (QCA/DfES 2000; Staggs 2000).

Curricular Guidance for Pre-School Education: Northern Ireland

In Northern Ireland all children have seven years of compulsory primary education, with children starting school in September if their fourth birthday falls on or before 1st July of that year. Some children can, therefore, begin their pre-school year when they are as young as three years and two months old, and move into primary education when they are just over four years of age.

There are no early learning goals in Northern Ireland. Rather, pre-school centres follow 'Curricular Guidance for Pre-School Education' (CCEA 1997). This document, in addition to giving guidance on promoting good practice, sets out the curriculum under seven areas:

- Personal, Social and Emotional Development
- Physical Development
- Creative/Aesthetic Development
- Language Development
- Early Mathematical Experiences;
- Early Experiences of Science and Technology
- Knowledge and Appreciation of the Environment.

These areas show links with the present Northern Ireland Curriculum for primary schools and are consistent with Northern Ireland Nursery Guidelines issued in 1989. The guidance describes the importance of each curricular area, and the opportunities and experiences that children should be given in the respective areas. It also contains a holistic description of the anticipated progress in learning that the majority of children will have made by the end of their pre-school year.

The Northern Ireland Curriculum is currently under review and one proposal presently under consultation is that children should spend their first year of primary school developing their dispositions to learn, their confidence and self-esteem and the ability to think for themselves and to show initiative. The second year would be a transition into more formal learning. The evidence for the benefits of this approach is supported by research, including research into how children's brains develop (Gopnik *et al.* 1999). We know that children's social and emotional development is vital to their success in later life and that young children are sensitive to feelings of failure. Therefore forcing children into formal learning too early can have a lasting effect on their whole education (Mills and Mills 1998).

This less formal curriculum is being piloted in a number of primary schools across Northern Ireland. Research has been commissioned to track the progress of children in twelve of the pilot schools over a four-year period. Initial reports from the researchers are very positive, with children showing increased confidence, independence, concentration and creativity. There is also early indication of marked improvement in children's oral language development (Sproule *et al.* 2001/2002).

Desirable Outcomes for Children's Learning Before Compulsory School Age: Wales

In Wales a Foundation Stage for children age 3 to 7 is to be introduced and the curriculum is being rewritten. It will however follow the principles highlighted in the current framework 'The Desirable Outcomes for Children's Learning' (QCAAW 2000). The discontinuation of league tables for schools and standard assessment tests for seven year olds are part of a move to avoid a 'downward pressure' into pre-school settings and to make the early years curriculum less formal. Jane Davidson, the Welsh minister for education and lifelong learning, is keen to ensure links between the childcare agenda and the early years agenda and plans to ensure that by September 2004 a part time place will be available for all three year olds (Barton 2002).

The Qualifications, Curriculum and Assessment Authority for Wales (QCAAW) (Awdurdod Cymwysterau, Curriculum ac Asesu Cymru) (ACCAC) first published the Desirable Outcomes guidance in 1996. It has since been re-issued following consultation with teachers and other education professionals during a review of the National Curriculum in Wales. Presentation of the document has changed but the content remains the same, reflecting the views of those consulted.

The document provides practitioners with guidelines for a curriculum framework appropriate for 3 and 4 year olds in a variety of settings across six areas of learning. These are:

- Language, literacy and communication skills
- Personal and social development
- Mathematical development
- Knowledge and understanding of the world
- Physical development
- Creative development.

It takes account of the best practice in Wales in pre-compulsory education and there is an emphasis on the process of learning. The importance of play is highlighted, as is the need for well-structured and purposeful activities. Play is seen as crucial to the development of self awareness, of learning the rules of social behaviour and for intellectual development. Early years professionals in Wales acknowledge that children learn most effectively when they are actively involved in first-hand experiences. The role of the adult is to help children to guide their play, to offer choices and also sensitive challenges so that their learning progresses. Early education is centred on the child; it requires adults to understand, challenge and inspire the child's talent to learn. 'The Desirable Outcomes for Children's Learning' document is written in both Welsh and English. Uniquely in Wales, the document requires all under-fives to be given opportunities to hear about Wales, about their locality, about customs, names, myths and legends and about people and events. This is referred to as the Curriculum Cymreig or Welsh Curriculum and forms part of a rewarding and lively learning experience that allows children in Wales to have their understanding of day-to-day life enhanced.

Curriculum Framework for Children 3 to 5: Scotland

In Scotland children under the age of five have access to a wide range of early education provision. Nursery classes, nursery schools, private partner provider establishments and playgroups offer a minimum of five two and a half hour sessions a week for three and four year olds funded by the Scottish Executive Education Department (SEED), but these places are not statutory. Funded provision can also be offered in other registered settings such as childminders and day nurseries. Children are admitted to compulsory education when they have reached the age of five in the February following the start of the school term in the previous August.

In 1997 at the beginning of the expansion of pre-school education 'A Curriculum Framework for Children in their Pre-School Year' (SCCC 1997) was commissioned by the Scottish Executive (at that time the Scottish Consultative Council for the Curriculum, now Learning and Teaching Scotland). As expansion progressed for three-year-olds it was necessary to consider widening the scope of the original curriculum guidelines to accommodate the learning styles of the younger child. Local authorities now have a duty to make a free part-time education place available for all Scotland's three- and four-year-olds. Therefore in 1999 'A Curriculum Framework for Children 3–5' (SCCC 1999) was produced and implemented throughout all provision in Scotland.

The principles that underpin the curriculum are:

- The best interests of children
- The central importance of relationships
- The need for all children to feel included
- An understanding of the ways in which young children learn.

There are five key aspects of children's development and learning:

- Emotional, personal and social development
- Communication and language
- Knowledge and understanding of the world
- Expressive and aesthetic development
- Physical development and movement.

Each aspect is described in terms of a number of features of learning. These set out a range of learning experiences to which all children are entitled during their pre-school years. The range of differences in children's development and learning is considerable in the early years. Nevertheless, all children should have the opportunity to participate in and enjoy the full range of experiences described.

The way in which children are grouped organisationally varies from provision to provision, but generally children meet in social groups with their own 'key person', particularly at arrival and departure times. During the session their own needs and preferences will be taken account of and staff recognise the need to respond to this and plan accordingly. There is no national assessment framework for children under compulsory school age. Learning and Teaching Scotland has produced a multi media pack to support transitions from the pre-compulsory to compulsory school stage 'Progress with Purpose' (Learning and Teaching Scotland 2002). This material seeks to highlight the important aspects of continuity of learning at the point of transition between the pre-school and primary school sector, but is not standardised assessment material.

Curriculum Guidance for the Foundation Stage: England

In England, educational provision for four year olds operates on the basis of being available to all children whose parents wish them to have it and this is to be extended to all three year olds by 2004. Children are not required to start compulsory schooling until the term after their fifth birthday, although many four-year-olds are in reception classes (Select Committee on Education and Employment 2000). In September 2000 a Foundation Stage of education was introduced for children aged three to the end of the academic year they are five, when most will be in the reception year, the first class in primary school. The curriculum guidance for this stage sets out the early learning goals across six areas of learning, which describe what most children are expected to achieve by the end of the Foundation Stage. All government funded settings are required to deliver a curriculum consistent with this guidance. The Education Act 2002 establishes the Foundation Stage as part of the National Curriculum. From 2003 new statutory assessment in the form of a Foundation Stage Profile at the end of the foundation stage will replace statutory baseline assessment on entry to primary school.

The areas of learning contained within the guidance are:

- Communication, language and literacy
- Personal, social and emotional development
- Mathematical development
- Knowledge and understanding of the world
- Physical development
- Creative development.

The early learning goals replace the age related desirable outcomes for children's learning on entering compulsory education (DfEE/SCAA 1996). The guidance provides an opportunity to draw on and celebrate and share existing good and effective practice in the Foundation Stage. Key principles and aims are promoted in the guidance through examples from real life settings. While welcoming the early learning goals, practitioners were concerned that without supporting guidance, those who worked with young children, parents and others might misunderstand their purpose and see them as goals for three- and four-year-old children, or a curriculum, or both. They were concerned that this would lead to a formal approach to learning, which would be at best unhelpful and at worst harmful to young children. The guidance has been developed to address those concerns.

The principles set out very clearly the values and beliefs that underpin the guidance and what they mean for those practitioners who work in the Foundation Stage. They emphasise the need for:

- all children to feel included, secure and valued and to be successful and develop a positive disposition to learning by building on what they already know and can do;
- practitioners and parents to work together in an atmosphere of mutual respect;
- a relevant and carefully structured curriculum, with opportunities for children to plan and initiate their own learning, as well as take part in activities planned by adults; with opportunities to become engrossed, work in depth and complete activities;
- a well-planned and organised learning environment within which children can explore, experiment, plan and make decisions for themselves.

All of these principles are dependent on practitioners who understand how children develop during the early years and who understand and can implement a curriculum that will help children make progress towards, and where appropriate, beyond the early learning goals. These principles require practitioners who understand well planned play, who do not make a distinction between 'play' and 'work' and who observe and respond appropriately to children, engaging with them in their learning and building positive relationships with children and parents.

In response to requests from practitioners, examples of children at different ages and stages are shown within 'stepping stones' towards the early learning goals. These set out children's developing knowledge, skills and understanding and attitudes to learning as they progress through the Foundation Stage. Diversity that responds to different needs of children, families and communities is reflected throughout the guidance. The establishment of the Foundation Stage in September 2000 gives this very important stage of education a distinct identity.

Conclusion

In this chapter authorities from the four countries of the UK have described how working within centrally developed national curriculum guidelines and frameworks, can provide all children with a balanced range of learning opportunities and experiences across diverse early years settings. Each country has responded to the debate about what and how young children should learn, through their published curricular guidance and through their reviews of early years provision. Although the documents discussed in this chapter vary in the way that expected outcomes for learning are expressed, in the ways these are assessed and in the degree of guidance offered to practitioners, all are underpinned by accepted principles (that is, a set of beliefs or values) that contribute to good practice. These include:

- the importance of play in learning
- relationships with adults
- an understanding of the ways in which young children learn
- including all children.

In the hands of knowledgeable and skilled practitioners, published guidance can assist in laying appropriate foundations for young children's learning.

References

Anning, A. and Edwards, E. (1999) *Promoting Children's Learning from Birth to Five*. Buckingham: Open University Press.

Barton, L. (2002) 'Better late', *Guardian Education*, 9 July, 2.

Bennett, J. (2001) 'Goals and curricula in early childhood', in Kamerman, S. (ed.) *Early Childhood Education and Care: International Perspectives*. New York: The Institute for Child and Family Policy at Columbia University.

Council for the Curriculum, Examinations and Assessment (1997) *Curricular Guidance for Pre-School Education*. Northern Ireland Council for the Curriculum, Examinations and Assessment.

David, T. and Nurse, A. (1999) 'Inspection of under fives education and constructions of early childhood', in David, T. (ed.) *Teaching Young Children*. London: Paul Chapman.

Department for Education and Employment/School Curriculum and Assessment Authority (1996) *Desirable Outcomes for Children's Learning on Entering Compulsory Education*. Department for Education and Employment/School Curriculum and Assessment Authority.

Gopnik, A., Meltzoff, A. and Kuhl, P. (1999) *How Babies Think*. London: Weidenfeld and Nicolson.

Hughes, J. (2000) 'A brief look at the early years curriculum in Northern Ireland and Wales', *Early Education* **32** (Autumn), 7.

Learning and Teaching Scotland (2002) *Progress with Purpose: Supporting continuity in children's learning 3–8*, Glasgow: Learning and Teaching Scotland.

Miller, L. (2000) 'Play as a foundation for learning', in Drury *et.al. Looking at Early Years Education and Care.* London: David Fulton Publishers.

Mills, C. and Mills, D. (1998) *The Early Years.* London: Channel Four Television.

Qualifications and Curriculum Authority/Department for Education and Skills (2000) *Curriculum Guidance for the Foundation Stage.* London: QCA/DfES.

Qualifications, Curriculum and Assessment Authority for Wales (2000) *Desirable Outcomes for Children's Learning before Compulsory School Age,* QCAAW.

Roberts, A. (2000) 'A brief look at the early years curriculum in Northern Ireland and Wales', *Early Education* **32** (Autumn), 7.

Scottish Consultative Council on the Curriculum (1997) *A Curriculum Framework for Children in their Pre-school Year.* Edinburgh: The Scottish Office of Education and Industry Department.

Scottish Consultative Council on the Curriculum (1999) *Curriculum Framework for Children 3 to 5.* Edinburgh: SCCC.

Select Committee on Education and Employment (2000) *First Report: Early Years.* http://www.publications.parliament.uk/pa/cm200001/cmselect/cmeduemp/33/3303.htm

Sproule, L. *et.al.* (2001/2002) *The Early Years Enriched Curriculum Evaluation Project.* Report produced for Northern Ireland Council for the Curriculum, Examinations and Assessment.

Staggs, L. (2000) 'Curriculum guidance for the early years', *Early Years Educator,* (October), 21–3.

Chapter 11

Approaches to curricula in the early years

Linda Miller, Jane Devereux, Alice Paige-Smith and Janet Soler

Introduction

In this chapter we explore five examples of curricula, which have influenced practice in early childhood education and care. They have been chosen to illustrate both recent and historical influences on early years curricula in the UK. Curricular guidance for the early years has become increasingly centralised in a number of countries, which has extended debates about what and how young children learn (Bennett 2001). However, alongside the development of this more centralised system practitioners have retained and woven influences from other approaches and models into their practice. These other approaches to curricula stem from research, from a particular set of beliefs or from a distinctive vision attributable to one influential figure.

Developing early childhood curricula involves making decisions and choices about what children should learn. Making these choices involves different groups such as early childhood practitioners, teachers, educational experts and policy makers. The early childhood curricula discussed in this chapter are based on official guidance issued by government and ministers, or are generated more locally for different early childhood settings, or have their origins in the distinctive vision of one educator – or they may embrace more than one of these influences. We have chosen these particular examples in order to illustrate the rich variety of approaches that early years practitioners bring to their work.

Two of the approaches discussed have been influenced by the work of great educators of the past, Rudolph Steiner (House 2000) and Maria Montessori (Montessori 1912). More recently the work of Chris Athey (1990) on Schema, has influenced early years practice in some settings. One example of curricula we focus on is 'Te Whaariki' developed in New Zealand (Ministry of Education 1996). This is a centrally generated national curriculum for early childhood, but is distinctive because it addresses both cultural and language issues in English and Maori and because of the involvement of stakeholders in its conception and development. In Italy, central government has traditionally been much less prescriptive about what children should learn at any stage of education. The

Reggio Emilia approach is an example of a localised system that offers a distinctive approach to teaching and learning in early childhood, and which has been extremely influential on professional thinking in countries throughout the world.

The influence of Steiner Education

Rudolph Steiner (1861–1925) established his first school in 1919 in Stuttgart for the children of the Waldorf Astoria cigarette factory workers. Steiner was approached by the factory owner to set up the school, as he was known as the founder of the Anthroposophy movement and a leading figure in the movement for social renewal and was concerned about the spiritual background of human evolution (Chalibi 2001). There are currently more than 770 Rudolph Steiner Waldorf schools and 1,200 kindergartens worldwide as well as many teacher training courses. Steiner viewed education as appropriate when it: 'allows the pupil's body to develop healthily and according to its needs, because the soul (of which this body is the expression) is allowed to grow in a way consistent with the forces of its development' (Steiner 1919: 3). He emphasised the nature of the whole human being, how the teacher should have insight into children, and that education was not just about knowledge but also about encouraging human beings to change existing social conditions. The approach is based on the principles of Steiner education as well as the individual creativity of the teacher (Stedall 1992).

Curriculum

The young child is seen as having a close relationship to nature and to the world about him or her. Early years educators' greatest tools are considered to be 'example and love' (Schweizer 2000: 23) and the young child is considered to be defenceless and trusting. Formal schooling does not begin until the child is aged six to seven. Until children are seven they are considered to need to develop their senses which may be over stimulated through urban living, and there is an emphasis on creative play, imagination and rhythm: 'What is right to offer the child under seven to learn when he absorbs so much so fast? The delicate senses are all embracing; the child absorbs willy-nilly the world around, recreating it through the divine gift of imitation in play, speech and behaviour' (Schweizer 2000: 23).

Hence Steiner education attempts to provide children with opportunities to explore nature and their senses and the world around them through the curriculum they experience in the early years. According to Schweizer, working with festivals brings children in touch with the seasons and develops a sense of rhythm in their lives. Rhythm is considered to be important for children and is brought into the curriculum through an awareness of the seasons, through a nature table for instance or through the rhythm of children's songs and rhymes, which are considered to stimulate the child's language beyond daily usage

(Britz-Crecelius 1972). The importance of rhythm and repetition is established through the daily, weekly and termly curriculum. Different days will be for special activities such as drawing, painting or cooking and the daily timetable will be routinely followed, punctuated by songs to indicate any changes in activity. The same songs or poems during ring time would be repeated every day for one month. The sharing of food prepared with the children begins with a grace and ends with thanks: 'They help of their own accord with the cooking or spreading, baking or chopping, serving, laying tables and washing up. It is a social occasion as well as nourishing' (Schweizer 2000: 25). Steiner proposed that children should learn to read and write after the age of seven, that writing should develop from drawing, that alphabet letters emerge from children's artistic sense and also that reading is considered to arise from writing. Alongside a curriculum based on the Arts such as music and painting, eurhythmic movement, or movement with meaning, is considered to be a way of encouraging children's development.

Play

Play is considered to develop children's ability to persevere and concentrate; it also allows the child to fill in time without being bored (Britz-Crecelius 1972). Within a Steiner perspective, games like hide and seek and peek a boo 'reflect the transition from there to here, the transition from the spiritual to the physical world, which takes place every morning on waking up' (Britz-Crecelius 1972: 18). Exploring the four elements is a part of the early years curriculum and children are encouraged to play with earth and water through digging in mud and sand and having access to a tap or buckets of water. Games with an element of air would include using kites, which create the opportunity for children to measure their own strength against the force of the wind. Children are also encouraged to join in with adult tasks such as cleaning and cooking as they are considered to learn through imitation. Pretend and imaginary play are encouraged as a way of developing the child's imagination and of conquering their surroundings. Some of the permanent play activities which would be available in a playgroup or kindergarten would include: a play house with rag dolls, doll clothes, covers, baskets to carry dolls (using soft colours such as pink and light purple), table with wooden and natural cups, pans, spoons, fir cones, water play, wooden bricks, natural wooden objects, wooden train set, knitted dolls which can be used as puppets, and wooden strollers.

The role of the adult

Steiner wrote about the ways in which teachers should educate children within the context of setting up the Waldorf school in the early twentieth century. At that time Steiner was concerned with the impact of the development of modern industry and what could be considered to be appropriate education, especially as the first Steiner school was set up for the children of factory workers. From birth to six or seven the child's soul is considered to go through a transformation when 'the human being naturally gives himself up to everything immediately surrounding him in the human environment' (Steiner 1919: 2). The role of the teacher who is entrusted with the education of the child is considered to be very influential: 'the child's soul becomes open to take in consciously what the educator and teacher gives, which affects the child as a result of the teacher's natural authority...whatever the teacher does should be sufficiently alive' (Steiner 1919: 2). Within Steiner playgroups and kindergartens there is a concern that the educator should nurture the child's individuality and creativity, and to also be a type of 'mentor' or supportive adult for the child. Rather than lead or control the children, the role of the adult is to guide young children through ritual activities that take place during the day. The adult would not instruct the children directly but would lead the child or children into activities through song – for instance 'Let's all tidy up now' would be chanted at clearing up time. The children are considered to learn through imitation and repetition of activities, songs, rhymes and story. During painting sessions the adult may sit and paint rather than instruct and when children play creatively they will allow the children to develop their own fantasy play situation only intervening to support the children's fantasy. House (2000) suggests that the importance of a Steiner approach in the early years is that it provides a central role to the importance of play which is unstructured by adults. He suggests that the Steiner approach to early years education should be publicised more widely as it is an 'effective alternative to the assessment-obsessed, anxiety-driven fare on offer in the state sector' (House 2000: 10) and this may be one of the reasons why parents choose Steiner playgroups or kindergartens for their children.

The Montessori approach

Dr Maria Montessori was born in 1870 in Italy where she studied engineering, before training as a doctor. In 1896 she was the first woman to graduate from the University of Rome Medical School where she worked in the psychiatric clinic developing an interest in the treatment of children. Gradually, she became interested in the education of all children and in 1907 opened her first 'children's house' in a poor area of Rome, San Lorenzo. Because of her medical training she initially approached the education of children from a scientific, rather than a philosophic or educational perspective; this significantly affected the way she worked and the structured materials that she developed. Throughout her life she travelled all over the world spreading her ideas and developing her philosophy until her death in 1952.

Underpinning philosophy

Montessori began by observing children and used the classroom as a laboratory to develop and test out her materials. She had a great love and respect for children and believed that each child is unique with a potential that needs releasing. Montessori saw the dignity of the child, along with freedom and independence, as cornerstones of practice. She believed that children had an inner and outer self and that the inner rhythm of the child's soul was crucial in helping children to grow and understand their world. She advocated that if the adult guided the child's outer self, the inner self would take care of itself (Montessori 1912). In Montessori's view this inner self helps the child towards independence, which she viewed as the ultimate goal for children. Montessori did not believe the child was an empty vessel that the parent or teacher had to fill up and felt that neither a nursery school nor the home offered children the kind of environment they needed. She set out to create 'a *natural* environment for the child' (that is, one suited to their nature) (Standing 1966: 4). Another way of describing the Montessori method is to say it is a 'method based on the principle of freedom in a prepared environment' (Standing 1966: 8).

Montessori based her work on the idea that children were very different from adults and used the term metamorphosis (meaning change of shape) to describe how children's minds and bodies were constantly changing. She developed a series of different didactic materials that she saw as leading to order, understanding and independence. According to Montessori, if children were inducted into this ordered environment and systematic ways of working, then 'active discipline' would be internalised by the child. Montessori practitioners do not discipline children in the traditional sense yet the environment is very controlled. Children are not free to wander but are encouraged to work with the materials, which for many practitioners may seem antagonistic to ideas of freedom.

The role of the adult

In Montessori settings the adult is seen as a guide rather than a teacher, with great emphasis placed on not intervening unnecessarily in what the child is doing. The child as the learner leads, the guide follows, thus respecting the child's inner life. Montessori believed that all children have a natural desire to find out and understand by doing, thus the guide inducts the child into the required way of working with each new piece of equipment, as appropriate to their age and stage of development. Each piece of equipment is designed to incorporate a specific learning purpose and must be used in a particular way. Children may repeat and play with the materials as much as they wish but the ways in which they can use the materials are clearly prescribed.

In training guidance is given to teachers on how to instruct children and model particular behaviours and ways of working; every teacher practises using each piece of apparatus in the correct way many times. As a child becomes more familiar with the material then the teacher steps back and observes.

Approach to practice

Within a Montessori setting children are placed in multi-age groups in three to six year spans, usually: 0–3, 3–6, 6–12, 12–15 and 15–18. Montessori viewed these mixed age groups as important for social development and for learning from peers. The environment is organised into subject areas and children are free to move around the room and work with a particular piece of apparatus without time restriction. Children work individually, with practitioners supporting one child at a time; group work is not a common feature of Montessori settings. Teachers or guides do not correct children as they work, but use observation to plan individual projects to support their needs.

The materials

The Montessori intellectual materials include the practical life curriculum, sensorial education, language and maths. Overlaying this is the cultural curriculum that includes geography, history, biology, music and arts. Within these areas Montessori devised structured activities and designed specific apparatus to develop children's knowledge, skills and awareness of the world. Equipment for all activities is child sized and children are expected to do most things for themselves. For example, practical life exercises such as pouring peas enable them to practise the skills needed to eventually get a drink independently. They are also expected to clear up after an activity. A typical piece of apparatus is number rods of different lengths, designed to introduce children to ideas of number. The first activity is to lay them out in order and if 'done properly, they form a sort of stair' (Standing 1966: 146). A series of set activities then follow as the guide observes the child's development. Using the apparatus in ways other than those prescribed is not encouraged.

This prescribed approach to practice highlights tensions for many practitioners between the espoused notion of freedom and the prescribed nature of the materials. Today there are many Montessori nurseries, but not all are staffed by Montessori trained practitioners and therefore may not follow the approach advocated by Montessori.

Schema

Chris Athey's work on Schema has its origins in the Froebel Educational Institute Project (1990), which aimed to provide information about the ways in which young children acquire knowledge. Athey was strongly influenced by the writings of Piaget. A key task of the project was to document the developmental sequence of behaviour in a group of young children, ranging from early motor behaviours through to thought and forms of representation. The project also aimed to provide an enrichment programme based on new kinds of collaboration between parents and practitioners.

What are Schema?

Athey worked with practitioners, observing children alone and interacting with others such as parents, to try to establish commonalities and continuities in their learning. Through her research (1973–1978) she showed how children's 'forms of thought' are fed by experiences provided in the home and in early years settings. According to Athey, children find their own match between the curriculum offered and their current cognitive concerns, which she describes as a series of patterns that children show in their learning and play. These patterns she called 'schema' and described each as 'a pattern of repeatable behaviour into which experiences are assimilated and gradually co-ordinated. Co-ordinations lead to higher-level and more powerful schemas' (Athey 1990: 37). So for Athey, schema are repeatable patterns of action that help children to make early categorisations and from that, to develop more logical and general classifications about the world around them. For example when babies apply a particular action or schema, such as sucking, to a variety of objects they gradually become more able to generalise about objects, which can be sucked. They may also, according to Foss (1974), use a series of schema with objects to explore such ideas as throwing, sucking and banging; from this behaviour they begin to generalise about which objects belong to which categories. As a child develops it then becomes the role of the adult to provide experiences that enable the child to use their existing schema. Further experiences are then assimilated into the child's cognitive structures and their breadth and depth extended. Athey (1990: 37) claims therefore 'increase experiences and schemas will be enriched'.

Athey's research (1990) found that schema manifested themselves in children's play. Examples of identified schema are:

- Trajectory – interest in up and down and along and back
- Rotation – interest in things that rotate
- Enclosure – interest in boundaries
- Enveloping and containing – covering and putting objects in containers
- Connecting – interest in joining things together in various ways and forms
- Transporting – moving things about in different ways.

Athey also identified three developmental stages relating to schema:

- Motor level – where the behaviours shown by the child do not appear to have any representational significance
- Symbolic representation – the child is able to represent events symbolically through their actions, play or in other forms such as drawing, modelling and painting
- Thought level – the child is able to give a description about an event or action after it has occurred.

These three different levels of functioning were found to relate to increasing chronological age – motor level was found in the youngest children and thought level in the older children.

Implications for practice and the role of the adult

The case study below illustrates Hannah's emerging patterns of behaviour over a six weeks period.

> Hannah (4yrs 3mths)
> Hannah played with lots of small equipment. She had her own bag in which she brought her teddy, wrapped in his special blanket, to nursery where he stayed until home time. Teddy was taken out of the bag when her mother came to collect her, then Hannah would wrap herself and Teddy together in the blanket before leaving. Hannah was frequently observed in the home corner playing with the dolls, wrapping them up and putting them in prams or cots and covering them with blankets. In the outside play area she was often seen hiding in the bushes setting up homes or dens; she always made a door that could shut. She collected and stored 'treasures' wrapped in tissue inside matchboxes. She would bring different wrapped objects to nursery and often covered her work or things she made. Her drawings of people were usually contained inside some kind of building. When she finished a painting, she often covered it over with a dark colour saying that it was 'night' or 'finished'.

These observations collected by the adults working with Hannah, show predominant patterns of play, which were driven by her interest in enveloping, covering and containing objects. Adults working with young children and using schema as a framework for their practice, seek to look beyond what children are playing with, to observe what they are doing with materials and objects. In Hannah's case the practitioners provided a range of 'enveloping' activities that extended her experiences. For example, they developed a wormery, which involved Hannah in digging for worms, putting them into the soil and wrapping the container with black paper. Thus she added to her knowledge of enveloping and adapted and modified her understanding through different experiences.

Within the schema framework, children's play patterns change and develop and they may show more than one dominating pattern. Sharing observations and understandings allows adults to be aware of children's predominant schema and to plan for these to be supported and extended by both parents and practitioners.

Athey suggests that 'where schemas have been well nourished by wide experiences, consistently accompanied by articulate speech, development has been accelerated' (Athey 1990: 204).

Te Whaariki

New Zealand has developed a national curriculum framework for early childhood, 'Te Whaariki' (Ministry of Education 1996). The developers of the

New Zealand early childhood curriculum were working in similar contexts to those involved in the development of the early childhood curriculum in England (Miller 2000) in that the curriculum was linked to the National Curriculum in primary schools. Despite this constraint, the developers of Te Whaariki developed a framework, which has implemented a bicultural perspective, an anti-racist approach and reciprocal relationships with the Maori community in New Zealand (Smith 2002).

The development of Te Whaariki

Margaret Carr and Helen May, who were responsible for co-coordinating the development of the New Zealand early childhood curriculum, wished to incorporate 'equitable educational opportunities and quality early childhood policies and practices' into the framework (Carr and May 2000: 53). Diverse groups of practitioners and representatives from different types of early childhood services were involved in consultations, as were people with nationally recognised expertise. Maori perspectives were a separate, but integrally related framework and the document is written in both English and Maori (Smith 2002). During consultations early childhood practitioners expressed a 'local, situated and often personal view of the early childhood curriculum' (Carr and May 2000: 53). This view did not necessarily fit with the government objective of establishing a national curriculum framework and many early childhood practitioners had difficulties with applying the word 'curriculum' to practice in early childhood settings. Nevertheless, Smith (2002) says that 'The introduction of holistic, open ended inclusive curriculum guidelines in New Zealand has been a success' (p. 17).

The curriculum

The New Zealand early childhood curriculum is usually referred to by its shortened title of 'Te Whaariki' (Ministry of Education 1996), which means a woven mat on which everyone can stand; this reflects the philosophy of the curriculum. It interweaves central principles, strands and goals into different patterns or programmes which each centre is expected to weave into its own curriculum. It is designed to cover the age range 0 to 5 years and is divided into three age groups, i.e. 'infants', 'toddlers' and the 'young child'.

The four broad principles which provide the framework are:

1. Empowerment – the curriculum empowers the child to grow and learn.
2. Holistic development – the curriculum reflects the way children learn and grow.
3. Family and community – the wider world of the family and community are an integral part of the curriculum.
4. Relationships – children learn through responsive relationships with people, places and things.

The five strands, which are underpinned by goals are:

- Well being – involving goals relating to health and safety.
- Belonging – involving goals relating to links to family and community, a sense of place, routines and customs and acceptable behaviour.
- Contribution – involving goals relating to opportunities for learning and a sense of self.
- Communication – involving goals relating to protection of the language symbols of their own and other cultures.
- Exploration – involving goals relating to play and active exploration of the environment.

'Te Whaariki' is mandatory in all government-funded early childhood programmes in New Zealand (Ministry of Education 1996, Smith 2002).

As with the Reggio Emilia approach in Italy, discussed later in this chapter, Carr and May argue that this curriculum cannot be imported as it stands into other countries, as it embodies bicultural and community values that are specific to New Zealand. The weaving metaphor of the mat embodies their bicultural vision of the New Zealand child which underpins this curriculum (see Carr and May 2000: 61).

The role of the adult

As in the 'emergent curriculum' of Reggio Emilia centres described below, Te Whaariki draws on Vygotskian sociocultural theory. Within this theoretical framework knowledge and understanding are socially constructed between the child and a more able 'other', rather than passively received. Teachers and practitioners have an interactive role and help to 'scaffold' the child's learning; hence relationships are highly important and children take an active role in their own learning (Smith 2002).

Reggio Emilia

Reggio Emilia is a community supported system of early childhood education and care situated in a small town in northern Italy. During the last two decades it has become internationally known for its provision for children under 6, through 'The Hundred Languages of Children' touring exhibition (Malaguzzi 1996) and through visits to the region from practitioners and authorities concerned with early childhood education. The wider influence of Reggio Emilia on early years practitioners throughout the world has been immense. The Municipality of Reggio Emilia operates the network of early childhood educational services; it co-exists alongside a publicly funded system of pre-schools for all three to six year olds. The network consists of 19 pre-schools for children aged 3 to 6 and 13 infant toddler centres for children aged 3 months to

3 years. The pre-schools serve a total of 12,999 children and the infant toddler centres serve 820 children. There are also three infant toddler centres managed by cooperatives and one infant toddler centre managed by parents, which have a special agreement with the local administration, catering for another 144 children. As a measure of its support, 12 per cent of the Town Council budget is devoted to funding the early childhood programme.

Loris Malaguzzi founded the Reggio Emilia system of early childhood education after his experiences in the Second World War; he strongly believed that a new society should nurture a vision of children who could act and think for themselves (Malaguzzi 1995). This led to an early childhood education system founded on the perspective of the child. Carlina Rinaldi, who has worked alongside Malaguzzi for many years, says that the cornerstone of the Reggio Emilia experience is based on the image of children as rich, strong, and powerful. Children are seen as unique subjects with rights rather than simply needs (Rinaldi 1995).

Approaches to practice

Malaguzzi drew on Vygotsky's theory briefly described above. Within this approach, knowledge is not 'transmitted' by the adult, but is co-constructed by the child and adult as they find meanings together. The nature of the relationship between the child and adult is central, as is listening to the child's views and ideas. A key feature of the work of Reggio Emilia centres is an ongoing dialogue which questions and challenges existing educational viewpoints and accepted teaching practices and approaches. This dialogue is shared with the children, parents, teachers, administrators, politicians and educators from other countries. Through this professional dialogue practitioners in Reggio Emilia centres have challenged the dominating ideas and accepted practices of early childhood teaching by 'deconstructing' (i.e. taking apart existing ideas and theories), to look at how they have shaped our ideas and beliefs about children and the ways in which we work (Dahlberg 2000). Time for this discussion and for planning and preparation is built into the working week. Time is also given to children to discuss ideas, develop cooperative projects, to research and problem solve and to revisit work and ideas already undertaken (Abbott and Nutbrown 2001).

The emergent curriculum

Within Reggio Emilia centres there is no written curriculum with prescribed goals and methods, the child is seen as a starting point for an 'emergent curriculum' (Rinaldi 1995: 102). This is a localised approach to teaching and learning that cannot be readily transferred and applied to another culture or context. The approach has evolved because the centres have not been constrained by external factors stemming from government objectives, the pressures of external assessment or the need to implement prescribed curriculum content. Malaguzzi refers to the 'hundred ways' in which he believes children learn and practitioners and other adults are urged to 'listen' to the many languages through which children communicate. Long and short term projects, which stem from the children's ideas, experiences and interests, serve as the main framework for the emergent curriculum. A criticism of the approach is that because there is no written curriculum there is a lack of accountability to the wider society. Advocates of the approach argue that there is a detailed recording of the curriculum process, which opens practice to criticism and scrutiny. This is achieved through documenting the children's work through photographs, slides and film and in the form of publications and the travelling exhibition.

The role of adults

In Reggio Emilia centres parents are seen as central to the programme and are closely involved from an early stage. The information they offer about their child is fed back into the children's activities and experiences, thus keeping the child as a learner at the centre. Adults working within Reggio Emilia view group work as an important form of social learning. Groups of children stay with the same teachers over a three-year period in order to create a stable and secure environment and to provide for continuity of learning experiences for the children. The adult is seen as a facilitator of children's learning, helping the children to explore ideas and to determine problems that arouse their interest. The 'pedagogista' works with parents and teachers towards educational aims and goals and has a co-ordinating role with many facets, including administration and training (Fillipini 1995). The artelier (artist in residence) is closely involved in project work and in the visual documentation of the children's work (Vecchi 1995).

The environment

A focal point of Reggio Emilia centres is the piazza, a central meeting place where children play and talk together. The visually appealing and stimulating environment of Reggio centres has had an influence on some early years settings in the United Kingdom; in particular the use of light, mirrors and reflective surfaces. Reggio Emilia centres have large windows and white walls and use mirrored surfaces, particularly the tetrahedron with a mirrored interior, where children can sit and see themselves from many angles. The work of the children is displayed and portrays the ongoing projects and research, which document the emergent curriculum (Abbott and Nutbrown 2001).

Conclusion: gaining insights into practice

Moss (1999: 8) has discussed how looking at other approaches to working with young children 'provides us with a sort of lens for looking at our own situations...a lens which helps to make the invisible visible and to see what is visible in a different light'. In other words, looking at the work of others allows us insights into our own practice and helps us to see this in a new light.

References

Abbott, L. and Nutbrown, C. (2001) 'Experiencing Reggio Emilia', in Abbott, L. and Nutbrown, C. (eds) *Experiencing Reggio Emilia: implications for pre-school provision*. Buckingham: Open University Press.

Athey, C. (1990) *Extending Thought in Young Children*. London: Paul Chapman Publishing.

Bennett, J. (2001) 'Goals and curricula in early childhood', in Kamerman, S. (ed.) *Early Childhood Education and Care: International Perspectives*. New York: The Institute for Child and Family Policy at Columbia University.

Britz-Crecelius, H. (1972) *Children at Play: Preparation for Life*. Edinburgh: Floris Books.

Carr, M. and May, H. (2000). 'Te Whaariki: Curriculum Voices', in Penn, H. (ed.) *Early Childhood Services: Theory, Policy and Practice*. Buckingham: Open University Press.

Chalibi, M. (2001) *Waldorf, Awakening to Tomorrow*. Berlin: Freunde der Erziehungskunst.

Dahlberg, G. (2000) 'Everything is a beginning and everything is dangerous: some reflections of the Reggio Emilia experience', in Penn, H. (ed.) *Early Childhood Services: Theory, Policy and Practice*. Buckingham: Open University Press.

Fillipini, T. (1995) 'The role of the pedagogista: an interview with Lella Gandini', in Edwards, C., Gandini, L. and Forman, G. (eds) *The Hundred Languages of Children: The Reggio Emilia Approach to Early Childhood Education*. United States: Ablex Publishing Corporation.

Foss, B. (ed.) (1974) *New Perspectives in Child Development*. Harmondsworth: Penguin Books.

House, R. (2000) 'Psychology and Early Years Learning: Affirming the Wisdom of Waldorf', *Steiner Education* **32** (2), 10–16.

Moss, P. (1999) *Difference, Dissensus and Debate: some possibilities of learning from Reggio*. Stockholm: Reggio Emilia Institutet.

Malaguzzi, L. (1995) 'History, Ideas and Basic Philosophy: An Interview with Lella Gandini', in Edwards, C., Gandini, L. and Forman, G. (eds) *The Hundred Languages of Children: The Reggio Emilia Approach to Early Childhood Education*. United States: Ablex Publishing Corporation.

Malaguzzi, L. (1996) *The Hundred Languages of Children: A Narrative of the Possible* (catalogue of the exhibit), Reggio Emilia, Italy: Reggio Children.

Miller, L. (2000) 'Play as a foundation for learning', in Drury *et al. Looking at Early Years Education and Care*. London: David Fulton Publishers.

Ministry of Education (1996) *Te Whaariki. He Whaariki Matauranga mo nga*

Mokopuna o Aotearoa: Early Childhood Curriculum. Wellington: Learning Media.

Montessori, M. (1912) *The Montessori Method.* New York: Frederick Stokes Company.

Rinaldi, C. (1995) 'The emergent curriculum and social constructivism: an interview with Lella Gandini', in Edwards, C., Gandini, L. and Forman, G. (eds) *The Hundred Languages of Children: The Reggio Emilia Approach to Early Childhood Education.* United States: Ablex Publishing Corporation.

Schweizer, S. (2000) 'Creating a meadow for childhood, education for a new millennium, what do young children need today?' *Steiner Education* **32** (2), 23–8.

Smith, A.B. (2002) 'Promoting diversity rather than uniformity: theoretical and practical perspectives', in Ffthenakis, W.E. and Oberhuemer, P. (eds) *Early Childhood Curricular Issues: International Perspectives.* Germany: Leske and Budrich.

Standing, E. M. (1966) *The Montessori Revolution in Education.* New York: Schocken Books.

Stedall, J. (1992) *Time to Learn, A film about Rudolf Steiner Waldorf Education,* A Hermes Films Production, Forest Row, Sussex.

Steiner, R. (1919) *An Introduction to Waldorf Education,* The Anthroposophic Press, www.elib.com/Steiner/Articles/IntroWald.phtml.

Vecchi, V. (1995) 'The role of the atelierista': an interview with Lella Gandini, in Edwards, C., Gandini, L. and Forman, G. (eds) *The Hundred Languages of Children: The Reggio Emilia Approach to Early Childhood Education.* United States: Ablex Publishing Corporation.

Chapter 12

Language and literacy learning

Angela Anning and Anne Edwards

[…]

The Review of the Desirable Outcomes (QCA 1999), was designed to lead 4-year-olds into a subject-based National Curriculum framework at school entry. For practitioners in the project with backgrounds in education (either within nursery nurse or teacher training) (see Anning and Edwards 1999) the goals set out in the framework were relatively easy to absorb. However, it was clear from our dialogue with practitioners from care sector backgrounds that for them the document was intimidating.

Frances, the manager of an independent day nursery, described her staff's reactions when she introduced the document at a staff meeting. One responded to the mathematics outcomes with an anguished 'I didn't even get me CSE in maths. I can't teach maths'; another to the descriptors for knowledge and understanding of the world with a worried 'I were crap at geography'. Other responses were more muted! We found that some experienced practitioners from day care settings were apologetic about their perceived lack of knowledge about educational practice and their unfamiliarity with words like 'curriculum' and 'topics'. Others took a more assertive line and argued that they did not want to be 'teachers'. For example, Sally, a deputy manager of a local authority family centre, argued cogently:

> Some of our 4-year-olds are here with us for a long day. They've got all their school years ahead of them. We're not teachers. None of us has been trained how to teach a child to write their name, or read, or count. We did the basic things on NNEB courses; but we are not teachers and we don't feel qualified to teach those kind of things to the children. You hear horror stories about nurseries teaching the children the alphabet and then teachers have to re-teach them sounds – you know, they've been taught 'ay, bee, cee' and they want 'a, b, k' – and we're not teachers. But we can give them all the opportunities they need to prepare them for school.

In fact the children in this setting were offered well-planned and stimulating activities covering a broad range of learning opportunities. There was evidence of the experienced staff responding quickly to and extending children's spontaneous episodes of learning. Again, Sally, the deputy manager clearly articulated the strengths of the provision for children's learning in the centre:

> We don't do much formal in the centre...but we cover the six [*Desirable Outcomes for Learning*] areas in play. We do science experiments. But we don't have the 4-year-olds coming out to do tracing or worksheets or whatever. It's all done through fun, practical, play activities – tie-dying, baking, whatever.

At first the staff panicked when confronted with the requirements of an education-based curriculum. Their confidence in what they were achieving was undermined. Fortunately, an experienced early years adviser in the local authority reassured them that what they were offering the children was fine.

This episode gives us an insight into the fact that curriculum models are socially constructed. They are designed by adults with particular beliefs about what constitute appropriate activities for children at a particular moment in history. [...] But most significant in shaping their beliefs about what children should do and learn before school are the culture and ideologies of their training, professional backgrounds and daily work experiences at the micro-level of their early childhood workplace settings.

It was the distinctive belief systems of 'education' that were exemplified in the 1996 *Desirable Outcomes for Learning* definition of what young children should learn:

> The desirable outcomes are goals for learning for children by the time they enter compulsory education. They emphasise early literacy, numeracy and the development of personal and social skills and contribute to children's knowledge, understanding and skills in other areas. Presented as six areas of learning, they provide a foundation for later achievement.

> (DfEE/SCAA 1996a: 1)

It is not surprising that those project members whose backgrounds were outside education felt threatened by the tone of *Desirable Outcomes for Learning*. The words were hard-edged – goals, compulsory education, literacy, numeracy, knowledge, understanding, skills, achievement. The definition was couched in terms of a 'high status' framework of preparation for academic achievements. Its focus was on the mind.

Contrast this set of goals for young children with one from the National Children's Bureau, where ideologies about childhood are framed in broader terms. The National Children's Bureau promotes the view that practitioners should draw families and communities into concerns about young children's development in a much more holistic way, and not just focus on their educational needs. A description of an appropriate curriculum for young children from one of their community of practitioners is 'investigation and exploration, walks and puddles and cuddles, books and blankets and anything that is part of a child's day, play and routines' (Rouse 1990). It is significant that there is a strong emotional component to this definition. The words used – cuddles, blankets, play – are about the physical and emotional needs of children, not just their intellectual needs. In this framework the body and the heart matter; the mind is just one part of the 'whole' child.

In the *Desirable Outcomes for Learning* (DfEE/SCAA 1996a) document 'play' was scarcely mentioned. The language used is an indication of the construction of childhood that dominates our policy in early years services in the UK. 'Happiness' and 'play' are derided by a male dominated society which emphasises the logical, scientific aspects of learning and the power of rational thought (see Anning 1994 for further discussion of play and the legislated curriculum). Play is dismissed as trivial or time wasting. Yet we argue that for early years practitioners play is perceived as the natural vehicle by which young children learn. Fromberg (1990) reviewed significant research evidence of the contribution of play to children's development. Yet, he points out, 'at the same time that the research literature on the value of play appears to expand geometrically the presence of play in early childhood classrooms has been dwindling' (p. 237).

It is significant that education has been assigned the lead role in the government's policy on integration of services for children. Current government policies on early childhood education prioritise children's academic achievements, not their emotional and social development, nor their physical well-being. Practitioners with educational backgrounds feel secure. So during the project, we never heard those with backgrounds in educational services apologise about their lack of knowledge and understanding of children's physical and emotional needs. We think these should be priorities. Even at a pragmatic level of measuring 'success', if children are not happy and comfortable, they are unlikely to feel good about learning and to make good progress in academic achievements. Equally, from a moral and ethical point of view, young children's emotional and physical well-being should be of paramount importance. It may be that those with educational backgrounds could learn from their colleagues in the care sector about catering for aspects of children's needs which are emotional and physical.

However, it is the discourse of 'school' subjects, not of children's general well-being, which has dominated curriculum reform for young children since the Education Reform Act of 1987. Of all the 'subjects' of the school curriculum, English is the one with which early childhood workers in all kinds of pre-school settings are most comfortable. However, depending on their backgrounds and belief systems, they will approach the 'subject' in rather different ways. For example, local authority funded day care settings have a tradition of prioritising language development in the activities they plan for their children. This emphasis is the result of the 'compensatory' framework of the care sector because historically their population has been skewed to 'disadvantaged' families and children 'at risk'. However, day care workers' approach to language development is very different from that in, for example, nursery classes in the maintained sector, where a particular 'school' view of language and literacy prevails. Their focus is on the development of spoken language.

[. . .]

Yet our education system is still geared to promoting literacy with a strong emphasis on 'conventional' reading and writing and this model is increasingly 'colonising' pre-school settings. The sign systems of school literacy – alphabet charts, words Blu-tacked onto doors, chairs and tables, workbooks and worksheets – which set the boundaries of literacy in the formal settings of many early years classrooms are infiltrating the informal settings of day care centres, childminders and even some young children's bedrooms or playrooms at home. Parents are pressurised into joining this version of 'the literacy club' by a burgeoning industry in 'out-of-school'/homework educational materials. In supermarkets parents are urged to invest in an array of workbooks, videos and educational games, all designed to improve children's basic skills in reading and writing. In 1998 all children in primary schools of compulsory school age were required to be taught a 'literacy hour' every day. From September 1998 even as children entered compulsory schooling (mostly at the age of 4) they were tested by baseline assessment systems on recognition of initial sounds in words, letters by both shape and sounds, and ability to write their names and words independently. Young children learn to position themselves within this dominant model of literacy. For example, reading is perceived to be about decoding text in books. So Scollon and Scollon (1981) report a young child explaining 'when my baby brother's hands are big enough to hold a book, he'll be able to read'.

We have to question both the appropriateness and effectiveness of this kind of curriculum model for language and literacy learning for young children.

[. . .]

The fact is that despite the current policy of promoting an early introduction to 'school' versions of literacy, British children, particularly boys, are scoring less well on measures of achievements in language and mathematics than children from systems in other European countries (for example, Hungary, Switzerland and Belgium) where pre-school experiences place an emphasis on talk and structured, active play which enable children to move more freely between enactive, iconic and symbolic modes of representation. In these countries children do not start their formal schooling with its emphasis on symbolic representation until they are 6.

Researchers for a Channel 4 programme, *Britain's Early Years Disaster*, argued that:

> The evidence suggests that Britain's early years education, far from helping young children, actually damages many of them. Unlike successful pre-school systems abroad – which move slowly from the concrete to the representational and avoid the abstract – British early years provision rushes children into abstract letters, words and numbers. While elsewhere primacy is given to developing confidence and precision in spoken language, here teaching is dominated by reading, writing and recorded arithmetic.
>
> While brighter children and those, from privileged backgrounds can cope with the demands this makes, less fortunate children suffer, lose confidence and probably

never recover. It seems likely that this helps explain Britain's long tail of under-achievement.

(Mills and Mills 1998: 17)

It is not only the curriculum content that appears to be inappropriate for our young children, but also the danger that the pedagogy of early childhood will become one of curriculum delivery. The current government emphasis on 'direct instruction' and 'whole class teaching' in primary education, exemplified in the arguments for the National Literacy and Numeracy Strategies, is impacting on Reception and even some nursery classes in England and Wales. Yet we have research evidence that young children who are exposed to too formal a schooling regime too soon may suffer long-term disadvantages. Much of this evidence was summarised by three women researchers in the early 1990s when pressure was building up from central government policy to introduce more formal styles of pedagogy into primary schools (see David *et al.* 1993). For example, results of research in the USA (Schweinhart and Weikart 1993), also reported by Sylva and Wiltshire (1993), indicated that three groups of children, one of which had experienced a formal pre-school curriculum and the other two playbased programmes (one a curriculum called High Scope and another less structured programme similarly based on active learning) showed increased IQs at school entry. However, in a follow-up study of the three groups at the age of 15, those that had attended the formal programme engaged more in antisocial behaviour and had lower commitment to school than those from the play-based programmes. In a more recent paper Sylva (1997) again used research-based evidence to argue that 'a curriculum in pre-school settings that is too formal will lead to poorer performance, disincentives to learn and low self-esteem' (p. 4). This takes us to issues about the significance of promoting positive 'dispositions' in the crucial formative stages of children learning to be learners, including learning to be readers, writers and speakers.

[. . .]

References

Anning, A. (1994) Play and the legislated curriculum: back to basics, an alternative view, in J. Moyles (ed.) *The Excellence of Play*. Buckingham: Open University Press.

Anning, A. and Edwards, A. (1999) *Promoting Children's Learning from Birth to Five: developing the new early years professional*. Buckingham: Open University Press.

David, T., Curtis, A. and Siraj-Blatchford, I. (1993) *Effective Teaching in the Early Years: Fostering Children's Learning in Nurseries and in Infant Classes*, an OMEP (UIC) report. Warwick: University of Warwick for Organisation Mondiale pour l'Education Prescolaire.

DfEE/SCAA (Department for Education and Employment/School Curriculum and

Assessment Authority) (1996a) *Desirable Outcomes for Children's Learning on Entering Compulsory Education.* London: DfEE/SCAA.

Fromberg, D. P. (1990) An agenda for research on play in early childhood education, in E. Klugman and S. Smilansky (eds) *Children's Play and Learning: Policy Implications.* New York: Columbia University Teachers' College Press.

Mills, C. and Mills, D. (1998) *Britain's Early Years Disaster* (survey of research evidence for Channel 4 television documentary *Too Much, Too Soon*). London: Channel 4 Television.

QCA (Qualifications and Curriculum Authority) (1999) *The Review of the Desirable Outcomes.* London: Qualifications and Curriculum Authority.

Rouse, D. (1990) The first three years of life: children trusting, communicating and learning, in D. Rouse (ed.) *Babies and Toddlers, Carers and Educators: Quality for Under Threes.* London: National Children's Bureau.

Schweinhart, L. and Weikart, D. (1993) *A Summary of Significant Benefits: The High Scope Perry Pre-School Study Through Age 27.* Ypsilanti, MI: The High Scope Press.

Scollon, R. and Scollon, B. K. (1981) *Narrative, Literacy and Face in Inter Ethnic Communication.* New York: Ablex.

Sylva, K. (1997) The early years curriculum: evidence based proposals. Paper presented at the SCAA conference 'Developing the Primary Curriculum: The Next Steps'. London: SCAA.

Sylva, K. and Wiltshire, J. (1993) The impact of early learning on children's later development: a review prepared for the RSA inquiry 'Start Right', *European Early Childhood Research Journal* **1**(1): 17–40.

Chapter 13

'Play is fun, but it's hard work, too!' The search for quality play in the early years

Lesley Abbott

Play that is well planned and pleasurable helps children to think, to increase their understanding and to improve their language competence. It allows children to be creative, to explore and investigate materials, to experiment and to draw and test their conclusions...Such experience is important in catching and sustaining children's interests and motivating their learning as individuals and in co-operation with others.

(DES 1989, cited in DES 1990: 11)

[...]

'Well,' said Daniel, aged 6, thoughtfully, 'play *is* fun, but it's hard work, too!' These words provide the focus for this chapter. Fun *is* what we all recall about our own play experiences, but in many cases play involves much more, and for play to be successful and enjoyable it often involves hard work.

At any one time in play children can be required to collaborate, negotiate, make choices, organise, explain, lead, communicate, share, take responsibility, ask and answer questions, record, interpret, predict, recall and reflect. No wonder, then, that Daniel considered play to be hard work! In the case study which follows, in which Daniel played a leading role, I would maintain that a range of quality experiences were gained by both children and adults. Defining quality, particularly in an area like play which itself seems to defy definition, presents us with problems.

[...]

However, we would be shirking in our duties as professionals if we made no attempt at all to pinpoint what it is about an activity or experience which makes us say we must have more of it. In that vein, therefore, when considering what is meant by 'quality' in play and what we should look for when attempting to identify those factors which contribute to a rich and meaningful experience for children and adults, a number of important points spring to mind.

The first is to do with 'ownership' and the degree to which children are involved, not only in 'playing', but in any decisions about the focus and planning of the activity. How often do adults and children talk about play? The second concerns the purpose and the degree to which views are shared and children understand the purpose of the activity. Third, quality play often depends upon quality resources and involvement on the part of the adults, yet research reveals both a lack of quality materials and play environments and a reluctance on the part of adults to become involved in play. The valuing and sharing of children's play by adults can only serve to increase the status of the activity and the self-esteem of the child. Finally, play must be capable of meeting curriculum requirements and of facilitating learning in a number of areas, including both cognitive and affective domains. It should provide for equality in terms of access and opportunity for all children, regardless of gender, race and special educational needs.

In answer to the question 'what are children learning through their play?', Atkin (1991: 11) suggests that we turn the question on its head and consider what they are not learning.

> In play children are not learning to fail, to seek right answers, to accept what adults tell them without question, to parrot rote responses, to stop doing something because they can't get it right, to become a spectator to others rather than a participant in whatever field of interest.

In examining the following case study of children at play, [in a structured play area] it is important to consider how far it is possible to identify some of these characteristics and factors which affect the quality of children's experiences in play.

Case study

'Welcome To The Dale Construction Site' declares the notice in the corner of the busy year 1 classroom in The Dale Primary School. Emma and Paul are 'on site' selecting, from a wide range on offer, the tools they will use to construct the building being designed by Daniel and Sarah at the drawing board in the office next door. A notice announcing that 'This is a hard hat area' reminds the builders of the importance of safety, and Paul takes a brightly coloured builder's hat from the appropriately labelled hook and places it on his head before he begins to study the plans.

In the drawing office the children discuss the client's requirements – consulting previously drawn-up plans, appropriately stored in plan chests, to help them decide where they should place the main entrance. Sarah pauses to answer the telephone – it is the 'boss' of the site, in the guise of the teacher phoning to ask for additional supplies of roofing tiles to be delivered to the site as soon as possible. The message, time received, quantity required and action taken, are recorded on the pad lying in readiness by the phone. In a voice which suggests that she has been at the job all her life Sarah deals with the request, adding 'Yes, I know – but we are working as quickly as possible and we will try to deliver on time'. Meanwhile 'on site' Emma and Paul discuss the relative strengths of the tile cement, reading accurately from the various tubs among which they must make a choice, and where a particular word eludes them, making an intelligent guess, applying the skills they have acquired in the more 'formal' aspects of their language work.

The 'builders' are supported by an environment full of information and displays which reflect exciting first-hand experiences covering a range of subject areas. Visits have been made to builders' yards, conversations have taken place, new vocabulary has been acquired, names of materials and 'builders' have been learned, as evidenced by Daniel's insistence on his change of name to Bob, 'cos it's more "suitable" for a builder'! Experiments have taken place in order to test the strength and suitability for the job of a variety of materials, and the results have been carefully and appropriately recorded.

[...]

Once the houses, carefully planned and designed in the drawing office, have been built on the adjoining site, 'For Sale' notices go up and adverts are drafted and redrafted in order to get the wording just right in order to attract 'first-time buyers'.

The children adopt a variety of roles as interested potential buyers come along to view the property, appropriately dressed and with mannerisms and accents carefully discussed and adopted. The language of negotiation, of buying and selling, vocabulary which includes words like 'conveyancing', 'contracts', 'surveyor' and 'mortgage' are used and the role of the building society is introduced.

Parents are involved in school and in the various fact-finding visits and excursions which take place. This type of involvement provides opportunities for discussion with staff and children and for observation at first hand of the potential for learning of this type of activity within the early years curriculum.

But the questions remain: What are the children learning, and how do we know? What is the purpose of this kind of activity which, if it is to be a 'quality experience', must be well planned and carefully thought out? It is important that teachers are able to justify the approach and for parents and children to see the meaning and relevance of what they are engaged in.

Let us examine this case study, of what I would call a 'quality' play experience, in the light of the claims made about play by HMI (DES 1989) at the beginning of this chapter and endorsed by the Rumbold Committee. The first claim is that 'Play that is well planned and pleasurable helps children to think, to increase their understanding and to improve their language competence'. There is no doubt that the play was well planned by both staff and children. National Curriculum requirements had been carefully considered and incorporated into an experience which was carefully discussed, was relevant, purposeful and of which the children had a sense of ownership. An examination of the variety of houses to be found in their area and a visit to the local builder's yard served to increase the children's geographical awareness in line with the programme of study for Geography at Key Stage 1.

> Much of pupils learning at Key Stage 1 should be based on direct experience, practical activities and exploration of the local area.

> (DES 1991: 31)

The detailed planning documents kept by the teacher ensured that curriculum balance was achieved and opportunities were provided for children to practice the skills they had acquired in the more 'formal' aspects of their lives. Witness Paul's experimentation with 'apostrophe s' as he lists the materials required in the builders' yard.

He had been taught a rule by his father and confidently applies it in his play. When questioned about the apostrophe he replied: 'Whenever you see an "s" at the end of a word you add that little squiggle!' We may question the wisdom of the teaching, but there is no doubting the fact that the play situation gave him the confidence to experiment and try out his newly learned skills, as in his use of phonetic spellings such as 'sment', something he might not have done in a more formal, teacher-directed activity labelled 'English' on the timetable.

[...]

Talking to children between the ages of three and seven about play, the recurring theme appears to be the relationship between freedom and fun and the opportunities for learning. 'You can write whatever you like in this big book', said Natalie as she sat at the desk in the 'office'. 'I know, look at this, it tells you the days of the week and the months and the year!' replied her friend as she discovered the wall calendar. Talking with the children revealed their pleasure in exploration and discovery and their joy in sharing their newly found knowledge with sympathetic adults in a non-threatening environment.

There is ample evidence that the children [...] are fascinated by the new words which they encounter listed in the 'office' and reinforced by the adults who play with them as they 'work' hard to understand the meanings. An example of playing with language occurred when Sarah was introduced to the word 'inventory' as she took stock of the materials. As she wrote she could be heard singing to herself 'inventory, story, gory', but [...] she revealed her understanding of the word as she explained to Paul what she was doing: 'I'm writing what we've got and how many so I'll know what to order – this is how it has to be done in this big book'. Increasing language competence is a major goal for all those engaged in the education of young children and, as we are informed by National Curriculum Council (1990) documentation: 'In role play areas children can practice recently learned and emerging skills.

[...]

It is clear that this was happening in the play of these five- and six-year-olds. It was also apparent that they were being creative, not only in their use of language, but also in the roles they adopted and in the imaginative ways in which they were using the resources. The second part of the quotation with which this chapter begins is worth examining in this respect: 'It allows children to be creative, to explore and investigate materials, to experiment and to draw and test their conclusions'.

The building site had been planned to provide the children with opportunities to make sense of what was happening in their immediate environment as a new housing estate was being built, and to meet National Curriculum requirements in science, maths and English. In reality it achieved far more than this; Atkin (1991: 34) observes that while

> good quality play is not a necessary condition for better achievement on traditional measures of performance, that is I.Q. tests and reading and maths tests, it does foster other competences that may be equally, if not more important, for example self-esteem, task orientation, attitudes to learning, persistence, flexibility and creativity.

There is no doubt that in the experiments which the children were required to conduct in testing the strength and suitability of a range of building materials and in recording their results they learned a great deal and met the required attainment targets. It is also evident that in solving the problems with which they were faced they became persistent and task-orientated, in accommodating the needs and wishes of others they learned to be flexible and creative, and as they experienced success their self-esteem increased by leaps and bounds.

[...]

An important factor influencing the quality of the children's learning and achievements is the trust placed in them by the adults with whom they worked. [...] In this case study the support rather than control offered to the 'builders' to explore and experiment with new skills without fear of failure or recrimination was instrumental in the success of the activity and is endorsed by the Rumbold Committee (DES 1990: 11) when they agree with HMI that: 'Such experience is important in catching and sustaining children's interests and motivating their learning as individuals and in co-operation with others.' They suggest that a key element in the search for quality in the play of young children is the adult – in particular, adults to whom they have easy access and who will 'stimulate and encourage dialogue...adults who offer views, ideas and observations and who "think aloud" elicit children's thoughtful participation more effectively than those who control the conversation, or those who do not intervene'.

[...]

It was heartening to discover that in this particular classroom play was seen as a high-status activity and acknowledged by staff, parents and children as a legitimate area in which all of them could be involved. It was also clear that careful thought had been given to ways in which the requirements of the National Curriculum would be met, how assessment would take place, where play featured in the development plan, and the school's commitment to continuity, progressing in learning and the endeavour to provide a broad and balanced experience for the children.

In order to provide successfully for play of this quality, the staff have to be both confident in what they are doing for children and able to justify the attention it is afforded within the school.

[...]

Despite the vast amount of research on and the contribution of many eminent educationists to our understanding of the importance of play in early learning, teachers are constantly having to justify – not only to parents but also to politicians and, sadly, to colleagues at other stages within the profession – children's play as worthwhile and not simply a pleasurable occupation or something to be done when 'work' is completed.

Atkin (1991: 30) suggests that adults are afraid of the messiness and unpredictability of play, in which neither the player nor the content are under their control. They distrust the irrationality of some kinds of play, the fact that it is not directly utilitarian and that assessing its outcomes is not easy.

This latter point is particularly important in the present climate when assessment has taken on new meanings and for some people is equated only with testing. Under the Education Reform Act 1988 assessment has become a statutory process, combining continuous teacher assessment with the results of Standard Assessment Tasks (SATs) in maths, English and science. It is important that early years educators continue to carry out their own informal and non-statutory assessments, because, as Drummond and Nutbrown (1992: 23) point out:

> The statutory requirements for the assessment of seven year olds, laid down in the Education Reform Act 1988, represent only a part of the whole process of assessment. There is much more to know about young children than their levels of attainment in Maths, English and Science at the end of Key Stage 1.

Close observation of, and interaction with, children in play will tell educators a great deal about their needs and development. Bruce (1987: 25) identifies a number of key principles which should underpin early childhood practice. She claims that: 'What children *can* do, rather than what they *cannot* do, is the starting point in the child's education'; 'and so,' as Drummond and Nutbrown (1992: 93) point out, 'by implication it is the starting point of assessment too'.

In drawing his plan for the house he was going to build, Daniel was able to show his teacher just how far his spatial awareness had developed, as well as his level of understanding of the task, hand–eye co-ordination, skills in using language, and social skills as he co-operated, negotiated and took on a leadership role. The diagnostic value of play cannot be over-emphasised; close observation of children in play guards against unrealistic expectations being placed upon them. Interaction with children in play that is well planned and purposeful allows staff to monitor not only the children's progress but also their own success in achieving the goals they have set. Careful recording provides evidence of progression and development in a whole range of areas which neither more formal methods nor simple checklists will pick up. [...] It is significant that on the building site children were much more open and honest in acknowledging what they could and could not do, and in recognizing and advertising the skills and achievements of others, than they were in other more formal learning situations.

[...]

Having eavesdropped on a group of children engrossed in and clearly enjoying their play, we may not be much further on in our quest to find an impeccable definition of either 'play' or 'quality'. What is clear is that the activity *was* purposeful and enjoyable, and that many of the processes identified as important within the framework and requirements of the National Curriculum were evident in this particular play activity. These include:

- collaborating;
- making choices;
- organizing;
- explaining;
- talking and communicating;
- sharing;
- taking responsibility;
- asking and answering;
- recording;
- interpreting, predicting, recalling and reflecting.

Those who claim that play and the National Curriculum are uneasy bedfellows are urged to think again.

[...]

References

Atkin, J. (1991) 'Thinking about Play' in Hall, N. and Abbott, L. (eds), *Play in the Primary Curriculum*. London: Hodder & Stoughton.

Bruce, T. (1987) *Early Childhood Education*. Sevenoaks: Hodder & Stoughton.

Department of Education and Science (1989) *The Education of Children under Five*. HMI Aspects of Primary Education Series. London: HMSO.

Department of Education and Science (1990) *Starting with Quality: The Report of the Committee of Inquiry into the Quality of the Educational Experience Offered to 3- and 4-year-olds.* London: HMSO.

Department of Education and Science (1991) *Geography in the National Curriculum – Programme of Study.* London: HMSO.

Drummond; M. J. and Nutbrown, C. (1992) 'Observing and Assessing Young Children', in Pugh, G. (ed.), *Contemporary Issues in the Early Years.* London: Paul Chapman.

National Curriculum Council (1990) *English Non-Statutory Guidance.* York: NCC.

Chapter 14

'What's it all about?' – how introducing heuristic play has affected provision for the under-threes in one day nursery

Ruth Holland

Introduction

> Too many books and training materials bunch the needs of under fives together but we must take care to perceive the needs of each child as unique, and to acknowledge that they each have special learning needs at different stages in their development.
>
> (Rouse and Griffin 1992:149)

The above statement describes a situation of which I have become increasingly aware. As co-owner/manager of a 60-place day nursery where over half the children are under 3, and approximately one third of children are under 2, part of my role is to oversee the planning of play and activities. Much of the material written about play is produced with 3- to 5-year-olds in mind, and does not specifically address the needs of younger children, with the result that play for children under 3 is often a watered down version of play aimed at 3- to 5-year-olds. For example a leaf printing activity may be carried out with a group of 3- to 5-year-olds with the aim of increasing the children's awareness of leaf shape or autumn colours and/or extending the children's painting skills, as well as many other possibilities. When this same activity is offered to a group of 18- to 24-month-old children who may be more interested in putting their hands in the paint, dripping paint from the brush or floating the leaves off the table, adults are often guilty of expecting the same response as they do from older children. We need to be careful that we are not guilty of fitting the child to the activity rather than the activity to the child.

One specific factor which should be considered when planning play provision for children under 3 is the tremendous rate at which development takes place. Two of the major milestones affecting children's play are mobility and speech acquisition; i.e. the needs of a small baby lying on a mat are going to be very different from the child who has just learned to walk, and again different from the child whose speech has become fluent.

[. . .]

Heuristic play

In my quest to discover more about play for children under 3 I have found work around the concept of heuristic play particularly fruitful.

'Heuristic play' is a term used by the trainer and educator Elinor Goldschmied to describe the early stages of play in which children's absorption is predominantly for putting in and out, filling and emptying containers and receptacles of all kinds. Here there is no question of success or failure. It is all new discovery and there is no 'right' or 'wrong'. The child learns from observing directly what these objects will 'do' or 'not do', in sharp contrast to much of the 'educational' equipment which has a result predetermined by the design which has been devised by the adult maker.

Part of the adults' role is to collect, buy or make a good quantity of objects such as empty tins and metal jar caps, woollen pom-poms, wooden clothes pegs, wooden and metal curtain rings and ping pong balls. The underlying idea is that these objects should offer the widest variety of materials and that they should be available to the children in large quantities.

Hair curlers of differing diameter; large and small corks; rubber door stops; varied lengths of chain, fine- to medium-sized links, not large chains; and large bone buttons can also be added to the collection (Goldschmied 1987).

The role of the adult

The role of the adult is partly that of organiser in collecting, caring for and thinking up new types of interesting items. They unobtrusively reorder objects and initiate the collecting by the children and the putting away of the materials in bags. They are essentially a facilitator, and as such they remain quiet, attentive and observant. They may study a particular child and note down all that he or she does with the materials, recording the quality of the child's concentration. The children are fully aware of their presence, though they do not encourage or suggest, praise or direct what the children do. (Only if a child begins to throw things about and disturb the others is it a wise plan to offer a receptacle and encourage her to place the things into it.)

It is important for the adult, during this heuristic play period, to sit on a chair. In this way she can be available to all the children and watch carefully what is going on. When the children are active in a group adults are likely to miss a great deal of what is significant in their behaviour if they are not seated. A child left free to choose what she wants to do in this secure atmosphere will tell a sensitive observer a lot about herself and so increase our understanding of her as an individual.

Staff who have experienced conducting this kind of play session have noted that:

- an atmosphere of tranquil concentration develops;
- children become absorbed in pursuing their own exploration of the

material for periods of half an hour and more, without direct reference to the adult;

- conflicts between the children are very infrequent because there are abundant materials, but at the same time there are many friendly interchanges between them, with gestures and early verbal comments;
- during the long nursery day this activity brings calm enjoyment both for them and for the adults. The staff have an opportunity to observe the children in a way which is not easy at other times in the busy day;
- where there are children under the age of 2 in a mixed age group, it is possible, when there is a staff member available, for her to give some special attention to a very small group. It offers a great advantage since often the younger children find they have to compete for attention with the older ones;
- as soon as a child begins to have some command of language the nature of her use of the material changes and items are put to an imaginative use as another, more complex, type of play emerges. Instead of 'What can I do with it?', the question moves to 'What can this object become?' For example, a wooden cylinder, instead of being popped through a hole, may be used as a feeding bottle for a doll. To link this to the treasure basket phase, the same cylinder has been used, by the seated baby, to grasp, suck and bang with.

[...]

Play and the under-twos

Some observations

Goldschmied (1987) recommends heuristic play for children 10 to 20 months old. As staff we made a conscientious decision to include this type of play in our curriculum. We decided that the most appropriate place to introduce this sort of play in our nursery was the Toybox room, where the children are 13 to 24 months old. One of my first observations involved two children, Richard and Harry (both 24 months), using the bobbins as trumpets, thus progressing along the continuum of learning from *What can they do with the objects?* to *What are they really for?* The use of the bobbins engaged the children's imagination and enabled them to make an attempt at deciding what the objects were really for, although at this stage it was quite clear that the former question was the more important.

[...]

I believe that Hutt *et al.* (1989) have made an immense contribution to our view of play, moving us from the simplistic notion of 'it is what all young children do' to a recognition that it is a complex, high level activity which, like all learning, is developmental. She argues that under the umbrella term 'play' there are many different behaviours, and only through close observation of, and involvement in, young children's play can the adult really understand what is going on and begin to help children move on to the next stage. The terms 'ludic' and 'epistemic' play are used to distinguish two very different kinds of play behaviours; they require different responses from adults.

Epistemic play behaviour
- is concerned with acquisition of knowledge and skill problem solving
- gathers information
- is exploratory
- is productive
- discovers
- is invention, task or work orientated
- is relatively independently of mood state
- has constraints which stem from the nature of the focus of attention
- needs adults to:
  - support
  - encourage
  - answer questions
  - supply information
  - be involved.

Ludic play behaviour
- is playful
- is fun
- is lacking in specific focus
- is highly mood dependent
- has constraints which (when they exist) are imposed by the child
- does not need to involve adults
- requires that adults should be sensitive to children's needs
- can be changed by insensitive intervention
- has the key features of enjoyment and fantasy
- is unconstrained
- is idiosyncratic
- is repetitive
- is innovative
- is symbolic.

Smilansky (1968) added a further category to Piaget's work, 'constructive play', in which objects are manipulated to construct or create something. I observed examples of such play during the session when Brittany (aged 23 months) stacked the bobbins, Lucy stacked the tins together, and Theo (13 months) placed the coat pegs all round the perimeter of the tin.

[... I also observed] the epistemic behaviour as described by Hutt *et al.* (1989), which is play that is exploratory, intent, attentive and assimilatory. This has important implications for adult involvement or at least, adult availability, if (as Hutt argues) the presence of the adult in epistemic, as distinct from ludic play, is crucial.

Important issues

I was so impressed with the quantity and quality of epistemic behaviour, as described above, that I turned my thoughts to two questions: how can we extend the opportunities for these children to gain learning experiences through exploratory play? Does this pattern of mainly exploratory play with some constructive and some symbolic play repeat itself if different toys are provided?

Taking my first question, I know the answer cannot just be 'more heuristic play', as we have found that if this play is offered more than two or three times a week to each child they begin to lose interest. I believe that this could be overcome if we had access to limitless new materials to add and swap with the existing materials but, as we don't, then other answers need to be sought.

In an attempt to answer the question I set up a water play session following the guidelines for heuristic play. Other toys and possible distractions were removed as far as possible and there was enough equipment to avoid conflict over sharing. Staff took on the role of observers and did not intervene.

The resources for the activity comprised ten shallow trays set out on tables. Each tray contained either warm, cold, clear or coloured water, with either ice cubes, corks or stones. After a while tea strainers and small beakers were added.

As I observed this activity I found, as with the heuristic play, that the behaviour was predominantly epistemic.

Another instance was when I observed this same group of children taking part in a gluing activity. As with the previous two activities all other toys were removed, each child had their own paper, glue, spreader and cut pieces of tissue paper, and staff intervened as little as possible.

The epistemic behaviour was repeated. The object of the children's intent was the glue. A great deal of time was spent stirring, dipping, spreading and making marks, with the glue and spreader on the paper. Sticking the tissue paper on was mainly ignored, unless suggested by staff, and then very often it was done quickly so the child could get back to exploring the glue. The children spent an average of 30 minutes gluing – Louisa (aged 24 months) spent 40 minutes at this activity and would have continued for longer had it not been lunch time! This is a significant finding given that researchers involved in the Oxford pre-school project (Bruner 1980) showed surprise when 3-year-olds concentrated on an activity for five minutes.

These observations led me to believe that these activities had succeeded in beginning to answer my first question: the waterplay session and gluing sessions had indeed provided further opportunity for exploratory play. My next step was to have a brainstorming session with nursery staff to produce examples of other exploratory play ideas, as my observations made me think there is certainly a need to provide this age group with plentiful opportunities for this type of play. As Abbott (1994: 80) points out, 'Hutt showed clearly that exploration is a powerful forerunner to full-blown play. Many teachers and other educators are guilty of hurrying children on to "production" when the joy, excitement, and learning to be gained from exploring the materials comes first.'

To help answer my second question – does the type of play change if the toys are different? – I set up two activities, deliberately choosing equipment aimed at play which Hutt *et al.* (1989: 224–5) found to produce ludic behaviour. The first activity was an outdoor physical play session with bikes, cars and trucks, and the second session was one in which imaginative toys were provided, such as small cars and a road mat, dinosaurs, farm animals, zoo animals, and play people.

What I observed from the outdoor play was that during the first five to ten minutes, play was relaxed and the children were at ease as they pedalled the bikes and cars around. After that the children became less boisterous, and I observed children examining pedals, looking closely at wheels, poking twigs between spokes and generally becoming more intent. What had begun with a group of nine children aged 13 to 24 months, all displaying ludic behaviour, changed after five to ten minutes to individuals behaving in an epistemic manner.

This pattern repeated itself during the imaginative play session. Again, to begin with, there were lots of examples of imaginative play – with the cars being rolled along the floor with 'brum brum' noises and animals being walked along with 'clip clop' noises – but again after five to ten minutes children began to examine the toys, turning them over, feeling them, placing them, examining them, etc.

So, therefore, from my observations the answer to my second question is that different toys and equipment can affect whether 1-year-old children play in an epistemic or ludic manner, but not as much as might be expected. But a third question might be – what exactly should be the adult role in these different kinds of play behaviours?

Staff involvement

I feel that children of this age in our nursery already have well-developed epistemic behaviour, and that while staff have an important role in providing the materials, equipment, a suitable setting and a calm atmosphere for exploratory play, there is little need for intervention during such play – this could well disturb a child's concentration or opportunity to learn through doing something for him or herself. I feel an important role for staff during such play is that of observer, thus enabling the future needs of the individual children to be assessed. However, this is something I will continue to monitor since Hutt clearly points to the important role of adult availability to support children's epistemic play.

However, in contrast to Hutt I felt that the children's play which displayed ludic behaviour – the physical and imaginative play – could benefit much more from adult intervention, as the children demonstrated their ability to initiate ludic behaviour play but were unable to sustain it for very long, unlike older children, who I have observed playing imaginative games over several days without adult intervention. It must be remembered that Hutt's research was with 3- to 5-year-olds, and clearly there are differences between this age group and the under-threes in their ability to sustain ludic play.

In order to support children I believe staff need to become fully immersed in the play, so that they are a part of it. It may be that staff initiate games such as chase in the garden, or perhaps they look to extend existing play, for example, by becoming the car park attendant when the children are playing on the bikes and cars. There may be instances where the staff play together themselves in order to provide model examples, such as holding telephone conversations using toy telephones.

However, in whatever way staff become involved in children's play, it is useful to bear in mind the conditions needed to ensure good quality play as identified in the Rumbold Report (1990) and described by Abbott (1994: 85):

1. sensitive, knowledgeable and informed adult involvement and intervention;
2. careful planning and organisation of the play setting in order to provide for and extend learning;
3. enough time for children to develop their play;
4. careful observation of children's activities to facilitate assessment and planning for progression and continuity.

[...]

Conclusion

Imaginative, exploratory and key workers' activities are now an established part of our nursery life for children under 3.

Of these activities it is the exploratory play sessions, I feel, that represent the biggest change. This would probably be the same for most pre-school establishments, as Hutt *et al.* (1989: 226) point out: 'Pre-school environments are structured in such a way as to encourage primarily ludic rather than epistemic activity...Free play, or ludic activity, clearly has an important effect on psychological development, but it requires appropriate counter-balancing by epistemic behaviour.'

I feel the quiet atmosphere and attentive behaviour of the children in exploratory play sessions can be likened to the behaviour of children when being taught in a whole-class situation – an idea to which I previously would have been averse.

However, my observations have led me to believe that the quiet atmosphere of these sessions and the attentive behaviour of the children provides them with excellent opportunities for learning.

References

Abbott, L. (1994) 'Play is ace!': developing play in schools and classrooms, in J. Moyles (ed.) *The Excellence of Play*. Buckingham: Open University Press.

Bruner, J. (1980) *Under Five in Britain*. Oxford: Grant MacIntyre.

Goldschmied, E. (1987) *Infants at Work* (training video). London: National Children's Bureau.

Hutt, J., Tyler, S., Hutt, C. and Cristopherson, H. (1989) *Play, Exploration and Learning*. London: Routledge.

Rouse, D. and Griffin, S. (1992) Quality for the under threes, in G. Pugh (ed.) *Contemporary Issues in the Early Years*. London: Paul Chapman Publishing/ National Children's Bureau.

Smilansky, S. (1968) *The Effects of Sociodramatic Play on Disadvantaged Preschool Children*. New York: Wiley.

Chapter 15

Great communicators

Marian Whitehead

The setting is a fine spring evening in a Cornish seaside town. A young couple with a child of around 12 to 15 months are sitting by the harbour. The child's buggy has been positioned as close as possible to the railings along the harbour wall and the child is leaning forward and gazing intently down at the rising tide, pointing at the lapping water, feet kicking excitedly, shouting 'sea', 'sea', 'sea'. The mother responds by saying 'Yes, it's the sea' several times.

It is all too easy to assume that an interest in children's language development must start with an interest in words and how children learn to use them. In the course of history many parents and scholars have believed just that and waited impatiently for infants to say their first words. Some legends suggest that an emperor with a taste for language study actually conducted an experiment to see if the first words of some unfortunate babies he had kept in isolation would be Latin! Even modern albums of the 'our baby' type, used for recording a child's development, usually include a page for 'first words'. But if we really do wish to understand more about language and support its development in childhood we need to start much earlier: we have to look at what is going on in the first hours and days after birth and not be misled by the excitement of words. Words rest on foundations that are laid down in the earliest communications between babies and their carers.

Communicating

For generations parents and carers have sensed that their newborn infants are attentive, playful and friendly, and modern research now supports such intuitions with clear evidence. It would seem that babies are great communicators from birth and have a range of pre-programmed abilities (instincts) which enable them to form close relationships with their carers. For example, babies prefer to look at human faces and eyes and pay attention to human voices. They actually spend remarkably long periods of time just gazing into the eyes of their carers (Schaffer 1977; Stern 1977). The recipients of this adoration are normally entranced and respond by smiling, nodding, talking and stroking the child's face, especially the cheeks, chin and lips. To an observer this behaviour can look remarkably like a real conversation, with turns taken to speak and gaps left for the 'speechless' baby to slot in comments. The adult partner behaves 'as if' this were a conversation and the slightest blink, squeak or squirm from the child is interpreted as a meaningful communication. But the infant partner is also very discriminating and will only give this level of attention to people. Although moving objects are tracked and watched, it is familiar adults who are usually treated to smiles, speech-like lip movements and arm waving (Trevarthen 1993). Furthermore, babies can set the pace for communications, making eye contact when they are feeling alert and sociable and dropping their gaze when they no longer wish to play this early language game. [. . .]

Continuing research into the sociability and communication skills of babies has demonstrated that they can imitate some interesting adult behaviours within minutes of birth (Trevarthen 1993). The list of actions imitated includes mouth opening, tongue-poking, eye blinking, eyebrow raising, sad and happy expressions and hand opening and closing. Perhaps it is not too fanciful to see these actions as crucial ones in the life of a social being who will live in groups, small and large, and communicate face to face by means of voice, expressions and gestures. We cannot dismiss these earliest acts of communication as insignificant flukes; clearly they are pre-programmed (in the genes) and therefore of some survival value to our species. Furthermore, adult carers solemnly imitate their babies and go along with the agendas they set. All this has been observed in recent years by professionals as varied as anthropologists, psychologists, linguists and educators, and the fascinating business of baby watching has attracted popular attention too (Morris 1991). There appears to be general agreement that early communication between babies and carers is a non-verbal form of 'getting in touch' with another person and crucial in the development of language, as well as of understanding and sympathy with others, and of social skills, cooperation and play.

In their earliest communications with a human partner babies also learn about themselves and how others see them. As they gaze into the eyes of their carers they see a mirror image of themselves and the responses of carers indicate how unique, human and lovable their infants are. This mirroring (Winnicott 1971), if it is a good experience, is the foundation of the child's own self-esteem and ability to love and inspire affection, and is yet another indicator of the significance of this period in a child's development when powerful communications take place without words.

Communicating babies and their carers do not live in vacuum packs and the worlds of particular cultures and communities shape their gestures, expressions, movements, talk and songs, so that from the start a baby enters a culture as well as a language. The basic patterns and timetable of language development are universal, but the fine details of gesture, talk, song and traditional care and beliefs about infants are as varied as the languages children learn. This is an important reminder that the roles of carers, families and cultural communities will always be of great significance in children's linguistic, intellectual and social development. Children do not just learn a language, they learn a way of life.

The kind of communication discussed so far is described by linguists as 'non-verbal communication': it helps to prepare babies for speech and underpins our use of spoken language for the rest of our lives. This wordless communication can also develop into sophisticated signing systems for the deaf, as well as complex signalling systems for occupations as different as dance and mime, racecourse bookmaking and aircraft landing control. The main characteristics of non-verbal communication in infancy are:

- face-to-face intimacy;
- strong feelings (from warm affection to rage and frustration);
- very dramatic use of facial expressions, especially eyes and eyebrows, mouth, lips and tongue;
- whole body movements (including dancing, for example), head nodding and shaking, arm and hand gestures;
- the use of 'mouth sounds' like clicks, whistles, hums, 'raspberries' and loud 'boos'.

The last set of characteristics may seem a little bizarre, but we all make use of 'tuts', grunts, 'mms' and even whistles in our talk, especially on the telephone when we have to keep in touch with our invisible talk partner. In the early days of infant communication, imitating these exaggerated mouth sounds may help the baby to practise a whole range of sounds used in the eventual production of words, but we should also note that such sounds may be funny, outrageous and even rude. Right from the start there is a strong current of playfulness, mucking about and teasing in communication – and babies do as much of the mucking about as do their carers (Reddy 1991; Trevarthen 1993). This teasing is a kind of fibbing, or playful deception, and is thought by some linguists to explain partly how language originated. In group life it was (and still is) important to be able to influence others, guess what was in their minds, and even 'change their minds'. Apparently the great apes, our nearest animal relatives, are 'extremely skilled deceivers' (Aitchison 1997: 26) – especially the chimpanzees – but for purely selfish reasons often connected with food. Human beings, however, can choose to tell a lie which is kind rather than brutally honest, and have turned fibbing into games and 'telling tales' into an art form.

Finding the words

First words, when they come, do not spring perfectly formed after months of silence. As examples of meaningful sounds they emerge from babbling which has been strongly influenced by the sounds of the language, or languages, used constantly with and around the child. As understandable and regularly used labels for people, objects, feelings and events, they can be traced back to the early months of non-verbal communication, when babies develop recognizable 'sounds' for significant people, toys and noisily impressive objects like lorries and aeroplanes. These personal labels evolved by an infant may start out as a 'gaa' or 'brr' but they gradually move closer to the standard words used in the home and speech community (Halliday 1975). In the course of this development they are often 'stretched' in their use by the child so that they can cover a whole range of similar events or ideas. For example, the sound or word for 'car' may be used for lorries, shopping trolleys and lifts; the early word for a significant male carer or parent may be used for any man seen in the street or on the local bus.

This gradual building up of a collection of important words for things is greatly helped by the behaviour of carers who communicate with babies and play the sorts of games which involve highly predictable routines with their own special sounds and words. For example, simply giving and taking things and saying 'please' and 'thank you', or waving and saying 'bye-bye', or pointing at and naming things in homes, streets, magazines, catalogues, picture books and on the television screen. All these important language games really get things going, but words are not just any old random sounds and identifying the first words of immature speakers is not easy (after all, they will have difficulty forming certain sounds for some years in early childhood). Because of this, modern linguists, unlike proud parents and carers, have a set of criteria for what is really a 'first word':

- it is used spontaneously by the child;
- it is used regularly in the same activity or setting;
- it is identified by the carer.

The emphasis on spontaneous use is important because with first words we are looking for evidence of the child's ability to identify and attempt to share meanings by using words – we are not interested in the skills of a well-trained parrot! The best evidence for meaningful word use is the child's reusing of the word in appropriate and similar situations. Treating the carer as the expert who can recognize and identify these first words is essential because only a regular carer has intimate knowledge of the child, as well as detailed knowledge of the contexts in which early words emerge.

The expertise of carers and the contexts in which children use their first words are interesting features of early language learning. Many studies of first words have been conducted and later published by linguists working with their own children – or their grandchildren (Engel and Whitehead 1993) – because carers are best placed to understand their children and their settings. This very powerful insider knowledge has revealed, among other things, that first words start as personal but highly consistent sounds (Halliday 1975); that first words are vivid records of the home life, culture and experiences of children; and that toddlers continue to practise language – especially new sounds, rhymes and words – on their own before falling asleep (Weir 1962; Nelson 1989).

Children's first words indicate how they are sorting out and making sense of their particular worlds and they also provide a guide to what really matters to them. When collections of first words are analysed it soon becomes clear that they can be grouped under such headings as: members of the family, daily routines, food, vehicles, toys and pets (Whitehead 1990). Clearly, people, food, animals and possessions are of great importance to babies and their obvious attractions drive the infants' search for labels. Having the right words for people and things is an almost foolproof way of getting others to help you get hold of, or stay close to, good things.

Also found among the first words are some simple instructions and requests such as 'up', 'walk', 'out', 'gone' and those really important little words in any language, 'yes' and 'no' (or their linguistic equivalents). All these kinds of words enable a small and fairly immobile person to manage other people, get help and make personal needs and feelings felt. During this 'first words' phase of language development it is obvious to parents, carers and professional linguists that children's single words frequently stand for quite complex sets of meanings, communications and instructions. A word like 'dirty' can in certain situations mean 'my hands are dirty', 'are you putting my paint-splashed T-shirt in the washing machine?' or 'I've dropped my apple on the floor'. Only the carer who is with the child at the time can understand and respond appropriately to such one-word utterances – and may still get them wrong! Human communication is always a sensitive and risky business and single words can only do so much. In order to unlock more of the power of language the young communicator must put words together in meaningful and unique combinations.

The power of language

Once young children begin to combine words together it is even more obvious that they are thinking for themselves and have some powerful understanding about how languages work. The evidence for these big claims can be found in the children's unique language creations which cannot have been imitated from adults and older children. We are likely to hear such requests as 'door uppy' (open the door) and 'no doing daddy' (don't do it daddy), and older infants go on to create new verbs out of nouns, as in 'lawning' (mowing the lawn) and 'I seat-belted myself' (putting on a seat-belt). Professional linguists get very excited about these examples (although other people often dismiss them as 'funny things children say') because they are evidence that all children are born with an innate ability to understand and produce appropriate and meaningful language (Chomsky 1957; Aitchison 1989; Pinker 1994). In fact, this remarkable ability to combine words together so that they make sense is grammar in action and indicates that a child is capable of thought, as well as able to be sociable and influence others.

Professional linguists describe 'grammars' in terms of the things they enable us to do with language (this may come as a surprise to readers reared on a strict diet of adjectives, past participles and the like) and the two highly significant functions of language are: getting things done especially with the help of others – and commenting and reflecting on the world (Halliday 1975). Young children certainly use their emerging skills as speakers in order to get carers and others to do things for them ('chair uppy': lift me onto the chair), and they also make statements which suggest that they can observe the world and comment on what happens ('no more miaow', said as the cat leaves the room). It is worth emphasizing that these early word combinations are evidence of thought, and of an innate ability to share and communicate meanings. Many people are convinced that language is for communication and socializing, which it is, but they overlook its role in our thinking and memory. Yet there is powerful research evidence, as well as common sense, to tell us that language creates and extends our ability to think about abstract and complicated ideas such as 'trust' and 'freedom', or things that are distant in time and space (dinosaurs; Australia; last week's visit to the cinema; my first taste of ice-cream), as well as the entirely invented and non-existent 'little green creatures from Mars', Paddington Bear and Jane Eyre.

These are examples of language as a symbolic system – that is, a way of letting words stand for things, ideas and experiences even in their absence, so that we can hold onto them and think about them. This is so central to human thinking that in cases where disease or genetic damage impair or prevent the development of speech and language other symbolic systems must evolve. The signing and touching 'languages' used by the deaf and the blind provide ways of sorting, ordering, recalling and reflecting on experience as well as gaining the cooperation of others. In early childhood the developmental patterns of affected children may show some personal and some general variations. The emergence of grammatical understanding will be in the normal range because it is pre-programmed and universal, but early word acquisition may show some delay (Harris 1992) because it is triggered and enriched by all the social and cultural naming and labelling games played with babies. It is important that infants who do have some form of sensory impairment have endless opportunities to touch, feel, move rhythmically, sign and name all the people, objects, materials and animals in their environments. We can still learn a great deal from the inspired teacher who placed the hands of the blind and deaf Helen Keller under a gushing water pump and constantly wrote the letter signs w-a-t-e-r on the child's palms as the water poured over them. Such support was left almost too late for Helen Keller who had to retrieve years of loneliness and frustration, but every impaired infant can be helped from the start with a range of stimulating sensory experiences linked to words or signs.

A timetable for speech and language?

In many ways learning languages never stops: we all increase our stock of words and continue to pick up the latest technical terms and fashionable slang of our groups and cultures. Many children start with more than one language, particularly in multilingual societies, or go on to acquire a second and third language at an early age. Some adults learn a new language for professional or social reasons, even to enhance their holidays in foreign countries, and schools in most societies are required to teach one or more other languages. The process of becoming literate and learning the written system of a language is also part of language learning, as is the skilled way in which we all adjust our language (dialect) and our pronunciation (accent) according to particular situations and audiences. But the earliest stages of learning to speak in childhood hold a great fascination for most adults who work with children and/or raise their own families, and some kind of developmental timetable is often asked for. However, such timetables can be rather dangerous if taken too seriously and interpreted with rigidity. Every child and every set of circumstances into which she or he is born is different, which renders timetables both unhelpful and potentially worrying for parents and carers. It is for this reason that no such timetable is included in this book.

A few notes on grammar

Some comments on grammar in this chapter may have seemed strange and require a brief explanation. A great deal of ignorance, prejudice and even fear surrounds the topic of grammar, and the modern study of language – known as linguistics – has not really changed this. The problems arise because there are two very different views of grammar, although few people understand or admit this. The most widespread view is rooted in largely discredited beliefs about what is 'correct' and 'good' in language and emphasises traditional rules of thumb which tell us how we *ought* to speak and write. This is known as the 'prescriptive' tradition because it 'prescribes' or 'tells us' exactly what the users of a language *ought* to do. However, the rules prescribed are mainly based on examples from Latin (historically the language of a very few educated and scholarly groups) and from written language, neither of which provide helpful guidance for young contemporary speakers of a living language, or their families. This rather illogical approach is aggravated by a general fear of change and of the ethnic and linguistic diversity in society, plus an excessive and persistent respect for privileged groups whose private education still values classical, 'dead' languages highly. This is sometimes at the expense of living languages, which are caricatured as having no grammar and not best suited for training the mind. Of course the situation is rarely described in such blunt terms, but the damage such unchallenged assumptions can do is considerable.

For example, the prescriptive approach has the effect of dividing a society into those who believe that they speak correctly and those who become convinced that they are bad speakers of their first language. It also promotes a rather nasty view of languages as ranked in league tables with some – mainly English and western European languages – at the top because they are supposedly more logical and sophisticated. This approach not only dismisses some languages (and by implication their speakers) as primitive and limited; it also seriously undervalues their young speakers' remarkable and creative achievements in early language learning.

The study of modern linguistics presents a quite different approach to grammar and actually sees it as a universal feature of human thinking, thus providing us with clues about how the mind works. The essential difference in approach stems from the fact that this linguistics is 'descriptive' not 'prescriptive', and aims to describe how we actually learn to speak and the rules we appear to be following when we speak and write a living language. In order to do this modern linguists attempt to be *scientific*: they look at what is going on in every aspect of language use. So, they observe, record, analyse and make informed guesses about what is happening in a language and what individual speakers and groups are doing with language in any given situation. They certainly do come up with rules for how a language works, but they get the rules from what speakers and writers are *doing* with language and they are always ready to change their descriptions over time as a language changes to meet the needs of its speakers.

Educators and carers need to understand a little about what lies behind the endless arguments about language and grammar, if only to realise that the disagreements are like the old quarrels between flat-earthers (a bit like prescriptive linguists) and those who accepted that the earth was round (somewhat like descriptive linguists)! The serious point here is that guidance and statutory regulations for the teaching of language, grammar and literacy are being imposed on early years settings, schools and even parents, and some of these regulations are very prescriptive and closer to a 'flat-earther' position than is admitted. For example, a long list of words to be learnt and recognised out of context are prescribed in the *National Literacy Strategy: Framework for Teaching* (DfEE 1998) for Reception year children, and these words are not memorable ones like 'elephant' or 'banana', but include the likes of 'and', 'my', 'it', 'was', and so on. Further lists of 'high frequency' words are also provided for the rest of the primary years. Other sources indicate more sensible, enjoyable and properly language-based approaches to helping young children build up their abilities to recognise such words on sight.

In conclusion, we need to be proud of young children's language, thinking and early literacy behaviours, and able to defend a sensible descriptive view of languages. We can point out that modern grammar is not an undisciplined free-for-all, but describes the rules of a language operating on at least three levels concerned with:

- the organization and patterns of *sounds* (known as phonology);
- the meaningful *combination of words* (known as syntax);
- the *meanings* of words and groups of words (known as semantics);

A fourth level, the *vocabulary* or stock of words in a language (known as lexis), is often included in grammatical descriptions.

This description of several levels of grammatical rules highlights the skill and complexity involved in the everyday use of language by any speakers and the remarkable achievements of young children in learning languages. However, it is not an easy guide to teaching grammar – in most cases these rules are far too complex for direct teaching – but it is a kind of ground plan for basing our approaches in the early years on children's love of language, their desire to communicate and their need to make sense of life and experiences. If simple rules are required, then we could do no better than suggest:

- raising the status of *talk* and *communication*;
- ensuring that any language use, spoken or written, is *appropriate for its purpose and situation*;
- drawing children's attention to print everywhere and *making print exciting*.

Supporting young communicators

Successful caring, parenting and educating is bound up with paying close and serious attention to young children and helping them to understand their world and manage themselves in it. But taking children seriously as people does not have to be grim and humourless – on the contrary, the best adult carers and educators are the most playful. The child watching the rising tide at the start of this chapter was already at the single-word naming stage of communication, but she (or he!) had been supported just enough to make talk about the sea possible: the buggy was as close as safety allowed to the edge of the harbour wall so that the child could peer down; time was made for uninterrupted watching; the child's recognition and naming of the sea was taken up by the mother and confirmed and expanded into a fuller statement. Above all, the sheer joy of watching the sea was communicated and shared. We can assume that this kind of communication had been repeated in other settings and circumstances many times before and had developed out of months of child and adult play, subtle body language, adult talk and shared communicative sounds and gestures.

We have to value all the non-verbal interactions which occur between infants and adults (or older children) in homes and group settings, create extra opportunities for them, and continue to value a wide range of non-verbal communications after spoken language is established. This will be particularly crucial for children whose first language is not English when they enter care and group settings, because they have to depend on picking up all the non-verbal communicative clues they can. The challenge this presents for the professional adults working with these young potential bilinguals can, however, lead to a wonderful freeing up and transforming of the procedures and curriculum in the setting.

Provision and activities

The following will help ensure rich linguistic beginnings:

- *People* Play, talk and interaction with other people are the key activities at this stage. At home, parents, other family, siblings, child minders and nannies are the key provision. In group care settings, key workers or stable carers for the youngest babies; a wider number of adults, young adults and older children, as well as same-age peers (babies who are able to sit up enjoy the company of other babies).
- *Places* In group settings some very small rooms and sheltered areas, inside and out, with cushions, carpeted areas and blankets to lie and sit on; the creation in homes and institutions of safe cupboards, dens (tables with floor-length drapes/cloths over them) or full-length curtains to hide behind; safe garden houses, trees, bushes and improvised tents (blankets, sheets and clothes-airers), and even sturdy fencing to peep through or imagine what lies on the other side.
- *Things to do* Face-to-face gazing, talking, gesturing, bouncing, singing, dancing, clapping; opportunities for listening and quiet watching (other children and adults, animals, moving trees, mobiles, out of windows, pictures, books); plenty of 'helping and talking' activities like food preparation, clearing up and domestic chores, bath times, getting dressed, gardening, shopping, walks and visits; opportunities to play with collections of natural and manufactured objects presented in 'treasure baskets' (Goldschmied and Jackson 1994) (e.g. wooden and metal spoons, fir-cones, shells, sponges, containers and lids, balls); also, saucepans and lids, rattles, squeakers, simple percussion instruments, wooden and plastic blocks (building bricks), soft toys and dolls; a small collection of picture, story, poetry and alphabet books.
- *Things to talk about* All the above provide ample opportunities for communication and talk and the development of complex forms of thinking.

References

Aitchison, J. (1989) *The Articulate Mammal: An Introduction to Psycholinguistics.* London: Routledge.

Aitchison, J. (1997) *The Language Web* (1996 BBC Reith Lectures). Cambridge: Cambridge University Press.

Chomsky, N. (1957) *Syntactic Structures.* The Hague: Mouton.

DfEE (Department for Education and Employment) (1998) *The National Literacy Strategy: Framework for Teaching.* London: DfEE.

Engel, D. M. and Whitehead, M. R. (1993) More first words: A comparative study of bilingual siblings. *Early Years* **14**(1), 27–35.

Goldschmied, E. and Jackson, S. (1994) *People Under Three.* London: Routledge.

Halliday, M. A. K. (1975) *Learning How To Mean: Explorations in the Development of Language.* London: Arnold.

Harris, M. (1992) *Language Experience and Early Language Development: From Input to Uptake*. Hove: Lawrence Erlbaum.

Morris, D. (1991) *Babywatching*. London: Jonathan Cape.

Nelson, K. (1989) *Narratives from the Crib*. Cambridge, MA: Harvard University Press.

Pinker, S. (1994) *The Language Instinct: The New Science of Language and Mind*. Harmondsworth: Allen Lane/Penguin.

Reddy, V. (1991) Playing with others' expectations; teasing and mucking about in the first year, in A. Whiten (ed.) *Natural Theories of Mind*. Oxford: Blackwell.

Schaffer, H. R. (ed.) (1977) *Studies in Mother-Infant Interaction*. London: Academic Press.

Stern, D. (1977) *The First Relationship: Infant and Mother*. London: Fontana.

Trevarthen, C. (1993) Playing into reality: conversations with the infant communicator. *Winnicott Studies* **7**, 67–84.

Weir, R. H. (1962) *Language in the Crib*. The Hague: Mouton.

Whitehead, M. R. (1990) First words: the language diary of a bilingual child's early speech. *Early Years* **10**(2), 53–7.

Winnicott, D. W. (1971) *Playing and Reality*. Harmondsworth: Penguin.

Chapter 16

Creative and imaginative experiences

Bernadette Duffy

Introduction: the dangers of a narrow approach

Too often young children are given access to a narrow range of creative and imaginative experiences which are limited and superficial. For example, opportunities to paint can be restricted to using a small number of ready mixed paints, with no choice of brush or paper texture, size or shape. As a 6-year-old boy told me, 'I like painting best *but* you can only paint at "choosing time". Miss says only one person at a time, no paint on the floor, don't mix the paints, one picture each so every one gets a turn *and* only if you've finished *all* your work. *I* don't think that's fair.' These sorts of conditions lead to impoverished provision and depressed thinking. If children are to become competent and use the media for their own ends they need the opportunity and time to explore a wide range of experiences.

The importance of access to a wide range of experiences

Tables 16.1–16.5 outline the different experiences that are part of the creative and imaginative area of learning. Each experience offers possibilities for learning and if we are not aware of these we may miss opportunities and impede children's progress. We need to ensure that the creative and imaginative experiences we offer are:

- *broad:* they must include the full range of experiences
- *balanced:* they must not concentrate on one area of experience and restrict or neglect the rest
- *accessible:* children's access should be monitored and their learning and development systematically assessed.

While some of the experiences described in Tables 16.1–16.5 will be available all the time and provide our core provision, others may be introduced for a limited period in response to children's interest and needs. By giving children access to a variety of experiences we offer them the opportunity to learn and develop:

- attitudes, feelings and dispositions
- knowledge and understandings
- skills and abilities.

and to use these in their own creative and imaginative ways. Each of these features of learning is important. For example, there is little point in teaching children the technical skills involved in drawing or music if they do not also have the desire to use these skills to create their own drawings or music, or to understand the work of others. Conversely, it is frustrating to have a burning desire to create a sound but to lack the technical skills necessary to achieve it. While knowledge and skills can be taught, attitudes and feelings cannot be learnt through direct instruction, but only develop in an environment that is encouraging and values these attributes. Creative and imaginative experiences encourage a wide range of:

ATTITUDES, DISPOSITIONS, FEELINGS

fun   appreciation   confidence   self-motivation   values

enthusiasm   experimentation   persistence   sharing

curiosity   perseverance   enjoyment   cooperation

willingness   acceptance   excitement   reflection   self-esteem

concern   self-discipline   evaluation   concentration

helpfulness   pleasure   lack of inhibition   respect for others

---

As adults we divide creative and imaginative experiences into the different forms of representation, for example, painting, drawing, imaginative play, and into knowledge, skill and attitudes to help us to plan and monitor children's access to a broad and balanced range of experiences. Children will not divide or perceive the experiences on offer in this way. For them, experiences are not compartmentalised and attitudes, knowledge and skills do not develop in isolation from each other.

Access for all

Access to creative and imaginative experiences are not only for those identified as gifted. Everyone has an entitlement to the full range of experience and to reach their full potential – the principles which underpin this chapter. But the society we live in assigns different value to different groups of people based on their:

- race, religion, culture, class and ethnicity
- gender
- special educational needs.

People in particular groups are seen as inferior, for example, people whose skin is not white, people who have certain medical conditions (HIV positive, mental illness), or people who come from particular religions (Muslims, Jews). Children who belong to families in these groups can find that their access to the creative and imaginative experiences they need is limited because of beliefs based on the view that they are inferior.

Children from some groups appear to display marked ability in certain aspects of creativity and imagination. However, we need to be cautious about ascribing this to innate ability. It is just as likely to be the result of upbringing and expectations. For example:

- Some groups of Chinese children have highly developed drawing skills at an early age owing to the value placed on and early instruction in these skills by the communities in which they live (Cox 1992).
- Boys often appear to be better than girls at creating three-dimensional representations with construction materials. While this may be partly the result of innate differences, most of the difference is due to the greater encouragement boys receive (Moyles 1989).

Children are aware of the values and judgements of the adults around them from a young age (DHSS 1989, *The Children Act: Guidance and Regulations*, Volume 2: 34). The distorted opinions that develop from exposure to beliefs that are based on prejudice and discrimination will stay with them. Young children need to preserve, develop and value their own worth and the worth of those around them. This does not mean treating all children in the same way but [rather] of ensuring that all children feel valued. If all children are to achieve this the adults who are part of their lives must be aware of:

- the prejudice that exists in society
- the ways in which beliefs based on prejudice affect children's opportunities to learn and develop their creativity and imagination
- the steps that can be taken to challenge and overcome prejudice and ensure equal opportunities for all children.

The range of abilities evident in any group of children make it extremely unwise to simply assume competence, or lack of it, on the basis of membership of a certain group. The abilities they display may be the result of innate ability but can also be the outcome of encouragement from the adults around them. We need, therefore, to ensure that all children have access to a broad range of experiences.

Leanne

Leeanne, aged 5 years, was involved in acting out the story of Cinderella. This had gone on over a number of days and with each retelling the narrative became more complex and detailed. She reached the point in her drama when she needed the ballgown. With the help of a nursery nurse student, Leeanne created the gown from lengths of cloth fastened with safety pins and decorated with stapled-on braiding. Once the gown was completed she returned to her imaginative play and continued the story. At the end of the session she chose to record her experience by drawing a picture of the ball, which she shared with her mother at home time. Leeanne's learning covered a number of creative and imaginative experiences. She engaged in imaginative play, used textiles and drew. She demonstrated a variety of attitudes, knowledge and skills. For example, cooperation, perseverance, knowledge of fabrics and their properties, knowledge of fairy tales, fine and gross motor skills. For Leeanne these were not experienced as separate entities, they were experienced as a whole.

Valuing children's race, religion, culture, class and ethnicity

The materials, equipment and experiences we offer should reflect a wide variety of cultural experiences. This is especially important for mono-cultural settings where children may not have the opportunity to encounter cultural diversity in their community, and when home cultures emphasize clearly defined roles for each gender. Creative experiences and imaginative play offer children the opportunity to explore lifestyles outside their immediate family and to gain an insight into the lives of others. It is important to avoid reinforcing stereotypes, for example, that all Indian women wear saris, or adopting a 'tourist' approach, such as only showing images of people from ethnic minorities in artificial and exotic settings. The aim is to increase children's understanding by showing images that reflect the real-life experience of families from a variety of cultures.

Stereotypical ideas of class may limit children's access. For example, some forms of creative expression, such as ballet and opera, are seen as not being relevant to working-class children. Children from different religious groups can also find their access curtailed, for instance it is sometimes assumed that children from Muslim families are not allowed to depict the human form. In fact, the depiction of the human form is only prohibited in mosques. There are many wonderful examples of Muslim artists representing the human form, for example in miniatures.

The experiences children have in their homes and communities will affect their uptake of the creative and imaginative experiences we offer. The experience of imaginative and creative play alongside an older sibling or friend can enhance younger children's play. In communities where they are part of an extended family or a network of close friends, young children will often have skills that children of a similar age, without access to these networks, lack.

Valuing children's gender

Young children are interested in gender differences and explore the roles adopted by each. While it is essential that children develop a positive self-image, part of which involves their identification with others of the same gender, we need to make sure that this does not limit their access to creative and imaginative experiences. The challenge is to confront stereotypes which limit access, and offer experiences which extend children's horizons. We need to think carefully about the labels we use, for instance, calling the imaginative play area of a classroom the 'Wendy house' or 'home corner' will not encourage boys to use it. Similarly, we need to monitor children's use of the physical environment to ensure equal access. For example, girls may be reluctant about using construction materials if these have been monopolised by boys and are therefore seen as 'boys' toys'. Bloom and Sosniak (1981) examined longitudinal studies of creative people and found that early experiences which de-emphasised traditional roles were significant.

Valuing children with special educational needs

Children with special needs are sometimes offered a limited curriculum with the view that they need to give all their attention to the acquisition of so-called basic skills – though what could be more basic than the desire to create? However, in many ways the experiences that form the creative and imaginative range have a particular relevance to children with special needs. These experiences encourage an open-ended approach to learning and enable children to use all their senses, including those which may be impaired. When children have a condition such as autism, art and music may offer a means of self-expression and creativity when spoken language fails them. Creative and imaginative experiences can offer children with special educational needs the opportunity to order their understandings and inner worlds and share these with others. Music and dance can express meanings which surmount the need for words.

Children who have marked abilities may also experience difficulties. Marked ability in one part of the creative and imaginative range of experience, for example music, may lead to an over-concentration on that area and neglect of other aspects of creativity.

It is essential to ensure that children with special educational needs are not intentionally or unintentionally excluded. The challenge is to adapt or expand the experience so that everyone who wishes can be involved.

Anderson

Anderson, aged 4 years 6 months, was visually impaired. His key worker observed his reluctance to engage in forms of representation which involved fine detail and confined locations, such as drawing while seated at a table. She responded by rearranging the outside space to include large sheets of paper attached to the wall for painting and drawing. Anderson responded with enthusiasm. He concentrated for long periods and returned to his drawings to refine and develop the images. The opportunity to work on a large scale enabled him to make full use of his available sight and the more spacious surroundings allowed him to move without fear of bumping into a person or object. By assessing Anderson's particular needs and altering the way in which he had access to drawing experiences his key worker helped him to engage in an aspect of creative expression he had previously been denied.

Two- and three-dimensional experiences and the possibilities for learning they offer (see Table 16.1)

Two- and three-dimensional experiences are often referred to as the visual arts. Two-dimensional experiences include:

- drawing – defining shapes and events with line
- painting – defining areas of surface colour
- printing – making marks by pressing
- textiles – creating woven surfaces and fabrics
- photography – creating images with the chemical action of light on film.

Three-dimensional representations include:

- constructions – forming representations by fitting together
- sculpting – forming representations by chiselling or carving
- modelling – working plastic materials into shape.

Experiences under this heading offer opportunities to represent using the elements of art:

- pattern – repetition of shape, colour, light
- texture – characteristics or quality of surface
- colour – hue (property of colour e.g. red, orange), intensity, saturation, brilliance, primary colours (red, yellow, blue) secondary colours (combinations of primary colours – orange, green, and violet)
- line, a mark, stroke, strip, dash
- tone – lightness or darkness, shade
- shape – outline
- form – three-dimensional experience of shape
- space – area between shapes.

Musical experiences and the possibilities for learning they offer (see Table 16.2)

Music is one of the performing arts and includes using voice, sounds, tuned instruments, untuned instruments, etc. to:

- produce musical sounds
- perform
- composing.

Musical experiences offer children the opportunities to explore and represent using the following elements:

- timbre – characteristics or qualities of sound
- texture – the way sounds are put together
- pitch – high/low, higher/lower
- dynamics – volume, loud/quiet, louder/quieter
- tempo – speed, fast/slow, faster/slower, rhythm, pulse
- duration – long/short
- harmony – two or more musical sounds produced together.

to provide:

- structure – the organisation of sounds, melody, combining musical phrases, and patterns
- composition – creation and formulation of work.

Dance experiences and the possibilities for learning they offer (see Table 16.3)

This is another performing art and includes using expressive movement to:

- produce dance
- perform dance
- compose dance.

Experiences under this heading offer opportunities to explore and represent using the elements of movement:

- basic actions – travelling, jumping, turning, rolling, balancing
- gesture – using face, fingers, hands, arms, feet
- stillness – frozen movement
- pattern – linking and repeating actions and gestures.

Imaginative play experiences and the possibilities for learning they offer (see Table 16.4)

Experiences under this heading offer opportunities to explore and represent:

- actions
- roles
- relationships
- situations
- characters from a variety of sources
- narratives and stories.

Sabrina

Sabrina, aged 3 years and 2 months, Elizabeth, aged 3 years, Maurice, aged 4 years and 1 month and Teddy, aged 4 years 6 months, were painting alongside each other mixing the colours they wanted using block paints in the primary colours and a selection of brushes. Each was involved in creating their own representation but was also aware of, and interested in, the work of the others. Sabrina was engaged in representing a house, she turned to Maurice:

Sabrina:	That doesn't look like a house.
Maurice:	That's because it's not a house it's a brown bear. I'm trying to get brown but it's gone purple.
Teddy [to Sabrina]:	Well that doesn't look like a house, it looks like a mermaid, look there's the tail.
Elizabeth:	You're looking at it upside down, that's the roof! Mermaids have legs!
Teddy:	No they don't...well, I suppose they might have legs inside their tails.
Sabrina:	I'll put the windows in...now it looks like a house.
Maurice:	It's the mermaid's house, that's what it is!

Table 16.1 Two- and three-dimensional representations and the opportunities they offer for learning

Experience	Knowledge, understanding, concepts	Skills and abilities
Drawing using a wide range of: • graphic and mark-making tools – fingers, pencils, charcoal, computer • surfaces – different textures and sizes of paper and card, chalk boards, computer screens, permissable walls and pavements • subject matter – physical attributes, abstract concepts such as the sound of a drum, recording movement • investigating marks and the qualities of lines, rubbings	• pattern, shape, line, tone, form, space, proportion • types of drawing materials and equipment • uses materials and equipment • drawing from a range of traditions • how to represent texture, shade, pattern movement, with marks	• observation • interpretation • estimation • measurement • experimentation • investigation • prediction • problem-solving • recollection
Painting using a wide range of: • hues – primary, secondary; shades – pastels, dark, light • sorts of paint – powder, block, natural dyes, ready mixed and self-mixed • techniques for applying paint – fingers, feet, a selection of brushes, marbling, spraying, splashing, stencilling • surfaces – paper and card of different sizes and textures	• colours, tints, shades, density • how to mix a range of colours • how to lighten and darken colours • the properties of paint texture • how to represent forms, texture, movement, colour by using paints	• recording • fine manipulation • gross motor skills • correct use of tools • equipment and materials
Printing using a wide range of: • objects – hands, natural and found materials, raised and embossed • surfaces – paper, card, fabric, walls, clay • forms – patterns (repeated and single), natural shapes, manufactured	• two-dimensional surfaces • the importance of flat surfaces when printing • properties of different surfaces • pattern	• communication • hand and eye coordination • tidiness • carefulness • accuracy • safety

Table 16.1 continued

Experience	Knowledge, understanding, concepts	Skills and abilities
Textiles using a wide range of: • techniques – plaiting, twisting, winding, sewing, dyeing appliqué, printing, knitting • cloths and threads – wool, canvas, hessian, linen, string, cotton, printed materials, raffia, straw, grasses, twigs	• textiles and their properties • weaving and sewing techniques • textiles from a range of cultures and times • use of clothing to represent membership of cultural, social or religious groups	
Photography using a range of: • cameras • light sources and images • light-sensitive paper	• know that cameras can take photographs • light sources • light sensitive paper • how to exclude light • the effect of excluding or increasing light	
Constructing – forming representations by fitting together using a wide range of: • commercial and found materials – bricks, blocks, Lego, wood • different ways of joining – using glue gun, gluing, tying, knotting, hammering, threading, looping, nailing, screwing, brass fastening, paper, clipping, stapling, treasury-tagging, binding, interlocking pieces • different ways of parting – cutting, tearing, sawing, punching hole • different forms – mobiles, collages, models	• names of shapes of the blocks and their relative sizes • properties of paper, wood, card • correct use of tools and implements, glue guns, staplers, scissors, etc. • balance • tessellation and pattern	• joining • parting • measuring • comparing size, shape, height • estimating volume • balancing blocks

Table 16.1 continued

Experience	Knowledge, understanding, concepts	Skills and abilities
Sculpting – forming representations by chiselling or carving using a wide range of: • materials – wood, salt, sand, stone • tools – hands, fingers, cutlery, saws, commercial tools • techniques – carving, hammering	• properties of materials • effect of removing portions from mass	• coordination of eyes, hands and fingers
Modelling – working plastic materials into shape using a wide range of: • materials – papier mâché, clay, dough • tools – hands, fingers, cutlery, commercial tools • techniques – moulding, pinching, scooping, flattening, rolling thumbing, squeezing, attaching, wedging	• of which materials can be: modelled • of the effect of manipulating plastic substances	

Table 16.2 Musical experiences and the possibilities they offer for learning

Experience	Knowledge, understanding, concepts	Skills and abilities
Producing a wide range of musical sounds and performing by: • using voice and mouth – shouting, humming, singing • body – hand clapping, finger clicking, feet stamping, rubbing • found materials – kitchen utensils, blocks, building textures (gravel, bricks, wood) • homemade instruments • keyboards – piano, organ • percussion – tuned (glockenspiel, bells) untuned (drums, shakers) • wind – trumpets, pipes, whistles • strings – violins, guitars, sitars • interpreting the work of others – from memory and simple scores • playing and performing with others	• things that make a sound • vibration produces sound • different sound effects of wood, strings, skin • tempo, rhythm, pitch, dynamic • names of instruments • correct usage of instruments • awareness of audience and venue • simple pieces and accompaniments • repertoire of songs from a range of cultures and traditions • instruments and music from a range of cultures and traditions	• listening, discriminating and memorising • experimenting with sounds – turn taking – voice control (breathing, singing, humming) • being part of a group • plucking, hitting, pressing instruments with accuracy • playing as part of a group – turn taking, patience • cutting, fastening, to make instruments
Composing and recording sound in response to a wide range of stimuli through: • opportunities to experiment with sound • memorising simple patterns to accompany songs • representing sounds and patterns using – child's own symbols and traditional notation • producing sound effects • improvising musical patterns • composing own pieces of music • recording own music • recording sound in different ways – memory, tape recorders, CD players, own marks, notations and scores	• that sound can be represented by symbols • that musical ideas can be communicated to others • ways in which sound can be represented • names of notes, their values and position of notes on stave • pentatomic scale • that major and minor chords can be related to moods	• recording sounds – operating tape recorders, making marks • reading music using child's symbols, colour coded and traditional notation • interpreting sounds and symbols

Table 16.3 Dance experiences and the possibilities they offer for learning

Experience	Knowledge, understanding, concepts	Skills and abilities
Producing and performing using movement expressively and creatively by: • moving the body – what can the body do and which parts of the body move? • moving in space – level, direction, pathways, sizes • moving in time – dynamics, tempo in terms of time, weight, space, flow • moving with others – with a partner, in a group, with an object • moving in response to music and sound • develop a repertoire of movements to express what is heard and felt • dances from different cultures and traditions • interpret and execute movements	• names of parts of body • spatial awareness • direction and position of words – left and right, up and down, backwards and forwards, side to side • sequence words – next, first, last • speed words – fast, slow, quicker • how to move body in a particular sequence of movement • movements related to tempo and mood • music can be interpreted in movement	• jumping and bouncing • swinging and swaying • stretching and arching • turning and bending • spinning and twirling • stepping and skipping • crawling and contracting • stopping and starting
Composing and recording in response to a wide range of stimuli by: • representing stories, music and ideas through dance • representing patterns that move • recording steps and movement using children's own symbols • recording steps and movement using traditional symbols	• movement can be represented by symbols • movement – line, form, pattern • way body moves – hands, feet, arms, legs, whole body • steps • use of symbolic movement • ways of recording movement	• tiptoeing and sliding • wriggling and twisting • rolling and balancing • dashing and diving • galloping and kicking • shaking and squatting • initiating • waiting turn • listening • discriminating

Table 16.4 Imaginative play experiences and the possibilities they offer for learning

Experience	Knowledge, understanding, concepts	Skills and abilities
Imitative play – copy *actions* of parents and carers using a wide range of: • small world toys, and puppets • props – real and miniature objects • dressing-up clothes	• suitable clothes for particular roles • sequence and characters of stories • appropriate props for different scenes • use of different body language and verbal • relationship and their responsibilities • household tasks – cooking, phoning	• listening and recalling • observing others • tidying up and dressing • writing, recognising signs • washing-up, mopping • squeezing and sweeping
Imaginative play – using experiences to create own scenario: • socio dramatic play – based on the adult roles children see around them, for example relationships (mothers), functional roles (shopkeepers) • character roles – based on fantasy characters from television, fairy and folk tales • using realistic props and models • using abstract and unstructured props – cardboard boxes • pretend props – finger for toothbrush • imagined props – miming	• community roles and responsibilities • a story has a beginning, middle and end • how to join in at appropriate times • how to negotiate • how to lead or be led • how to improvise • how to develop a narrative	• fine manipulative skills • gross motor skills • drying up, cleaning • estimating, measuring • caring for clothes • sorting and matching • using face paint • joining in, negotiating • leading and being led

Appraising and appreciating and the possibilities for learning they offer (see Table 16.5)

Experiences under this heading offer children opportunities to:

* watch, listen and feel
* respond to and comment on
* to appraise and evaluate
* appreciate

their own expressions of creativity and imagination and those of others.

Depth

Not only do we need to make sure that children have access to broad and balanced provision, we also need to be aware of the importance of ensuring that children are able to deepen their understanding. There is a danger that in trying to ensure that children have access to the breadth of provision listed above, our approach becomes superficial and they end up with a series of activities rather than the opportunity to delve into an experience. Children need time to explore and opportunities to repeat and return to experiences, so as to deepen their understanding.

Each form of creative and imaginative medium has its own properties and offers its own solutions. Access to differing experiences allows children to increase their understanding by solving problems in different ways. Representing the same experience or idea through the different media enables children to explore it in depth. Using an unlikely medium to represent an image or idea, for instance, drawing a loud sound or making the sound of sunshine, challenges children's thinking and skills. The medium they finally choose reflects:

* their mastery of that medium
* the properties the medium brings to solving the problem they wish to solve.

For example, children can explore and deepen their understanding of pattern by encountering the same concept in a variety of media:

* *pattern you can hear* – music, for instance rhythm – ta, taa ta, taa, ta or repeated phrases in a song
* *pattern that moves* – dance, for instance – up and down, up and down or a sequence of steps
* *pattern you can feel* – texture and textile, for instance – under and over, under and over, in and out, in and out, or the feel of the weave
* *pattern you can see* – draw, model and paint, for instance, light and shade, decoration, repeated sequences of colour or shape.

Table 16.5 Appreciation and appraisal and the possibilities they offer for learning

Experience	Knowledge, understanding, concepts	Skills and abilities
Opportunities to experience a wide variety of creative and imaginative representations including: • their own • other children • their own culture and tradition • other cultures and traditions • their own time • other times • through recordings and copies • live performance – music, dance • hearing the work of others • paintings, sculpture, drawings	• the properties of material • the elements of art, music, dance • the creative process – for example, in printing • how things are constructed and deconstructed • the values, concerns and preoccupations of others • intentions of others and gauging their success • purposes of creative and aesthetic expression • the way representations and artefacts enhance the environment in which we live • the role of dance, music, art in life • the role and work of artists and crafts people • history and cultures • vocabulary to describe and discuss what they see, hear and feel	• listening • watching • feeling • responding • articulating • commenting • critical skills • appraising • evaluating • appreciating • valuing

Children can also deepen their understanding through opportunities to represent their experiences and ideas using action, images, and traditional symbols. Bruner (1982) describes these three ways of processing information as:

1. *The enactive mode* – based on action, learning through doing, for example, children representing fast and slow using their body movements.
2. *The iconic mode* – replacing the action with a drawing or using an image to stand for an object or concept, for example, children representing fast and slow using marks and signs they have devised themselves.
3. *The symbolic mode* – using traditional symbols (musical notation, writing, numbers) for example, children using music notation to represent fast and slow.

Through these modes children are able to produce their own representations, store and retrieve information. At different ages different modes will predominate. For example, young children will readily use actions to represent their experiences, whereas they are less likely to use codes such as music notation. There is sometimes a tendency to neglect the enactive mode as children grow older, but it is important to ensure that all the different modes continue to be available to children as each can offer new insights and deepen understanding.

If children are going to have the opportunity to delve into experiences and deepen their understanding they need:

- access to materials and equipment
- time to explore materials, equipment
- an understanding of the properties of materials and equipment
- the chance to develop their skills and understanding
- time and opportunities to use their skills and knowledge to create their own representations
- a variety of social contexts: working alone, alongside others, in pairs, in groups.

Differentiation

While it is essential to ensure that all children have the opportunity to experience a wide range of experiences, it is also crucial to recognise that the needs of individual children will vary over time and that the needs of the children in any group will vary at any one time.

Children's learning needs will vary according to their:

- ability
- stage of development
- interest.

In response we need to differentiate the experiences we present, to match the experience we are offering to the learning needs of the individual children we are offering it to. For example, through the questions we ask, and the responses we expect from different children, we can increase the complexity of the experience on offer. By breaking the experience and explanations we give into smaller more manageable steps we can maximise understanding for less able children. Creative and imaginative experiences offer children the freedom to use the materials in an open-ended way. As there is no pre-prescribed end product, individual children are able to use the materials in a way that matches their own learning needs.

The adults' expertise is in enabling children to develop mastery and the freedom to explore at their own level by finding ways to develop the skills and concepts children need at the time they need them. To do this we must be sensitive to be aware of:

- what to introduce, and when, by being aware of the typical stages children go through and what is developmentally appropriate
- the processes involved in creativity
- when to intervene and when to stand back.

Conclusion

Children are not empty vessels. They have their own ideas and thoughts, their own desire to create. Our responsibility is to ensure that we build on children's current skills and understandings and expand this by providing new opportunities that develop their attitudes, skills and knowledge across a broad range of experiences.

[. . .]

References

Bloom, B. S. and Sosniak, L. A. (1981) 'Talent development vs schooling', *Educational Leadership* **27**, 86–94.
Bruner, J. (1982) 'What is representation?', in M. Roberts and J. Tamburrini (eds) *Child Development 0–5*. Edinburgh: Holmes McDougall.
    Bruner explains the concept of the enactive, iconic and symbolic modes.
Cox, M. (1992) *Children's Drawings*. London: Penguin.
DHSS (1989) *The Children Act: Guidance and Regulations*, Vol. 2. London: HMSO.
Moyles, J. (1989) *Just Playing?* Milton Keynes: Open University Press.

Part 3
Growing and developing

Jane Devereux

Introduction

The final section of *Working with Children in the Early Years* aims to provide insights into the healthy growth and wellbeing of young children. The World Health Organisation (1984: 1073–6) described health as:

> the extent to which an individual or group is able on the one hand to realise aspirations and satisfy needs; and, on the other hand, to change or cope with the environment. Health is therefore seen as a resource for everyday life, not the object of living; it is the positive concept emphasising social and personal resources as well as physical capacities.

This inclusive definition of health sets a firm direction for all and underpins the approach of the authors in this section. Each author sees the all round growth and development of the child as important with the emotional, social and physical dimensions having as important a part to play as health.

The first chapter in this section by Jane Devereux, 'Observing Children', provides a rationale for observing children and offers ways of observing that have implications for practice. Information gathered by watching children at play or involved in other activities, provides insight into their current interests and ways of learning, their next steps and possible concerns. Such insight will help early years practitioners to support healthy growth and development.

The next two chapters relate directly to the health and wellbeing of children. The first, 'Children growing and changing' by Patti Owens, explores the interpersonal world of the growing child and describes how children develop as individuals and how they relate to the wider world. The second, by Angela Underdown, 'Health inequalities in early childhood' highlights the very different start in life that some children have owing to the circumstances into which they are born. The case study in the chapter raises issues about children's emotional development and their attachment to parents or carers. It also discusses related issues such as supporting parents in difficult circumstances, child protection and cultural differences relating to health and wellbeing in families. It offers insights into the difficulties some families have in accessing services. Understanding the complexities that exist in some children's lives from an early age is crucial if inequalities are to be minimised.

Finally Christine Macintyre's chapter 'Studying play from a developmental perspective' uses play as a means of describing how young children grow. She explores how they grow physically and links this to their emotional and social wellbeing. Ideas and theories about the nature of play are developed and provide a useful context for practitioners to reflect on their own provision and practice – a key aim of this book.

References

World Health Organisation (1984) *Health Promotion: a WHO discussion document on the concepts and principles*. Summary report in: *Community Medicine* (1985) **7**(10), 73–6.

Chapter 17

Observing children

Jane Devereux

[...]

Introduction

[...]

Observations can help teachers and other adults working with children to develop their knowledge of the child and of their developing competences, schemas and personal interests. Key questions that I have asked myself throughout my teaching career, are: Why am I doing this activity or action with these children in this way? Is it the best way to enable the most learning to take place for all of the group? Why do I want them to learn this now? Is it informed by my knowledge of the learners' interests, needs and wishes? How do I know this?

[...]

This chapter will explore how watching children provides the core and basis for all future actions. It will provide a clear rationale for planned observations of children's learning and for the need to keep objective records of that achievement in order to best serve the needs and interests of the learner. This knowledge provides an informed basis from which to work to support, challenge and extend children's learning.

Why observe?

According to Stierer *et al.* (1993) there are four key purposes for observation. These are:

1. gaining knowledge of children's strengths and areas for development;
2. reviewing provision;
3. forward planning;
4. for summative reporting.

The DES Report *Starting with Quality* (1990) supports these with its emphasis that observation-based assessment should be a fundamental part of the process of understanding children's learning and of reflecting on the effectiveness of the provision, as well as having both a formative and summative role. OFSTED Criteria for the Inspection of Education for Under Fives (1993) also stressed the importance of observation as crucial to 'ensuring breadth, balance and continuity of learning'.

We can look at some of these possible reasons in more detail.

A. *Observations can provide formative evidence of children's competence.* This is defined by the PROCESS team (Stierer *et al.*, 1993)[1] as 'the gradual building up of a picture of young children's learning and development, through everyday observation of them engaged in classroom activity and through discussions with parents' (p.1). Observations provide the information on which to base future action and develop our knowledge of how children think and learn, as well as providing evidence of their developing competences, persistent interests, dispositions (Katz and Chard 1989) and schemas (Athey 1990; Bartholomew and Bruce 1993). [...] For teachers of young children, therefore, it is important that observation is seen as a fundamental part of the process of teaching and learning if the goals described above are to be achieved. It is not an end in itself, because some kind of action should normally be a consequence of those observations, even if it is a decision to do nothing, yet, or to gather further observations before planning changes in provision.

Watching children at play and work I am constantly surprised by their creativeness, inventiveness, persistence and talent. While watching a student practitioner on placement in a nursery I heard the following discourse between two girls at work in the writing corner, set up by the student. Having noted an interest in teddy bears by a group of children, she had provided some teddy note books which these two girls were using and discussing as follows:

> Victoria (3 yrs 8 mths): What's that you've put in your writing? [Points] There!
> Louise (3 yrs 11 mths): Oh! That's a full stop. [She makes it bigger and darker]
> V: What's it do?
> L: It stops my writing going on.
> V: Oh I think I need one of those! Let me put one here. [Puts in large full stop at end of her writing.] That's stopped that writing. Good.

(personal observation)

For me, this was a magic moment – being in the right place at the right time. It is only a short observation but provides a whole wealth of evidence about young children as learners and also of possible lines of development to take

---

1 'PROCESS' is an acronym for the project 'Profiling, Recording and Observing Competences and Experiences at the Start of School', carried out jointly by the London Borough of Merton Education Department and the Faculty of Education at Roehampton Institute London.

with those two girls. It does not imply that one must prepare a formal lesson on the use of full stops, but it does suggest that it would be valuable to gather more evidence of the children's understanding of their use, e.g. to collect samples of their writing over the next few days and weeks to see if there was any consistency or pattern in the use of full stops. I may have done some shared writing with groups, including the two girls, and talked about full stops there. I may also have read some familiar big books at story time, encouraging children to help me with the reading. This would have created opportunities to talk about features of written language, such as full stops.

B. *Observation raises our awareness of our own beliefs and values, and encourages us to be more conscious of how these affect the interpretation of what we see.* Differences in children's experiences, for example, in relation to gender and culture, will be highlighted by observing what they do. Our expectations of the children will also be influenced. It is therefore vitally important in early years' settings that all adults are involved in the process of gathering observations so that a range of voices can inform the team's approach to provision and interaction with the children. Included in this notion of 'all adults' must be the parents and carers of the children. They have been the foremost influence in the child's life and have provided the crucial basis of their early learning. [...] But important to note at this time is the way that our observations and those of the parent and/or carers can help provide continuity in the learning of the child between home and school. Each can inform the other of concerns and developments that can enable all to enhance the learning experiences of the child.

C. *Gathering observations of competence will provide practitioners with evidence* to report to parents, receiving teachers, heads, LEA inspectors, OFSTED and other outside agencies concerned with the child's progress. This summative use of evidence allows for 'a stock-take' (Stierer *et al.* 1993) at significant points in the child's educational life, such as the transfer from nursery to reception or from one school to another. It can inform the discussions that take place between some or all of the above groups.

Vital within this justification for observation is the need for evidence if there are concerns about a child's progress or lack of development. For example, children who have difficulty settling into a new setting, find it hard to relate to others, have difficulty communicating with others or have speech difficulties may benefit. Practitioners may need to seek expert advice and support for the team and/or the child. Gathering information about children will help to refine our understanding of any problem, or alleviate our anxieties by refuting our initial concerns. Having information and detailed observations enables us to approach the appropriate agency(ies) from an informed basis and so initiate action as quickly as possible.

At all times in our work with children we should be able to justify the actions we take, on the basis of our detailed knowledge of their needs and experiences. Observation is, therefore, a vital skill that practitioners need to develop from the very beginning of their careers. However, many experienced practitioners will admit that it is not as easy as it sounds. How, then, do we get started and what do we do with the observations as they are gathered?

Factors to consider when observing

Getting started

Who, how, what, when and where to observe are important questions to address in getting started. This can seem a rather daunting list and inhibit some from even attempting to observe. It will be different for each practitioner as it depends on individual experiences of observation and on the skills already developed. The most important thing is to make a start, and to reflect on that experience and learn from it. Sharing experiences with other team members or colleagues in different situations will help clarify the process of observation and may highlight needs.

Who should do the observations?

The whole team should be encouraged to be involved, but some members may need support and encouragement to begin. First, it is important to just have a go. Watch an individual who interests you or causes you concern. Record what you see on some form of note pad or proforma. The more people who are involved in the observing the more varied will be the evidence about each child. If that produces a consensus of evidence then the assessment of that child's competence is stronger, and decisions about ways to extend and challenge that child will be better informed. Parents, as has already been mentioned, should be part of this process too, but it is important to be sensitive to the different ways that parents both want to be and can be involved in their child's education. The start of a child's time in an early years setting is a crucial one to be in contact with parents, to welcome them but also to share their knowledge of their child's learning up to that point. Parents are the first educators of the child and do not stop being such when children start school, but their role is, different and complementary to that of the school.

Both Bartholomew and Bruce (1993) and Stierer *et al.* (1993) offer ways of involving parents that allow them to contribute their observations in order to help build up a comprehensive picture of the child as a learner. The Parent Discussion Book explained in *Profiling, Recording and Observing* (Stierer *et al.*, 1993) is an example of one of many different versions of parent consultation that have been developed by practitioners in different localities and educational settings and which provide opportunities for parents to share their understanding and knowledge of their children as learners, through informal discussion with the teacher and practitioner. It does not replace the initial home visit which may sometimes be carried out prior to starting school, as the purpose of this is quite different. Bartholomew and Bruce (1993) develop this idea and show how parents can feed observations into the early years setting to help inform the school's assessments. This is, of course, a two-way process and school-based observations may help and inform parents/carers, facilitate learning beyond the classroom and provide continuity for the child.

This discussion may also help assess whether or not observations are providing the information needed about the child as a learner. If the information from parents does not concur with the teaching team's developing picture of the child it may indicate possible areas for further observation, or changes or additions to the provision already on offer. It may be that the quality of provision does not allow children to operate at an appropriate level, important questions may need to be asked about how the environment is organised, about how children are able or unable to access resources, and about the support and interaction that takes place between children and adult. Tightly prescribed tasks with control in the hands of the teacher may limit children's opportunities to display their creativity, imagination and expertise, and discussion between children and adults where children's efforts are directed towards guessing what answer is inside the teacher's head may affect the development of their own thinking strategies and skill in solving problems.

Play is a vitally important part of a child's activity. The provision of opportunities for play can allow children to practise and develop new skills and competences, to explore emotional situations, to experiment with ideas, to take risks and to solve problems. Involving all those who work in the early years team in observing children at play and work is therefore vital to gain a clearer picture of each child's competence.

When is the best time to observe?

In reality, as soon as we enter an educational setting, we begin to watch and look. At first this is to gain an overall view of what is happening within the room, and the provision that is on offer. This will include noting the areas of provision, the adults involved and their location and the forms of interaction that are taking place. However, it is very important that our observations go beyond this, since 'understanding the process of assessing children's learning – by looking closely at it and striving to understand it – is the only certain safeguard against children's failure, the only certain guarantee of children's progress and development' (Drummond 1993: 10).

For the very reason that observation is part of the process of teaching and learning and is happening all the time as we listen to and interact with children, it is important to take care that its vital role is not lost. If observation is not planned for specifically, then it often does not happen. How will we know what children are achieving, if we do not spend time watching and listening to what they do and say? At times we will want to observe as we interact with the children, and many of our questions and actions will be in direct response to the children's actions. The more we know about individuals and about child development in general the better will be our observations and, ultimately, our judgements. Planning for observation is, therefore, important and should be part of the general routine. Questions about how many observations can be made during a session, and by whom, need to be considered. In particular, the goals set for the number and type of planned observations must be both realistic and achievable, if they are to stand any chance of happening.

Many nursery teams meet briefly each day or regularly during the week, to share significant information, including observations about children, provision and resources and to plan the next day's provision in the light of the day's events and the children's experiences. The allocation of people, and time, to observe as well as who or what is to be observed, may be some of the decisions taken at such meetings. Observations can be made:

- at regular intervals during a day;
- at incidental or opportune moments;
- at the start and end of sessions/activities;
- during activities while participating with children;
- during activities but not participating.

The timing of the observations and the form they take will be determined, to some extent, by the kind of information it is hoped to collect, and we shall consider *what* to observe later in this chapter.

How can observations be made?

In observing the current interests and schemas that dominate the child's interactions and actions in school or nursery we need to look at the whole child and the interplay of intellectual, social, emotional and physical aspects that are vitally important and feed and support each other. We need to be aware that we can and do bring our own experiences and expectations to bear when we observe any action. The old saying that 'what we look for is what we see' carries an important warning for all those working with children that we try to see what the children are *actually* doing and not what we *think* they are doing, or even what we *want* to see. As DES (1990) suggests, it is important to remember that the context within which our values and beliefs operate may be different from that of the child and we must respect this difference and individuality.

Observations should be as objective as possible given all the influences that can come in to play as we watch. The use of language is, therefore, very important. There is a world of difference between recording that a child 'wrote his name from right to left in the top right hand corner of the paper starting with the first letter in the extreme corner and moving along from the right to left' and saying that 'he wrote his name in the top right corner of the paper but it was written wrongly as it was back to front'. The first is both more factual and less judgemental than the second entry. Judgemental language may work to lower teacher's expectations for individual children, and close down options for them. In this example, use of the word 'wrong' does little actually to describe what the child has done and to provide information about how his understanding and competence can be developed. It may also be that this child's first or home language is one in which reading and writing *are* carried out from right to left.

Ignorance or insensitivity to such factors are ways in which our observations can be affected.

Statements such as 'has difficulty in concentrating', 'is a slow reader', 'has poor gross motor skills' sometimes appear in children's profiles. What evidence, though, can be given to justify such comments? To reach such conclusions the observers would need to have seen things which led them to believe them to be 'true'. To write such statements, however, sometimes even based upon a single observation, suggests that general conclusions are being drawn too easily. For example if we take the comment 'is a slow reader'. The child in question may have had difficulty with a particular text or been called away while in the middle of another activity in which s/he was deeply involved.

At this stage it is useful to consider two types of observation – participatory and non-participatory. The use of either will be dependent on such issues as staffing levels, resources and the information that is being gathered.

Participatory observation

All teachers, as part of their everyday work with children, are involved in participatory observation, but this does not always lead to written entries in the child's record. Participant observation may initially seem more difficult to manage, in that notes must be made either at points during work with the children, or immediately afterwards if the knowledge and evidence is not to be lost. We think that we will remember something and will be able to note it down later. Given the pace at which events can develop in the nursery, however, these observations can easily be lost or inaccurately remembered. Having 'post-it' notes, clipboards with paper or note pads, placed strategically around the room will help provide both the incentive and the means with which to record the incident, briefly, as it happens. Another practice is to ensure that you always carry a notepad with you, from place to place. Such pads often become the focus for children's attention, too, with them leaving messages and writing their own 'notes' down.

Observations made in this way may often be incidental and unplanned, e.g. the writing corner described earlier. Like the planned observations, these can be incorporated into the general system of observations which add to the developing picture of a child.

The habit of recording observations almost automatically comes with practice and notes often become shorter, but more telling in their content, with increasing experience. One teacher in the PROCESS Research Project (Stierer *et al.* 1993) said that as she became more experienced at observing she wrote less but it told her more!

Non-participatory observation

Non-participatory observation means that the observer stays outside the activity in order to concentrate on the child or aspect being watched. If a single child is the focus it allows the observer to watch that child both as an individual and in the setting of an activity. Similarly, a focus on an aspect of provision or on a particular activity, allows the observer to concentrate on that aspect of the nursery alone, without having to keep an eye on anything else.

If the observation is to be non-participatory, children need to know which adults are available for help while that person is busy observing. One teacher in the PROCESS project (Stierer *et al.* 1993) used to wear a hat when observing, and the children knew that they had to go to the other adults while this hat was being worn!

Where to sit while observing in this way is also important, but becomes less of an issue as children become used to seeing adults watch them. Sitting too near or far from an activity may affect the quality of what is seen or heard, and even the observer's ability to do so. What is most important is that where an adult sits does not have a limiting effect on the children's activity.

A range of formats or ways of observing are also possible, which may be appropriate for particular purposes and at specific times.

Time sampling

Time sampling involves making observations at pre-specified intervals, for example, every ten minutes during a session, of a targeted child, group or area of provision. Possible questions one might have in mind when observing a particular child, for example, might be:

- Where is he?
- Who is he with?
- What is he doing?
- What is he saying?

Similarly, in observing an area of provision, or piece of equipment, the observer might be considering the following:

- Who is using the equipment?
- What are they doing?
- What are they saying?
- Are adults involved?

Time sampling is particularly useful for tracking children's activities and interactions over a period of time, for building up a picture of particular children, and for appraising the value and use of equipment.

Frequency sampling

Frequency sampling is a way of tracking incidences of particular aspects of behaviour in a child or group of children. In this, the observer identifies a feature of behaviour and notes whenever this occurs. For example, a child may appear always to play alone in the nursery. Observations would focus on whether or not this was indeed the case, and would include looking at whether s/he approached another child, children or adults, whether s/he initiated any interaction, how any interaction was initiated, and where in the nursery this occurred. As its name suggests, frequency sampling can be useful in giving an accurate picture of the frequency of aspects of behaviour, and can be used to monitor both progress and concerns.

Duration observation

Duration observation is a way of accurately tracking how long children spend at particular activities or using certain equipment. It may seem sometimes as if a child or group of children spend *all* of their time in the construction area or riding the bikes: duration observation is a good way of establishing just how much time they *do* spend in these areas, and can help to ensure that the observations we record are accurate. 'Kuldip spends all of his time on the bikes' may, in reality, be Kuldip chooses the bikes first, generally spends half an hour on them and then moves on to other activities.'

Focused observation

In this method, the observer selects an activity, child or children and records everything that happens for a pre-specified period of, for example, five minutes. Focused observations can be helpful in giving a complete picture of children's activities and achievements.

Who and what should we observe?

Decisions about who or what to observe will be driven by the individual's or team's responsibility for the children in their care, and their interests. The following list shows something of the wide range of possibilities:

- new children;
- individual children or groups – gathering general information;
- children giving cause for concern;
- areas of provision;
- use of particular areas;
- resourcing of areas;
- movement around areas.

How these are to be observed will vary, according to the reasons for the observations, and in relation to the information needed. A look back at the previous section, on how observations can be made, will help in reaching decisions about the most appropriate forms of observation for particular situations. Whether observations are to be of one child, several children, or an area of the nursery or classroom that is being monitored to assess the effectiveness of provision, as was stressed earlier, it is important to write what is actually seen and heard.

Providing a rich and varied environment plays an important part in the observation process. Quality observations are supported by quality provision. What constitutes quality provision will be briefly discussed here. Young children's learning is deeply embedded in the context in which they are operating. Hughes (1986) describes the higher levels that children can operate at when that learning is in a context meaningful to them. A responsibility for professionals working with young children, therefore, is to provide contexts that will facilitate such learning.

DES (1985) describes nine areas of experience – linguistic, mathematical, scientific, aesthetic and creative, human and social, technological, physical, moral, and spiritual. Children need experience within all of these areas if they are to develop as well-balanced individuals. Again, it is part of the role of teachers to ensure sufficient knowledge of the children, in order to support, challenge and extend their learning in the above areas of experience, in ways appropriate to each individual child. Observation in each of these areas of experience is a vital way of getting to know the child's needs and competences. Stierer *et al.* (1993) suggest the following aspects on which to focus, all of which may occur in those nine areas: children's interactions, attitudes, investigating and problem solving, communicating, representing and interpreting, and any particular individual needs.

Keeping a record of the areas in which a child has been observed should raise questions for the professionals involved. A question such as why a child does not go to some areas is worth asking. It will be useful then to look closely at that provision: is it not interesting to others as well? Is it that the child has not had access to that kind of experience and thus may need the support of an adult to initially explore its potential? What *are* the particular interests of that child? From these records it will be possible to see the balance of observations one has of all of the children and build into planning the times necessary to observe children for whom there is less evidence.

Which children are confident with books? Does Simone ever go into the block area or outside to play? Does Jane settle at a task for more than a few seconds? Does Kuldip use provision other than the bikes? Who does Marcus play with? How good at solving problems is Hassam? Does he persist? Does he ask for help? If so whom? These are all questions that can arise about individuals, for which planned observations may help to find answers.

What happens to the observations?

Management and storage

As the notes and 'post-its' and pieces of paper accumulate it is important to have some way of managing the volume, both in the short and long term. These pieces of paper initially provide support and information for the planning of future work with the children: they have a *formative* purpose. They are also needed for the *summative*, report-writing stage, when statements are made about the child's progress, often for communication to others, in particular to parents or carers, and other practitioners. In the long term, developing a manageable form of filing system for the observations is important if all of these observations are to be most useful, and are not to be lost. A pocket file for each child, ring binders and a section in a filing cabinet are all possibilities, but solutions will be individual, dependent upon available space and storage facilities and the time to support them. Keeping these samples of evidence is, however, very important both in order to inform planning, and for when it comes to the summative stage(s) in a child's time in the nursery or class. They give insights into the child that can inform the understanding of parents, headteachers, inspectors, educational psychologists and other agencies, and provide evidence that can support statements made of the child's competence, in a wide range of contexts and areas of experience.

The short-term management of observations includes the sharing of these with other staff at the end of day or at team meetings so that everyone is aware of the successes, efforts and concerns about individuals, areas and resources. Gaps in professionals' knowledge about particular children can be identified, and plans can be made to fill these gaps.

Sharing observations

How these observations and records are shared with parents/carers is an important aspect to consider, and ways of doing so need to be developed. Not all parents are able to collect their children at the end of a day or session. This does not, of course, mean they are not interested in their child or do not care about supporting them. In order for all parents to have the opportunity to share such observations on a regular basis the school may have to examine ways of making time available for teachers to do so, time which may involve extra resourcing and have staffing implications. Having another adult come in to take a story session at the end of the morning or afternoon for half an hour a week, or putting groups of children together for a period at the end of the day, may give some time, but a range of options need to be considered if as many parents as possible are to have the opportunity to participate. Bartholomew and Bruce (1993) describe how parents who cannot come in actually contribute observations to the records via a parent observation sheet, which feeds in to the nursery's records.

At summative stages, at the end of the school year, not all of the observations themselves will go forward to the following teacher or setting. They do, however, form the basis for formal records and report-writing, with evidence for the statements being drawn from the observational records. The summative statement or report then goes forward, the observations that fed it are stored or discarded, and the process begins again with the next intake.

Summary

Watching children explore and make sense of their world provides valuable insights into their developing competences. In exploring observation as part of the role of the adult working with young children it is hoped that its vital role in relation to many aspects of early years work has been articulated. Collecting evidence of competence, creativity, persistence, imagination and socialisation gives us insights into the child's growing intellect and personality, and enables professionals to provide the best supportive learning environment for each individual. As Drummond (1993: 10) says about the early years professional's roles and responsibilities: 'Paramount among them is the responsibility to monitor the effects of their work so as to ensure that their good intentions for children are realised.'

References

Athey, C. (1990) *Extending Thought in Young Children*. London: Paul Chapman.

Bartholomew, L. and Bruce, T. (1993) *Getting to Know You*. London: Hodder & Stoughton.

Department of Education and Science (1985) *The Curriculum from 5–16: curriculum matters 2*. London: HMSO.

Department of Education and Science (1990) *Starting with Quality* (Rumbold Report). London: HMSO.

Drummond, M. J. (1993) *Assessing Children's Learning*, London: David Fulton Publishers.

Hughes, M. (1986) *Children and Number*. Oxford: Basil Blackwell.

Katz, L. G. and Chard, S. C. (1989) *Engaging Children's Minds: the project approach*. New Jersey: Ablex Publishing.

Office for Standards in Education (1993) *First Class: the standards and quality of education in reception classes*. London: HMSO.

Stierer, B., Devereux, J., Gifford, S., Laycock, L. and Yerbury, J. (1993) *Profiling, Observing and Recording*. London: Routledge.

Chapter 18

Children growing and changing: the interpersonal world of the growing child

Patti Owens

What is so important about interpersonal development?

As an early years practitioner for over twenty years, I have had the opportunity to observe a lot of young children and adults interacting as they spend time together. Nowadays I also work as a psychotherapist with adult clients. Time and again I hear stories of love and care offered to these people as children by nursery nurses, nannies, teachers and playgroup workers, as well as parents. And, of course, I hear the bleaker tales of rejection, humiliation and sometimes abuse at the same hands. Our responsibility as early years practitioners is a serious and important one in human terms; we play a key role in both the *intra*personal and *inter*personal development of human beings. Our work with the youngest children has a profound effect on the way they come to feel intrapersonally, or 'inside themselves', and on the manner of being they adopt as adults, in interpersonal relationships with others.

Interpersonal development is, perhaps, an area of human development that we could be more aware of. As a result largely of political factors, 'child development', as it has traditionally been called, has come under some suspicion in current educational thinking. In teacher education, with its emphasis on 'academic subjects', child development has been widely relegated to a special 'option'. Even amongst early childhood educators there has been a tendency simply to keep teaching the major theorists from the past (Davenport 1991, Owens 1997).

These trends seem doubly unfortunate. First, poorly informed professionals can not adequately support a child's interpersonal development, and we pay the cost in society as children grow up into adults who do not relate effectively to others, or even feel good about themselves. Secondly, despite the great contribution made by past theorists, it is easy to criticise some of their ideas from a modern perspective. Without an understanding of important research conducted more recently, early years practitioners can be left feeling that it is better to trust one's intuition in these matters, rather than a faulty or mistaken developmental theory.

A new approach to developmental theory

In this chapter I want to argue that some of the more recent research on children's development is worth knowing about because it can help enrich our observation and understanding of the inner world of children. [...]

I have identified three themes which together inform current developmental theory and create a background for my discussion, later on in this chapter, of Daniel Stern's model of interpersonal development in very young children (Stern 1985).

1. There is now an emphasis on 'whole' child development. In effect this means that we are no longer easy with the notion of separating out areas of development. When I focus here on interpersonal development I keep in mind that this is only one, though a very important, aspect of every child's experience and perception. The notion of 'whole-ness' also transcends old-fashioned terms like 'phase' or 'stage' of development, favoured by earlier theorists. We concentrate on young children, but of course interpersonal development continues throughout human life, and it is often experience rather than ages, phases or stages, that triggers off new learning at a particular point.
2. The old debate about 'Nature versus Nurture' does not in fact get us very far, much as this has preoccupied past theorists (Bee 1992). We now give due recognition to the fact that human development takes place in a social context. The process whereby a child grows in human character and understanding is more like a 'transaction' than a battle where one side is dominant. We are learning much more about the complexity of neonate and infant experience (Kagan 1984, Berry Brazelton and Cramer 1991). Recent researchers, furthermore, have identified the critical influence that even young children bring to bear on their carers and their environment, so changing the course of their own development (Woodhead *et al.* 1991).
3. Unlike major theorists such as Freud, who seems never to have actually observed an infant whilst constructing his theories about human developmental psychology, recent researchers base their theoretical models on close, detailed infant and child observation. Whilst accepting that observations provide the evidence for ideas about how children develop, most researchers also see the practical impossibility of a totally objective 'scientific' stance. The observer will be influenced by, amongst other things, their own early experiences, often seeing events through the filter of their own childhood memories (Houston 1995). Modern researchers try to take account of this unavoidable subjectivity. Daniel Stern (1985), for example, uses the notion of the 'participant observer' where he checks out his own observations and intuitions against those of any other adults, usually parents or carers, who are participating in the observation.

Without a theory, such observations and intuitions can be very interesting and rewarding to follow up, but they remain un-grounded. Current researchers, therefore, construct models of development that offer a kind of map, or template against which we can orient our observations. Unlike past developmental theorists whose work has often been presented as scientifically true, or even proven, modern researchers tend to take a more humble attitude, but one that enables them to continually check their theory against what they actually observe, revising the model in the light of further research. In this way, a theory can only ever be more or less 'useful', not more or less true.

These three characteristics of modern developmental theory are evident in the work of Daniel Stern, and it is to that research I now turn.

Daniel Stern's model of infant interpersonal development

Daniel Stern draws on two perspectives in constructing his model of infant development: psychoanalysis and developmental psychology, notably attachment theory (Bowlby 1965, Barnes 1995). As a developmental psychologist he is a committed infant observer; as a psychotherapist he makes some inferences about the infant's 'inner' psychological world, based on his experience of taking adults through the process of psychoanalysis. Stern gives a detailed account of the first two years of life, during which period he argues that the infant goes through the process of developing four distinct 'senses of self'. Each sense of self begins its development only when the infant has particular experiences and gains particular human capacities, during the process of wider growth and change. Stern refers to these sets of experiences as 'domains of experience'– not stages or phases of development.

In the first eight weeks or so of life the infant's sense of self is 'emergent' and the primary need seems to be for 'relatedness' with the primary care giver, usually the parent(s). Stern sees as crucial the infant's capacity at this point to perceive events and experiences with their 'whole' self. Think for a moment of a baby feeding: he or she touches, smells, sighs, desires to be fed, experiences satisfaction. These experiences do not distinguish between the physical and the emotional, for the infant's perception of the world takes place using their whole being. Correspondingly, Stern notices the importance of a key 'parental assumption', namely that this infant is a person with developing human characteristics. Consider how we might say to a very young infant things like, 'You want your nappy changed don't you?', or 'I bet you wish your sister was here.' Stern thinks, rightly in my view, that past developmental theorists have been wrong to see this neonate behaviour as purely based on physical survival needs. In doing so they have 'looked right past' what was happening in front of their eyes, as infant and parent/carer make those significant initial contacts; the beginnings of human relatedness. Hence Stern's labelling of this first domain of experience, the 'domain of emergent relatedness'.

Then between about two and six months of age, the infant develops what Stern calls a 'core sense of self', based on experiences and perceptions in the domain of 'core relatedness' to another human being, usually the parent or carer with whom the infant spends most interactive time. If we imagine for a moment that the infant could speak, he or she might say, 'I am a being with a physical presence. I can feel physical sensations, which for me are not separate from my emotional feelings. If I am happy I feel good in my body; if I am distressed I feel pain. I am aware that other beings (parents/carers) can influence how I feel.'

What is more, Stern's observations lead him to hypothesise that the infant begins at this time to remember the most often repeated events, and then make generalisations based on these rememberings. Stern calls this process the establishment of RIGs, or 'Repeated Interactions that are Generalised'. The experience of, say, having a bib put on comes to be associated in the infant with nourishment, which is a physical need. But the experience is also strongly associated with closeness to the parent/carer, and with that more of a sense of himself or herself as both distinct from, and related to, that other person. If the physical nourishment goes along with welcome, appropriate interaction from a parent/carer who tunes in to the infant on more than just a physical level, these experiences can be generalised to form special RIGs that will persist very strongly throughout their coming life. Good experiences of this kind, which include the special interaction with another person who gives emotional, as well as physical, nourishment, can help the infant to experience what Stern calls an 'evoked companion', or the experience of being 'not alone' psychologically, even when this is materially the case. Work with insecure children and adults suggests that where this process has not happened for some reason, the individual can not 'evoke a companion'; they can not believe that they will be protected and nurtured, however safe they are in fact (Gillie 1999).

The third sense of self, the 'subjective' sense, begins to be experienced, according to Stern's observations, around seven to nine months. This is the domain of 'inter-subjective relatedness' where, all being well, the infant comes to trust that his or her own feeling states are both unique to himself or herself, and capable of being understood by significant other people, mainly parents or carers. The infant realises for the first time, perhaps, that 'I have a mind, and so does this other person'. Intimacy can be more or less deep and fulfilling for the infant, depending on how he or she experiences the other person in relation to himself or herself. Crucial to this new development is the 'care-giver's empathy', or indeed lack of it. This is the first time, says Stern, that the care-giver's 'socialisation of the infant's subjective experience' becomes an issue. The parent or carer has responsibility for affirming or denying the infant's inner, subjective experience. A child can learn that some of their feelings – the need to weep, the urge to reach out and love another, for example – are, or are not, acceptable. These attitudes, as Stern notes, tend to move forward with us into adulthood, as strong and persistent RIGs.

All three domains of experience and perception continue through infancy and beyond, and we need to bear in mind that these are not stages or phases of development like those traditionally outlined, but ways of experiencing ourselves and other human beings that have their beginnings in our infant histories. These early experiences become part of our adult ways of being; part of how we experience ourselves in relation to others, helping to form our habitual attitudes and predispositions to the ever changing circumstances of ordinary human life.

The fourth domain of 'verbal relatedness' depends on language acquisition and comes to the fore, according to Stern, at around fifteen to eighteen months. The infant becomes capable of making clear to others that they know things, using symbols and words. This gives them another way of thinking about themselves, others and the wider world; they begin to develop a 'verbal self'. Central to this process is the forging of 'we meanings'. Think of the kind of example where a toddler tries to make himself or herself understood; fails at first, then succeeds. Such verbal agreement, though necessarily symbolic (words are in themselves abstract entities) adds a kind of concrete-ness to the child's reality. Before words, a lot depends on the child's ability to respond to, then initiate, interactions with their parents and carers, in conjunction with the parent/carer's empathetic and welcoming response to the child's efforts. Now, says Stern, words can be used to solidify the sense that 'we' understand things together. The child can gain enormously in confidence and ability to relate and communicate with others, in generalising from these verbally supported RIGs. As with the other domains of infant experience, however, there is also the possibility to distort or fracture the child's experience. Words add another even more powerful dimension in such cases. An all too common example is the child who experiences violence or abuse from a 'carer' who at the same time speaks kind words like 'I love you, I don't want to hurt you, but...'. Or there is the example of the child whose attempts to reach out in affection to another person are met with words that should express reciprocation, but do not; the child instead hears harshness of tone, or experiences emotional coolness, not the warmth the words alone might suggest. As psychotherapists know, there are many ways in which the experience of 'words not matching my reality' can become part of the adult's way of being in the world, and their habitual expectations in relation to others.

Some implications of Stern's research for early years practitioners

So what are we to make of Stern's model of infant interpersonal development, as early years practitioners? Many of us will have dealings with infants and very young children so the relevance may be immediately apparent. Others will be working mainly with older children in the 0–6 years age range. It might be interesting then to notice how Stern's notions of 'domains' of experience, and development of different 'senses of self', for instance, can inform your observation and understanding of older children's interpersonal development.

With these issues in mind, I want to finish this chapter with an infant observation I recently undertook and analysed in the light of Stern's model of infant interpersonal development.

Observation of Thomas

I observe Thomas in June 1999 when he is ten months old (43 weeks). He is with his father, who shares childcare with Thomas' mother; both parents do paid part-time work. They are at a toy library group close to their home, which Thomas has visited twice before with his mother. Thomas and his father are playing on a large mat where four other children, all under a year, are using the selection of colourful and soft toys set out by the toy library leader and her assistants.

Observation method

As the observer, I have known Thomas' parents for several years. Thomas is their first child, and I have observed Thomas in the home setting on a number of occasions since his birth. I try to keep myself in the background, though if Thomas approaches me I will interact with him as normally as possible. Thomas' father has agreed to be a participant observer, and discuss the observation with me after it has been completed. The observation lasts about 5 minutes.

Record of observation

Thomas has been sitting near an eleven month-old girl, picking up and dropping squares of coloured felt fabric. He rolls from a sitting position into a crawl, moving across the mat for a couple of metres. He sits up, head turned to the right, and points, making excited 'Ee-ee-ee-ee!' sounds. Thomas' father, who has been watching him, looks in the direction of Thomas' pointing finger. Thomas first looks at his father's face, then back in the pointing direction. Thomas' father says, 'What do you want, Tom? Yes, cubes...they look exciting, don't they?', and pointing at them himself, says, 'Ye-e-e-e-eh – cubes!'. Thomas looks at his father's face again and chuckles, then points, looking at his own hand, then at his father's face again, then his father's hand. Thomas suddenly lurches into a crawl, going over to the soft, coloured cubes. He sits up again, and bangs his hand down a few times on one of the cubes, making the 'Ee-ee-ee!' sound again. Thomas' father comes over. 'Bang, bang, bang!' he says, tapping his fingers on the cube. Thomas watches him do this then looks away, this time pointing in front of himself towards another cube. He makes as if to crawl towards it then stops and looks up at his father's face. Seeing his father look away (he has noticed another child throwing toys in a rather dangerous looking manner) Thomas whimpers then starts to cry, banging his arms and kicking his legs. 'Oh, what's the matter?' whispers Thomas' father, 'Wasn't I looking at the cube with you?' He strokes Thomas' face and Thomas stops crying and points again to the cube in front of him. 'OK Thomas,' says his father, 'This cube is a yellow one – Ye-e-e-llow!' Thomas laughs and looks up, touching his father's smiling mouth.

My response to this observation, in the light of Stern's research

This observation reflects very clearly some of the key points in Stern's model of the development of a 'subjective sense of self'. Thomas is apparently seeking what Stern calls a 'shared subjective experience' with his father. He is not content merely to enjoy his own knowledge (That's a cube over there!) and mastery (I can sit, crawl, grasp, be excited, feel happy, be worried, point my finger and make daddy look...). He wants to do what Stern calls 'sharing the focus of attention' with his father. Being 'preverbal', Thomas needs experiences of the kind that do not require language, though his 'Ee-ee-ee-eeh!' sounds communicate excitement effectively enough. He uses pointing himself, to make his father look in a particular direction, as well as looking in the direction that his father points, rather than simply looking at his hand as a younger infant might have done. All this indicates a shared experience where Thomas is both aware of his own physical and feeling state, and trusting that his father will understand that too, because somehow the father seems to have similar feelings.

These early interpersonal experiences rely on a special kind of empathy that Stern labels 'affect attunement'. I noticed that Thomas' father responded to his son's excited 'Ee-ee-ee-eeh!' sounds with words spoken at a similar vocal pitch: 'Ye-e-e-eh, cubes!', accompanied by a sort of wriggle in his upper body. When I asked Thomas' father why he might have done this, he said that although he had not thought about it at the time, on reflection this 'wriggle' was another way of letting Thomas know that his excitement was 'contagious' – a shareable human experience. Stern thinks that these experiences of affect attunement 'recast the event, and shift the focus of attention to what is behind the behaviour, to the quality of feeling that is being shared'. So here Thomas learns that he can have feelings of excitement, enthusiasm, concern, fear, all of which are capable of being understood by this important other person, his father. And further, Thomas can know more about his own inner feelings now, as well as responding to more overt parental behaviour.

Of course, Stern's model leaves some things unanswered and may generate some objections. Stern himself wonders if 'different societies could minimise or maximise this need for intersubjectivity'. He is aware that in a society like many in the West, where individualisation of human experience is highly valued, we run the risk of losing out in interpersonal terms. Certainly the many signs of personal and social breakdown seem to point to this trend, so it is not surprising that Stern, like myself and others in the field of psychotherapy and counselling, should see a need to attend to the interpersonal, as well as the individual development of the infant (PCSR 1997, AHPP 1999). Stern's model, however, may not be generalisable across the spectrum of different human societies.

Conclusion

Writing as an early childhood educator, I can see that Stern's ideas lend more weight to some of the principles we already hold dear, such as the guidelines on appropriate adult to infant childcare ratios enshrined in the Children Act (1989), or the principle that 'children need relationships with significant responsive adults' at the foundation of the 0–3 *Educare* curriculum (Rouse and Griffin 1992). If we are to have infants and very young children in institutionalised childcare situations at all, these must be centres not just of excellent educational practice, with trained professionals to care for the children in a well resourced environment, but also places where these 'unseen' interpersonal processes can be nourished in the growing child. Whether an infant or young child is cared for in their own home, by a trained childminder, or in some other early years setting, 'what is at stake here is nothing less that the shape and extent of the sharable inner universe of the child' (Stern 1985).

Writing as a psychotherapist, I see daily the effects of neglecting the interpersonal world of the growing child, in favour of other kinds of 'success'. The majority of people who attend my practice are outwardly successful and have achieved a great deal 'out there' in the world. Their lameness is internal; their pain is often silent and hidden from others. Long ago, they lost the trust that others will be capable of understanding how they feel; as adults their apparent self confidence is not supported by the internal strength that can only grow, it seems, in the company of another person who affirms and encourages interpersonal efforts.

I make use of Stern's idea that the 'domains of experience' go on developing throughout a human life. It is never too late, I suspect, to experience another's empathy and attunement to one's inner world; this experience can bring healing, even to adults quite advanced in years. How much better then, to show our children that feelings matter as much as mental arithmetic; that caring for each other is no less important than learning to read (QCA 1999). Our support for the interpersonal development of young children is no 'optional extra'; it provides the solid ground on which to build a healthy and happy human life.

References

AHPP Publications (1999) *Association of Humanistic Psychotherapy Practitioners*. London.

Barnes, P. (1995) *Personal, Social and Emotional Development of Children*. Milton Keynes and Oxford: Open University and Blackwell.

Bee, H. (1992) *The Developing Child*. New York: HarperCollins.

Berry Brazelton, T. and Cramer, B. G. (1991) *The Earliest Relationship*. London: Karnac House.

Bowlby, J. (1965) *Child Care and the Growth of Love*. Harmondsworth: Penguin.

Davenport, G. C. (1991) *An Introduction to Child Development*. London: Collins.

Gillie, M. (1999) 'Daniel Stern: A Developmental Theory for Gestalt?', *British Gestalt Journal*, December 1999.

Houston, G. (1995) *The Now Red Book of Gestalt*. London: Gaie Houston.

Kagan, J. (1984) *The Nature of the Child*. New York: Basic Books.

Owens, P. (ed.) (1997) *Early Childhood Education and Care*. Stoke-on-Trent: Trentham.

PCSR Publications (1997) *Psychotherapists and Counsellors for Social Responsibility*. London.

Qualifications and Curriculum Authority (1999) *Investing in our Future: Early Learning Goals*. London: Qualifications and Curriculum Authority.

Rouse, D. and Griffin, S. (1992) 'Quality for the under threes', in Pugh, G. (ed.) *Contemporary Issues in the Early Years*. London: NCB/Paul Chapman.

Stern, D. N. (1985) *The Interpersonal World of the Infant: A view from psychoanalysis and developmental psychology*. New York: Basic Books.

Woodhead, M. *et al.* (1991) *Becoming a Person*. London and New York: Routledge.

Chapter 19

Health inequalities in early childhood

Angela Underdown

Jason and his mother, Jacky, have recently moved into a women's refuge to get away from Jason's father, Ned, who has become increasingly violent. Jacky has always been short of money and lately Ned has been spending most of his wages on alcohol. Jacky's depression started when she was pregnant and, although she loves Jason, she found it difficult to form a close emotional bond with him. Jason has frequent temper tantrums and has become very aggressive with other children. Jacky is finding it hard to get Jason to the new nursery since they moved and he has missed even more sessions because of chest infections. The health visitor thinks that Jason's cough would improve if he wasn't always in a smoky atmosphere and if he lost some weight. Jacky has been trying hard to cook healthy food but Jason will only eat burgers and chips.

The effect of poverty on children's health

Jason is not experiencing the emotional, social or physical health that we might expect for a young child living in the United Kingdom (UK) in the 21st century. The fact that Jacky has little money and is living in temporary accommodation, causes added stress and impacts on all the family's health. There has been a sharp increase in the number of young children living in poverty in the UK over the past twenty years. In 1979, 1 in 10 children lived in a household with below half the average income, but by 1999 this had risen to 1 in 3 children (DSS 1999). This dramatic increase in children living in families with insufficient income has had a devastating effect on children's health, with the gap between health experienced by those in highest and lowest income groups becoming ever wider. Issues such as disability often put added financial pressures on a family. Parker (cited in BMA 1999) concluded in his study that 55% of families with a disabled child were living in or on the margins of poverty. The BMA report (1999: 103) also highlights the severe disadvantages of ethnic minority families with disabled children:

> The barrier of inadequate information and lack of interpreters, the reluctance to offer some services, such as respite care, because of misunderstandings about the role of the extended family and the poor housing and poverty exacerbate any problems of care.

Many children face situations where their health is compromised, but living in a family with insufficient income frequently compounds these difficulties, as can be seen in the following overview.

Children who live in families experiencing relative poverty are:

- Less likely to eat a healthy diet.

People in lower socio-economic groups shop more carefully to obtain more food for their money but they are more likely to buy foods with high levels of fat and sugar because they are richer in energy and cheaper than fruit and vegetables (Acheson 1998, Leather 1996).

> Why do children from poor families consume such a lot of fizzy drinks, milk and white bread? Penny for penny, a chocolate bar provides more calories than carrots, even from a market stall. If the child refuses what is offered there may be no money in the budget for an alternative.

> (Thurlbeck 2000: 809)

While poor families are understandably concerned with ensuring that children's stomachs feel full and that they have sufficient calories for energy, repeated studies have shown that coronary heart disease, certain cancers and obesity are linked to nutritionally poor diets in childhood. For children like Jason, adult ill health may well be the legacy from his poor childhood diet. Lack of money for iron-rich food such as red meat and green leafy vegetables have also led to outcomes such as iron deficiency anaemia, leading to reduced immunity and greater susceptibility to infection (BMA 1999).

- More likely to have a childhood accident.

Child accidents are the major cause of death for children aged over 1 year in the UK and children from the lowest social classes are four times more likely to die from an accident and nine times more likely to die from a house fire than a child from a more affluent home (OPCS 1994, Roberts 2000). Children in poorer neighbourhoods are also likely to have less safe places to play and often face increased danger from traffic. The reasons for such a wide differential in morbidity from accidents between the socio-economic groups has been the cause of much speculation. It is most likely that a wide combination of contributory factors interplay in these outcomes. For example, a smoke alarm may seem an unnecessary expense when struggling financially to provide food for the family and perhaps factors, such as depression or lack of awareness of child development, may mean that risks to children are evaluated differently from one family to another.

- Less likely to be breast fed for any length of time.

Despite the benefits of being breast fed being clearly shown by numerous research studies, there is a dramatic contrast in the incidence of breast feeding, with women in higher socio-economic groups being twice as likely to breast feed as women in lower social groups (BMA 1999). Research indicates that the physical, cognitive and emotional benefits of breast feeding are many, including fewer allergies, fewer infections, less diabetes and the promotion of brain and intestinal development (Jenner 1988, James *et al.* 1997).

- More likely to have parents who smoke.

Women from social class 5 are four times more likely to smoke in pregnancy than women in social class 1 (Foster *et al.* 1997), resulting in lower birth weight, and an increased risk of sudden infant death syndrome (Leather 1996). In addition, other research has linked parental smoking, in low income families, to less balanced diets. In families where both parents smoked, 26% reported that they were unable to afford essential dietary items such as vegetables and fruit compared with 9% in low income families where the parents did not smoke (Marsh and McKay 1994). In addition the prevalence of asthma and chest infections is higher where children passively inhale cigarette smoke (Upton *et al.* 1998). In the case study, Jason's health visitor was clearly concerned about his repeated chest infections and the possible links with passive smoking.

- Are more likely to have a parent suffering from depression.

Although at least 10% of all mothers suffer post natal depression (Cooper 1991 cited in Roberts 2000), studies indicate that the long-term effects of maternal depression on the cognitive and emotional development of children are more marked where there is socio-economic disadvantage (Murray and Cooper 1997; Petterson and Burke Albers 2001). Some children, like Jason, may find themselves living in a family where a combination of problems such as lack of money, domestic violence and maternal depression constantly interact to negatively influence health.

- Less likely to achieve well at school.

Children from disadvantaged backgrounds tend to have lower educational attainments and recent research studies (Duncan *et al.* 1994) have shown clear, deleterious links between poverty and children's cognitive abilities, from as early as two years of age (Smith *et al.* 1997). Acheson (1998: 40–1) recommends that more high quality pre-school education should be developed:

> ...so that it meets, in particular, the needs of disadvantaged families. We also recommend that the benefits of pre-school education to disadvantaged families are evaluated and, if necessary, additional resources are made available to support further development.

The effects of domestic violence on children's health

Domestic violence is prevalent in all socio-economic groups. Studies have indicated that in homes where there is violence towards women, there is also violence towards one or more children in 40–60% of cases (Hughes *et al.* 1989). Between 75% and 90% of violent incidents in the home are thought to be witnessed by children, in itself constituting emotional abuse. Pre-school children living in violent situations may present with behavioural problems or physical responses such as headaches, stomach aches or diarrhoea as well as erratic nursery attendance and poor concentration (Hilberman and Munson 1977). Abrahams (1994) also found a range of emotional health problems, from being frightened and withdrawn to being angry and aggressive. However, the results of trying to leave a violent home often lead to health consequences for children. Living in a refuge or bed and breakfast may well expose children to a change in economic resources, they may have to leave their friends and neighbourhood, and some children, especially from ethnic minority groups, may face bullying (Mullender and Morley 1994).

How can these health inequalities be addressed?

The government commissioned an 'Independent Inquiry into Inequalities in Health' and the committee chaired by Sir Donald Acheson produced their report in 1999, highlighting three key areas for health improvement:

- all policies likely to have an impact on health should be evaluated with regard to their impact on health inequalities
- a high priority should be given to the health of families with children
- further steps should be taken to improve the living standards of poor families.

The government has pledged to tackle health inequalities and to end child poverty within a generation and raise the threshold for defining poverty from 50% to 60% of median income (DSS 1999, Howarth *et al.* 1999). The government policy agenda includes a whole range of initiatives to improve the health of children. The plan is to ensure that a combination of national policy and local action encourages new and innovative partnerships to tackle inequalities. The policy agenda includes:

- reducing child poverty by reforming benefits and tax systems;
- raising awareness of healthy behaviour through the Healthy Schools Programme;
- setting up The National Family and Parenting Institute to value and support family wellbeing;
- introducing a National Service Framework (NSF) for children's health to ensure consistency of health services for children in all areas and that children and families are consulted about services;

- strengthening the support available to families in disadvantaged areas through Sure Start for families with children under four years of age;
- setting up the Children's Fund to allow local projects to provide preventative services for 5–13-year-olds and their families;
- improving the health of children in care through the Quality Protects Scheme;
- improving access to healthy food through school breakfast clubs in disadvantaged areas and the National School Fruit Scheme (see example below).

Examples of three interventions to improve children's health

The National School Fruit Scheme – a national government scheme

During 2001 the Department of Health piloted a National School Fruit Scheme in a cross-section of 500 primary, infant, special and nursery schools. The scheme aims to ensure that every child between four and six years of age is offered a piece of fresh fruit every day. The scheme has been evaluated positively so far, recording comments from teachers like the following:

> It has challenged our misconceptions that children won't eat fruit.

> An excellent filler between breakfast and lunch, especially as certain children have little or no breakfast.

Following early evaluations the Government plans to ensure that by 2004 every child will be entitled to a piece of fruit every day at infant school.

Bright Beginnings – a voluntary sector project

The Children and Young People's Participation Project Warrington aims to promote healthy eating and child safety. This Children's Society group meets once a week and is open to anyone in the area who cares for a child of under 5 years. The group has a rolling programme of activities and carers decide which session they would like. Sessions include:

- Healthy eating
- Eating ideas for children
- Cookery on a budget
- Fun with food.

This project is a partner to Warrington Child Accident Group, who recently carried out a campaign called 'Careful that's Hot' in response to statistics from Warrington Accident and Emergency Department in 2000 showing the extremely high number of injuries to children due to hot drinks and hot fat. The project supports this safety campaign by offering a 'SAFE (Safe Affordable Family Equipment) Buy' outlet, selling safety equipment and offering advice on safety to families. This scheme aims to offer families the knowledge and skills to make their own informed decisions about child safety.

Development of home zones – a local authority safety intervention

Some local authorities are launching 'Home Zone' schemes aimed at ensuring that the local neighbourhood is for people rather than transport. The Northmoor inner city estate in Manchester based their home zone on a consultation with local people. The area is now planted out with trees, there are safe play areas and an improved road layout with traffic calming measures.

A *partnership approach*

The schemes described above are innovative attempts to try to improve the health and safety of children, but they can only have a real impact on health if they are part of an integrated range of measures aimed at meeting individual and community needs. Jacky, for example, may need more support with parenting Jason, help with finding suitable accommodation and help for her depression. Every initiative can add another part to the puzzle of meeting health needs in a holistic way. So, to use the example of developing home zones: this not only provides for safe play in a pleasant environment, it also involves consulting with children, young people and adults to find out what they think will work. By actually participating, people can 'own' the changes and develop personally through meaningful contributions. By actively contributing, children and adults feel valued and competent, whereas those living in deprived situations often feel powerless and unable to influence. Sure Start projects are attempting to redress this power imbalance by actively listening and consulting with the community so that services are flexible to fit what parents and children want and need.

References

Abrahams, C. (1994) *The Hidden Victims: Children and Domestic Violence.* London: NCH Action for Children.

Acheson, Sir Donald. (1998) *Independent Inquiry into Inequalities in Health Report.* London: HMSO.

BMA (British Medical Association) (1999) *Growing up in Britain: Ensuring a healthy future for our children.* A study of 0–5-year-olds. London: BMA.

Duncan, G., Brooks-Gunn, J. and Klebanov, P. (1994) 'Economic deprivation and early childhood development', *Child Development* **65**(2), 296–318.

DSS (Department of Social Security) (1999) *Opportunity For All: Tackling Poverty and Social Exclusion, The First Annual Report.* London: HMSO.

Foster, K., Lader, D. and Cheesborough, S. (1997) *Infant Feeding.* London: HMSO.

Hilberman, E. and Munson, K. (1977) 'Sixty battered women', *Victimology: An International Journal* **2**(3–4), 460–70.

Howarth, C., Kenway, P., Palmer, R. and Miorellie, R. (1999) *Monitoring Poverty and Social Exclusion.* York: Joseph Rowntree Foundation. London: New Policy Institute.

Hughes, H., Parkinson, D. and Vargo, M. (1989) 'Witnessing spouse abuse and experiencing physical abuse: a double whammy?', *Journal of Family Violence* **4**, 197–209.

James, W., Nelson, M. and Ralph, A. (1997) 'Socio-economic determinants of health. The contribution of nutrition to inequalities in health', *British Medical Journal* **314**, 1545–9.

Jenner, S. (1988) 'The influence of additional information, advice and support on the success of breast feeding in working class primiparas', *Child Care Health and Development* **14**, 319–28.

Leather, S. (1996) *The Making of Modern Malnutrition: An Overview of Food Poverty in the UK*. London: The Caroline Walker Trust.

Marsh, A. and McKay, S. (1994) *Poor Smokers*. London: Policy Studies Institute.

Mullender, A. and Morley, R. (1994) *Children Living with Domestic Violence: Putting Men's Abuse of Women on the Child Care Agenda*. London: Whiting and Birch.

Murray, L. and Cooper, P. (1997) (eds) *Postpartum Depression and Child Development*. New York: Guilford Press.

Office of Population Censuses and Surveys (OPCS) (1994) *Child Accident Statistics 1993*. London: HMSO.

Petterson, S. and Burke Albers, A. (2001) 'Effects of poverty and maternal depression on early child development', *Child Development* **72**(6), 1794–1813.

Roberts, H. (2000) *What Works in Reducing Inequalities in Child Health?* London: Barnardo's.

Smith, J., Brooks-Gunn, J. and Klebanov, P. (1997) 'The consequences of living in poverty for young children's cognitive and verbal ability and early school achievement', in Duncan, G. and Brooks-Gunn, J. *Consequences of Growing Up Poor*, 132–89. New York: Sage.

Thurlbeck, S. (2000) *'Growing Up in Britain'* (Review), *British Medical Journal* **320**, 809.

Upton, M., Watt, G., Davy Smith, G. *et al.* (1998) 'Permanent effects of maternal smoking on offsprings' lung function', *Lancet* **352**, 453.

Chapter 20

Studying play from a developmental perspective

Christine Macintyre

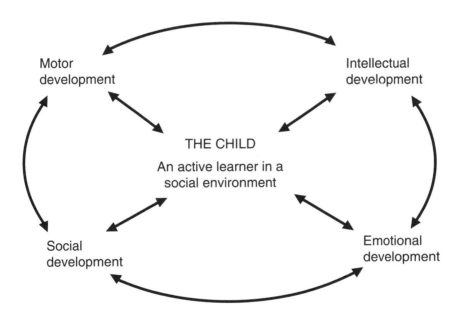

Figure 20.1 Aspects of development

The study of play and that of child development naturally complement each other. Those who seek to understand early child development can find many examples of each aspect of development in play, for 'as in the focus of a magnifying glass, play contains all the developmental tendencies in a condensed form' (Vygotsky 1978), and because it does, it is helpful to have a structure which can make this complex study more manageable. The one suggested here is to subdivide the study of development into four aspects, namely:

1. Social development, or the study of how children build relationships and learn to interact in groups,

2. Perceptual-motor development, or the study of how children learn to move efficiently and effectively in different environments,

3. Intellectual or cognitive development, or the study of how children learn to be logical and rational thinkers, and lastly,

4. Emotional or affective development, or the study of how children's feelings and perceptions affect their behaviour and learning.

Of course the four aspects interact and so progression or indeed regression in one aspect impinges on all of the others.

For example, a boy just able to swim will have taken a huge stride forward in the perceptual-motor domain, but progress also spills over into the others. Now that he is able to swim, he can interact with friends, a social gain; he has learned the names of different strokes and when they are best used, i.e. an intellectual gain; and possibly best of all, he has become more confident in his own ability to learn a new skill and this is an emotional gain.

The arrows in Figure 20.1 linking the different subdivisions of development are there to remind those who observe children, assess their progress and plan learning activities on that basis, that progress in one area is likely to benefit other areas as well. In a similar vein, new or unhappy experiences can cause children to regress to an earlier developmental stage. Then they will appear unable to do something which they had mastered before. This explains why parents can be flummoxed to find that their toilet-trained youngster has been having accidents in his new school! This may be a more common occurrence as more three-year-olds come into nursery, especially as being toilet trained is no longer one of the criteria for entry!

It can be difficult at times to know where to place different assessments. If a child is able to get dressed after P.E. in an acceptable amount of time where previously that was really difficult, what kind of progress is that? Is it intellectual? (the child can now understand the order of putting clothes on and gauge the time to be spent on each action), is it perceptual-motor? (the child has now developed the coordination to be able to do up buttons and tie laces), is it emotional? (the child has gained confidence from not being last). In my view, considering progress across the spectrum and weighing up all the advantages is more important than recording observations in the 'correct' place. In fact, different viewpoints can form the basis of rich discussions about children's progress.

And sometimes, just as different people have different reasons for doing things, so children can put greatest value on the less obvious benefits, e.g. 'When I can swim I'll be allowed to go to the pool without Mum!' This child is eager to be free!

A more detailed look at the rationale for choosing these aspects of development as key contributors to learning follows.

Social development

Many parents and teachers would say that the social dimension of learning is the most important one because if children are happy in school they are likely to be more receptive and confident and therefore able to take new learning on board, or at least they will not be afraid to ask for help. Moreover, sociable children are able to interact and learn from their peer group as well as from their parents and teachers. Many important researchers (e.g. Wells, Wood) emphasise the importance of active children learning in a social setting. Vygotsky's (1978) concept of 'the zone of proximal development' and Bruner's (1966) idea of 'scaffolding' both claim that if children are supported by more knowledgeable others as they learn – and these need only be one step ahead – they will be able to move forward more quickly than if they tried to learn alone.

Social development is therefore vitally important as it enables children to:

- learn from others,
- interact appropriately with adults and children,
- cooperate in group situations,
- take the lead role in decision making,
- at times take the subsidiary role,
- become aware that others also have needs,
- learn to empathise, i.e. understand different perspectives,
- understand how events affect others,
- develop socially acceptable behaviour in different circumstances,
- make decisions (social and/or moral) and stay with them,

- appreciate the value of friendship,
- develop altruism, i.e. caring for others at some cost to oneself.

Perceptual-motor development

The perceptual-motor aspects of development concern the acquisition of practical skills through developing abilities such as coordination, balance, strength and speed of movement. The underlying skills of planning movements so that they are efficient and effective, involve much perceptual learning based on making spatial and kinesthetic decisions. These depend on the other senses (i.e. visual, auditory and tactile), interpreting environmental cues accurately, so that feedback into the sensory system guides decisions about when to move, what to move and where to go!

Planning movement, that 'knowing what to do when', is also known as ideation. Large movements involving the large muscle groups are known as gross motor skills while the smaller muscle groups contribute to fine motor control.

N.B. If children have a learning difficulty, it can often be spotted first in poor movement coordination.

Example

Children who don't crawl very often can't crawl. As a result they lack early sequencing and coordination practice, and experience in stretching forward and making spatial decisions while in a secure position. Picture a child in a prone kneeling position, i.e. ready to crawl. Imagine one hand stretching forward to go into the movement. As this happens the body weight must shift to be completely supported by the other three points. This is good practice for learning to balance. If children don't experience this, and parents not understanding may be pleased that their children have 'jumped a stage', they are missing out a fundamental stage in learning to move effectively in different environments, for balance is essential to stability in both stillness and movement.

Often children who haven't crawled have reading difficulties, sometimes dyslexia. This is because they have missed out on sequencing practice, i.e. moving their limbs in the correct order imprinting a pattern of sequential movement into their brain. These omissions are also regularly found in children with dyspraxia (Macintyre 2000).

It is important that due attention is given to perceptual-motor development, because this enables children to:

- control their movements with increasing dexterity,
- move effectively and safely in different environments,
- develop spatial and kinesthetic awareness,

- develop the abilities that underlie skilled performance,
- know how to organise sequences of movement,
- become involved in health giving activities,
- enjoy participating in sports, gymnastics and dance,
- be confident in tackling new movement challenges.

Intellectual development

The intellectual, or cognitive aspects, of development concern the acquisition of knowledge and understanding about all aspects of everyday life and in all areas of the curriculum. Children need to develop this so that they can learn:

- to develop knowledge and understanding of the world,
- to develop language and communication skills,
- to develop the capacity to think logically and rationally,
- to make informed decisions,
- to develop mathematical and scientific concepts,
- to solve problems,
- to think creatively about new ways of doing things,
- to concentrate on the task at hand,
- to cope with specialised learning in the classroom and at home.

Emotional development

This is perhaps the most difficult area to understand, possibly because the development of confidence as one example, is only apparent in carrying out another task or perhaps in changed non-verbal behaviour which is always difficult to assess. Other things like appreciation or imagination are less tangible than, e.g. getting a sum right and making progress in mathematics, but this is a hugely important aspect of development for it allows children to:

- pretend to be someone else,
- approach new situations with confidence,
- express feelings and emotions,
- cope with anxieties and be more resilient,
- enjoy open-ended problems,
- appreciate works of art/music/dance,
- cry if they want to,
- understand the perception of other people,
- develop altruism,
- appreciate the atmosphere, e.g. in a church,
- be innovative and imaginative.

As all of this terminology becomes clear, there are two other very important factors to remember. First, one aspect of change may be dominant at one time and affect the others. Think of sudden growth spurts. At these times children who have grown have to make physical and emotional adjustments especially if they are 'the first' in their peer group. The children who are waiting to grow have similar hurdles and the emotional upheaval can act negatively on other aspects of learning. Growing children all pass through the same stages but the pace of so doing is different and this can cause anguish and uncertainty. Perhaps this is particularly true in the early years when parents are apt to make comments, such as 'He's very shy,' or comparisons which the listening child interprets as criticisim, e.g. 'Goodness, isn't he big, much bigger than my boy.' It is not hard to imagine the impact on the child's self-esteem!

Second, the children at the centre of all of this are not passive recipients, but people who make decisions and react to teaching in their own way. Children always surprise by how much they can learn but they will bring their own experiences and be influenced by their genetic endowment and their context – their previous learning, their environment and the quality and quantity of the opportunities they have had. Perhaps they will learn best if their own ways are recognised and respected.

> Each child is a unique individual. Each brings a different life story to the early years setting. Growing up as a member of a family and community with unique ways of understanding the world creates an individual pattern and pace of development.
> (Scottish Consultative Council on the Curriculum 1998)

This being so, parents, teachers and nursery nurses must understand that there are key factors interacting to influence development and how children learn. They are heredity, growth, maturation and environment (Figure 20.2) and will be considered in turn.

Heredity

Bee (1999) describes heredity as 'a genetic blueprint which influences what we can do.' The influence of the nature (inherited/genetic) component of development against that of the nurture (environmental) one has been hotly debated for many years. The conclusion has always been that a constant and complex interplay of both factors determines the child's behaviour. Nonetheless, trying to understand the starting-off position, i.e. what the child has inherited, and how home and preschool, i.e. environmental influences, have shaped a child's attitude towards play and learning, is a fascinating study. And of course it is essential if we are to understand if and how we can help children build on the favourable aspects of both.

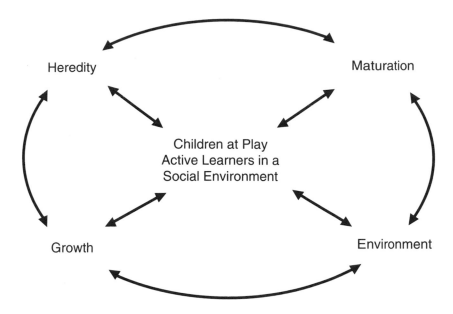

Figure 20.2 Influences on development

Where does it all begin?

Unless there is some genetic abnormality, e.g. in Down's Syndrome, the nucleus of each cell in the body has 46 chromosomes arranged as 23 pairs. These hold all the genetic pointers for each individual and determine the factors shown in the following list:

- height,
- aspects of personality, e.g. temperament,
- aspects of intelligence, e.g. the ability to empathise with other people's feelings,

- body build,
- patterns of physical development,
- vulnerability to allergies,
- possibly dyslexia and/or dyspraxia

The only cells which do not contain 46 chromosomes are the sperm and ovum. They are known as gametes. Each has 23 chromosomes, not 23 pairs. Each chromosome is composed of a chain of molecules of a chemical (DNA) which can be subdivided into genes and each gene is responsible for an aspect of development, e.g. which blood group, what hair colour or even what diseases the child inherits. At conception the 23 chromosomes from the father and 23 from the mother come together. They can hold similar 'instructions' or very different ones. Researchers are still trying to explain the part each plays when different instructions come together. If, for example, a child inherits one which signals shyness' (a temperamental trait) from one parent and 'outgoingness' from the other, what then? Bee (1999) explains that typically, one gene will be dominant and this will influence the child's behaviour while the other, the recessive gene, is dormant and has no visible effect. However, this dormant gene can still be passed on to the next generation.

These are 'either/or' characteristics; there is no blend. This explains why children in the same family, brought up in the same environment can be 'chalk and cheese' with parents amazed at the very different characteristics the children display. Even when two siblings look alike, they can still have very different temperaments – one may be happy-go-lucky and resilient and appear to weather storms unscathed, while the other is sensitive and vulnerable and has a harder time coping in what, to the outsider, would be seen was the same set of circumstances. Of course the siblings may learn from one another and behaviours can be altered by copying or modelling, but fundamentally the temperaments stay different because they depend on inherited genetic material. At the same time the inherited genes do not absolutely determine the pattern of any child's development. In Bee's (1999) words 'they influence what can be done.' The specific set of instructions contained in the genes is known as the genotype whereas the phenotype is the name given to the child's observed characteristics. Figure 3 shows that both the genotype and the environment influence the phenotype. Additionally they also work together to further influence the phenotype.

Example

A mum-to-be may conceive a child with genotype 'high IQ', however unwise use of drugs or alcohol during pregnancy may damage the child's nervous system so that the initial potential cannot be realised. These damaging environmental effects are called teratogens. Others are rubella in early pregnancy which may result in sight, hearing or heart problems, or AIDS (although only 25% of babies born to mothers with full blown AIDS, as opposed to IIIV, will develop the disease). Viruses can also attack the placenta reducing the nutrients which sustain the embryo.

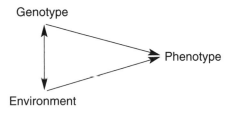

Figure 20.3 Influences on the phenotype

Distinct from teratogens are genetic errors. One example is the chromosome abnormality which results in Down's Syndrome, which holds a degree of intellectual retardation as well as particular physical characteristics. Another is phenylketonuria, a metabolic disorder which cannot be detected prenatally and which prevents the metabolism of a common amino acid. Treatment is a rigid diet, essential to prevent the onset of mental retardation.These errors occur at the moment of conception and are permanent although new technology may be able to change this. Most people will regard this as a most welcome intervention.

Personality factors or temperamental traits are other inherited factors, but they may be more amenable to environmental influence.

Example

If a child inherits the temperamental trait 'impulsiveness' and so tends to act without considering the consequences, then a home and school setting which models 'slowing down' and thinking through the outcomes of actions could be very beneficial. If, for example, adults help the child practise 'crossing the road drill', calmly pointing out the dangers, then later the child may be less likely to dive into the road. Of course one example won't do much to change usual ways of behaving. Constant and consistent examples are needed to influence temperamental traits which house relatively enduring characteristics. Although children may well learn to slow down in familiar situations, when new ones arise, they tend to instinctively respond in their own temperamental way. Impulsivity does tend to diminish as children mature, and this together with the learning which comes from daily experiences means that they can be 'trusted to be safe' and need less supervision as they play.

An impulsive child in a household of impetuous adults however, has no different role model and will have a harder time becoming reflective and cautious.

At the other end of the impulsive continuum is 'reflectiveness' and generally this is seen as a welcome trait. People who are reflective take time to consider options and therefore often choose the best one. Taken to the extreme of course, these individuals can be confused by visualising too many alternative ways and never get anything done! There are times when snap decisions need to be made and other times when there is time to make an informed choice. Maybe the skill comes in recognising which is which.

Understanding development in this way is important, for theoretical knowledge houses practical implications. Realising, for example, that parents with higher IQs are likely to pass on the wherewithal to do well in school *and* provide a stimulating learning environment, means that less-favoured children are doubly disadvantaged. This knowledge can justify early intervention programmes specifically designed to overcome the double deficit (both genetic and environmental) which less fortunate children face. If this happens early, children can begin primary school on a more level playing field. Without this understanding, teachers could expect children with very different backgrounds and experiences to learn the same things together and this could further compound the inequalities.

While growth and maturation are sometimes used as synonyms they are subtly different.

Growth

Growth is a change in quantity, for example, the increased size of the body with age or the number of words in a child's vocabulary or the range of skills a child has. In other words growth denotes change in a quantitive, descriptive way. It says 'this is what occurred', but provides no description of why.

Of course, these growth changes have associated psychological changes. Young children usually want to be big because they associate this with being clever or independent or grown up. Moreover, researchers in schools have found that teachers give more responsibility and independence to children who are big for their age. They appear to consider size as an indicator of competence rather than chronological age, even over ability. Or perhaps they consider that they need to protect the wee ones more. Bee (1999) certainly claims that 'large and robust children elicit different kinds of care giving than fragile ones.' For whatever reason 'big' children appear to be seen as being 'ready' or more reliable earlier and they are given more complex tasks. Usually they respond well and the parents' and teachers' expectations are met.

Large children are also more likely to be chosen as leaders by their peer group (Lerner 1985). This is important even in the earliest years, for the tallest boys and girls can be six inches taller than the smallest ones. Perhaps realising this, i.e. the tendency to favour one group, parents, teachers and nursery nurses can help the smaller children by remembering that size does not always equal competence and ensure that responsibilities are more equally given out.

Heredity has a very strong influence on growth. When healthy children have supportive environments, their genetic influence explains their height. Tall parents usually have tall children, while short parents have shorter ones, although there is some regression to the mean. Furthermore, children can't eat to be tall or starve to be short as many an aspiring jockey or ballerina has discovered. However, growth rate can be affected if the environment is really poor because malnutrition or abuse does cause the growth rate to drop. Some recurring illnesses such as asthma can also affect growth. The effects of regular medication on growth are being investigated at this time.

Estimating final height

The final height of children can be predicted with some accuracy. The correlation between height at age two and final height is .78 (Tanner 1990). However, this works best for children of parents of average height. The calculation will need amending with two tall parents or two small ones. Length at birth has a much lower correlation, only .3 because conditions in the womb, i.e. environmental influences, have a strong effect. The timing of puberty also affects final height. Those who go through it early tend to be shorter. And so although the genetic influence in growth patterning is strong, there are other factors which need to be considered (Table 20.1).

Table 20.1

Children who reach their height potential, tend:	Children who do not reach their height potential, tend:
to come from an 'advanced' background to have consistent security and support to have escaped illnesses such as asthma necessitating drug therapy	to come from a disadvantaged background to have erratic support to have been laid low by illnesses to be from larger families

A combination of factors – genetic/environmental and personal – work together to influence height.

Maturation

The term maturation means 'genetically programmed patterns of change' (Gesell 1925). These include changes in body size and shape, muscle control and hormonal changes at puberty. These patterns are genetically programmed, they are inbuilt. They begin at the moment of conception and continue until death. Understanding these changes is important because they explain development rather than describe it.

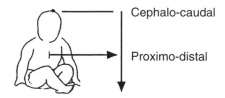

Cephalo-caudal

Proximo-distal

Figure 20.4 Early physical development

All children in all cultures pass through the same patterns of change. Physical development is cephalo-caudal (i.e. progressing from head to toe), and proximo-distal (i.e. progressing from the centre to the periphery). This is why babies can hold their heads up before their back muscles are strong enough to let them sit, and why they can sit before they are able to pull up to stand. Most children crawl, even up stairs before they walk, for this is the same action. The instructions for these sequences are built in at the moment of conception, they are not taught. Even anxious parents can't teach their children to walk. They won't walk till they are 'ready', i.e. till they have the strength and balance and coordination, and the maturity to allow them to try. The fact that most children walk between 11 and 18 months establishes one detail in a timetable of age-norms and this is often used as an assessment device to measure progress. For example see Table 20.2. It must be remembered however that the span of 'normal' development is wide.

Table 20.2 Developmental Norms

Age 6–8 months	– should be able to reach and grasp, but still will have difficulty 'letting go' – should be 'nearly sitting' unsupported for a short time – may be rolling over sideways
Age 9–12 months	– pulling up on furniture, attempting to stand with support – will be moving around – hopefully crawling
Age 1 year – 18 months	– walking and crawling intermittently – lots of bumping down Some will scribble using a finger thumb pencil grip but often a clutched grip is used. No hand dominance at this stage.
Age 2 years	– immature running pattern evident now- may be little control in stopping Climbs stairs in a step feet together pattern. Can unscrew lids, thread beads and chat in longer phrases. Understands what is being said. Will rebel if displeased! Shows clear hand preference although some jobs can still be done with either hand.
Age 3 years	– confident running now. Jumping to have 2 feet off the ground still difficult. Combines movements, e.g. running to kick a ball – not always successfully. Attempts stairs with the mature fluent pattern. Catches a large soft ball.
Age 4 years	– pedals a trike now. Can run and jump to land on two feet. Can pour juice from a jug and wipe dishes. Can hammer nails and do jig-saws. Has a large vocabulary. Still concerned with 'own' events rather than appreciating other people's but developing altruism and empathy especially if role models are at hand.
Age 5 years	– can skip and follow a clapping rhythm now. Enjoys stories and rhymes. Likes to look after others and take responsibility. Likes to help organise and can tidy up. All the basic motor patterns should be achieved now.

N.B. the 'normal' age span for the development of the basic movement patterns is wide, but children markedly different from their peers should be checked out to see if extra help is required.

Children who don't crawl may not have the sequencing and coordination to allow them to do so. Instead of allowing them to miss this stage, crawling games and analysing the crawl pattern for the children can be helpful in giving the kind of balancing and reaching experience which they otherwise would have missed.

Maturation and perceptual development

For many years it was thought that genetically determined development was preset regardless of the environment. One interesting phenomenon which appeared to support this was the child's developing language. Many develop strange past tense word forms, e.g. 'I goed to bed', despite never having heard such usage. However it is now accepted that maturation is enhanced by a stimulating environment. Sadly, children from severely impoverished environments do not develop the same density of neural connections in the brain as those who have rich experiences, such as interacting with people who are interested in children and who encourage them to learn. Trevarthen (1993) claimed that these must happen at the right times 'when the brain is thirsting for new experiences', if they are to be readily assimilated.

There are also social and cultural differences which impact on maturation. Being allowed, or being constrained, to do certain things at certain times, e.g. getting out to play unsupervised, going to nursery at age three, 'big' school at age five in Britain, and not until seven in Germany, i.e. at an age when the authorities decide it is the best time to begin formal education. These socialising events accompany the biological/maturational changes which occur. Again, the effects of heredity and environment work together to influence the individual development of children.

In comparison to the limited motor development which prevents very young babies from carrying out more than seemingly random, or uncoordinated movements, their perceptual development is quite advanced at birth. They can see, and are especially well-focused at about eight inches, which is nursing distance; they can hear and recognise family sounds and can respond to these to ensure that their caretaking needs are met; they know their mother or their caretaker's smell, and can recognise this source of security; they can readily discriminate between the four basic tastes of sweet, sour, bitter and salty, and by making their preferences felt, they can ensure that they are given the correct kinds of food. With these capabilities in place they are all set for learning.

Observation of newborns allows researchers to claim that not only do they have these capacities, but they are able to make associations between them. Babies, hearing their mother's footsteps, for example, will begin the searching and sucking actions which precedes feeding. Likewise, if someone who usually plays with them approaches, they will open their eyes wide and by increasing the activity of their arms and legs, indicate that they too are ready to play. This is called schematic learning. The babies are building a repertoire of patterns or schemas from their experiences and using them to make judgements about their future behaviours. Rovee-Collier (1986) suggested that these kinds of linkages are in fact the development of expectancies in children, i.e. the beginnings of the process of intellectual development. Bandura (1992) also shows that, 'The development of memory skills helps children to remember what actions in what situations produced what outcomes.'

In this way children build a bank of information so that when they meet a new situation they can make judgements about the most appropriate response. Others may help the children in this decision-making process by providing reinforcements: smiling, nodding or other rewards which indicate that the demonstrated behaviour is approved.

Beyond the baby stage, the development of the different modes of perception has a marked influence on how children *can* learn, and this of course influences the best ways for them to be taught:

- Visual
- Auditory
- Tactile
- Kinesthetic
- Proprioceptive
- Vestibular

Visual

The most obvious benefit of vision is to be able to see clearly and recognise people and objects and the distances between them. To do this the eyes must work together with no condition, e.g. astigmatism or cataract, which could take objects out of focus and make any sort of spatial judgement difficult. If children have visual difficulties, they can be seen peering closely at their book, screwing up one eye to cut out distractors, even shaking their heads as if to clear away a foggy image. Sometimes opiticians may give children the 'all clear' because they can see ahead quite clearly and recognise letters instantly, however their functional vision can still be impaired. If it is, the letters on a page may wobble or run together, even jump out of sequence, making identification and reading difficult. These children are also likely to have difficulty in tracking objects, e.g. the path of an approaching ball. If they lose the flight path, then their fingers don't have time to make the necessary spatial adjustments to let them catch and the ball drops at their feet.

If the eyes don't follow the letters smoothly in the correct sequence, learning to read is bound to be problematic. Tracking difficulties may make it very difficult for children to identify 'which line' and 'where on the page' they should begin. In maths too, faulty tracking can cause figures to jump out of line, meaning that while the children understand what it is they have to do and can do it orally, getting the right answer on paper is a different story. When copying from the board is necessary, these children have real difficulties. Then, they have to find the correct place on the board, leave that, and then find the right place on their page, and perhaps do this several times in each lesson. Giving the children an inclined board can make a huge difference, because one of the adjustments, i.e. transcribing from the vertical to the horizontal and back, has been eased.

Another difficulty arises if the children have poor three dimensional vision. This means that they see objects flat against their background rather than protruding from it. As a result, the children's spatial judgements are impaired. They walk into things, get bumped and bruised and possibly even scolded at the same time. Very young children may not be able to see their shoes on a patterned carpet because they don't stand out. Any complex design is confusing.

Tables at school need to be covered with plain cloth to ease identifying and sorting objects, e.g. jigsaws or matching shape puzzles. Finding hidden pictures in a background of other lines is impossible. It is not difficult to see why children who bump into things and feel clumsy and uncoordinated have associated confidence difficulties and feel misunderstood and sad.

Sometimes children with visual perception problems cannot bear their personal space to be invaded. They are extremely protective and become very upset if others come in too close. As they also misjudge distances, they can be upset by children who come too near and upset them, even when these others had no such intention.

A last word on visual perception concerns children whose vision does not cut out distractors. Their attention is constantly interrupted by movements in the environment, e.g. fluttering leaves, which others manage to ignore. They are often scolded for not paying attention when visual distractibility is the cause. Self-esteem is hit again!

Auditory

Hearing clearly allows children to be alert to everything that goes on in their environment. It is also the most important requisite for listening, and children who listen well have a good chance of learning well. Children who don't listen well give a late response to instructions and this can cause problems from the moment they rise till bedtime. The problem often is that these children can't cut out background noises. Most children do this filtering out automatically, and this lets them concentrate on the most important things being said. But those with auditory difficulties strain to hear through the rustle or the buzz that is going on around them and can become understandably tired and irritable as they do. Relief comes from switching off all noises, and when teachers say 'He is in a world of his own', maybe this is why. The other world is too frantically busy. And so these children miss the teacher's instructions and often have to follow a neighbour to catch up. Their responses are delayed and if the neighbour's actions are faulty, theirs are too.

Finding a quiet spot for them is not easy in a busy classroom and writing simple instructions rather than calling them out takes time. Establishing quite a rigid routine so that the children know what comes next is a great help. These quite simple moves to assist the children can be very productive in the improved quality of the response that is received. They also stop the frustration of having to repeat instructions over and over again.

Tactile

This is a less obvious source of trouble for some children. There are really three aspects to consider. The first is to understand that some children can't bear to be touched. Even inadvertently brushing against them can cause them to over-react, possibly hitting out. The second is that touch may cause children to jerk as in a reflex action. The children may be sitting quietly listening to a story when one with this sensitivity jerks and disrupts the quiet mood. The child can be just as surprised as you for what has happened is that a T-shirt has rubbed his back and caused a reflex, just like the knee jerk. This is beyond the child's control but he gets the blame! The third is that some children require what is called hard feedback from the environment. These children crash around. They don't know their own strength, and put far too much of it into every action. When they run they go too fast and can't stop unless they crash into a wall or anyone standing by; they press their pencil too hard and it breaks; things just come apart in their hands. They have difficulty in interpreting the feedback from the environment unless it is strong and to get this feedback they need to 'bang hard'.

Kinesthetic

Some children have little awareness of their bodies, i.e. kinesthetic awareness. They are not aware of the effect moving one body part has upon the others. They have difficulty moving just one part in isolation, with children under three especially tending to move the body as a whole instead of in separate parts. This is wasteful of energy and makes the movement appear clumsy and uncoordinated. They also tend not to be sure where they end and the outside world begins and this lack of a clear appreciation of body boundary makes fine movements, e.g. holding a pencil, difficult. Of course hands still tend to be chubby which can make refined actions problematic too. Gradually as the children mature the movements become more refined.

The kinesthetic sense can be subdivided into three parts:

1. Body awareness – Do I know where my feet are without looking? Can I feel how close my back is to the wall? Do I know how to push my hand through my sleeve?
2. Body boundary – Do I know where I end and the bat I have in my hand begins? Do I know how far I am from the edge of the pavement?
3. Spatial awareness – Can I judge how far the car is from the zebra crossing? Can I put the jug of juice on the table without knocking the edge and spilling the juice?

I hope these questions show how difficult the day is for children who have not a well developed sense of space and where they are in it. They get bumped and bruised and soon, because they have difficulty moving accurately and quickly, no one wants them to play.

Luckily young children love games which help develop body awareness, e.g. Simon says 'Put your hands on your heads', or use rhythmical phrases, e.g. 'hands on heads, push them tall, hands on knees then curl up small'. These can gradually include elbows, knees and backs to enlarge the children's body awareness. This training all helps in activities like forward rolls, for how can children 'make a round back', if they can't feel where their back is? How can they be safe if they don't know how far they are from the wall?

Proprioceptive

The proprioceptor cells which are in the muscles and joints of the body work with the kinesthetic groups to tell where the body is in relation to outside objects. They help movement to be segmented and efficient. Children who have a sound proprioceptive sense can sit down without looking at their chair – they sense where it is, how high the seat is and so they can judge the amount of effort needed to sit down. They can do all their usual movement patterns without looking – fastening buttons, even tying laces can be done by feel alone. Those who can't must compensate by turning to see and/or bending to feel, i.e. movements which take time and need added coordination and concentration. Proprioceptors also help maintain balance and control, especially when different amounts of fluctuating strength are required, e.g. in bicycling over uneven grass instead of on a smooth pathway. Children with a poor proprioceptive sense are less skilled in these types of movements, and need to use their other senses, particularly visual, to compensate.

Vestibular

Vestibular receptors are situated in the inner ear and work to coordinate movements which require balance. This is why children with an ear infection sometimes find their sense of balance is affected. Some children just love to go on the waltzer at the fair; the whirling action temporarily confuses their proprioceptors and they feel giddy, almost out of control. They enjoy this sense of losing and regaining balance. Others find this kind of sensation unpleasant, to be avoided at all costs. But even those who seek this temporary sensation of vertigo would not wish to have it continuously, because then carrying out even everyday movements would be extremely stressful.

The vestibular sense responds to changes of position of the head, automatically coordinating the eyes and body. It also helps children recognise the midline of their bodies which is important in understanding directionality.

Environment

The child is born into a family system which may be nuclear, i.e. two parents and possibly brothers and sisters, or extended, i.e. including other relations like grandparents or long-staying friends, or transient, i.e. with different people arriving and departing at longer or shorter intervals. The child may be very important or not important at all to those who make up the group. The group itself may be stable, e.g. having the same sorts of values which stay the same over time so that the children gain a clear picture of what is 'right' and 'wrong' in that context, or the value systems may fluctuate like the people who come and go. The atmosphere in the group may be pleasant or filled with acrimony. And so you can understand how children come to school with very different expectations of security and awareness of the kind of behaviour which would be acceptable in a new setting.

The family in turn exists within a larger cultural system or community with different traditions, values and beliefs which may be more or less important to the smaller groups within it. Children absorbing the mores of their culture will expect staff to understand all the aspects of their different beliefs and value systems, e.g.to know and appreciate important festival days, or any food limitations or friendship patterns. Part of children's learning is to broaden their awareness of and come to respect different perspectives. They have a lot to learn.

Many complex questions about the effect of the quality and quantity of a child's environment are constantly being asked, e.g. to what extent does providing a rich stimulating environment in school compensate for deprivation at home and if it does, at what age does it need to be provided? Or, if this kind of environment is essential, how is it that so many highly successful people overcome severe disadvantages? Why is there the adage that a certain amount of disadvantage appears to spur some people to high levels of achievement? Does this depend on personality factors, e.g. grit and perseverance, or cultural factors, e.g. athletes being 'valued' and acting as role models for children who can practise without expensive equipment? Or have both positives to be in place if adversity is to be overcome? Is there a danger that children given everything on a plate as it were, will have nothing to work for? Or do humans always want something they do not have?

Those who provide education work hard to compensate for the disadvantages of both genetic and environmental deprivation that children encounter and no one would wish that any child was denied opportunities to flourish. The question of whether and to what extent a learning environment can compensate for a poor home environment is a difficult one to answer. Morally, children can't be denied access to a better learning environment for the sake of carrying out research to find out. Considering the level of disadvantage and the form it takes, the length and timing of any malnourishment or abuse adds to the complexity. Certainly the environmental factors are hugely complex just as the genetic ones are!

Moving now from more general considerations to more personal ones we find that the genetic factors which children inherit can, in turn, profoundly influence their environment. For instance children with sunny temperaments and smiling faces tend to receive more positive feedback than more sombre children. Children who spot any opportunities and go forward to take advantage of them tend to be favoured over those that are withdrawn and hold back. This shows how children themselves can positively or negatively affect their environment. Their own interactions, based on temperament as well as coping skills, significantly affect any outcome.

Long and Valiant (1984) studied 456 boys from inner-city schools and identified protective factors which appeared to overcome environmental disadvantages. They were:

- as preschoolers they had been affectionate, easy children
- they had a positive bond with at least one carer
- they had reasonable language and mathematical skills.

In other words they had some positives to begin with and these endured to help them.

A high-quality environment is a stable one where children have love and security and lots of appropriate stimulation. Given these circumstances, both resilient and vulnerable children are likely to do well. Resilient children can even do well in unfavourable circumstances. It is when vulnerable children have a poor environment that the outlook is bleak. The important issue is that neither a poor environment nor a vulnerable personality alone causes a poor outcome. The crippling factor is when the two negatives come together as a double blow.

It seems, however, that resilient children can do better than others in poor environments because they look forward rather than dwelling on things past. They recognise and seize opportunities. Perhaps knowing this, teachers and nursery nurses could help 'other' children by pointing out what possibilities there are. This links with helping the children plan rather than always concentrating on the thing that they are attempting to make.

What then are the implications within this nature/nurture debate? There is a lighter side and a darker side to this in my view. It is one thing for parents to note and enjoy mannerisms which they see passed on, or real or imagined potentials for achieving certain distinctions, provided they are realistic and do not stress the children or attempt to mould them into images of what their parents themselves would have liked to be. It is another if parents and teachers make poor prognoses about their children and justify their lack of input and encouragement on that basis. Time and time again children who are motivated surprise, sometimes amaze by their sustained commitment and their level of achievement, while others with seemingly greater gifts switch off and do not fulfil their potential at all. And so while the genetic endowment of individuals supplies a potential development, the fulfilment of this is facilitated by the kind of environment which provides stimulation and learning possibilities. Today, those who are concerned by the nature/nurture division usually say that it is most fruitfully seen as an interactive, interdependent process rather than a posing of opposites.

In the new century, one major intervention in the 'nature' field is genetic engineering, when the scientific modification of a baby's genetic code is possible. Identifying genetic disorders which cause severe illnesses or handicaps in the foetus leads to the complex questions which surround pre-natal intervention, even abortion. In a radio phone-in Mary Warnock, co-author of The Warnock Report (1978), pleaded that only parents of a child whose quality of life would be severely affected should be given the choice of having an abortion, while another mother of two healthy boys claimed that her desire for a girl was so strong that she would be prepared to abort a boy! When such possibilities exist, different people will obviously have very different views on the extent to which they should be able to determine the characteristics of their child, or indeed whether that child should be born at all.

As more and more children are spending time with childminders, at play groups and nurseries so the responsibility for much of the children's day is shifting. Children from very different environments are coming together earlier and for longer. Understanding how they develop and ensuring that learning opportunities 'match and extend' is therefore even more complex and more important than ever before.

References

Bandura, A. (1992) 'Social cognitive theory', in Vasta, R. (ed.) *Six Theories of Child Development*. London: Jessica Kingsley.

Bee, H. (1999) *The Growing Child*, 2nd edn. London: Longman.

Bruner, J. S. (1966) *The Process of Education*. Cambridge, MA: Harvard University Press.

Gesell, A. (1925) *The Mental Growth of the Preschool Child*. New York: Macmillan.

Lerner, R. M. (1985) 'Maturational changes and psychosocial development: a dynamic interactional perspective', *Journal of Youth and Adolescence* **14**.

Long, J. V. F. and Valiant, G. E. (1984) 'Natural history of male psychological health: escape from the underclass', *American Journal of Psychiatry* **141**.

Macintyre, C. (2000) *Dyspraxia in the Early Years*. London: David Fulton Publishers.

Rovee-Collier, C. (1986) 'The rise and fall of infant classical conditioning research: its promise for the study of early development', in Lipsitt, L. P. and Rovee-Collier, C. (eds) *Advances in Infancy Research*, Vol. 4. Norwood, NJ: Ablex.

Scottish Consultative Council on the Curriculum (1998) *Promoting Learning: Assessing Children's Progress 3–5*.

Tanner, J. M. (1990) *Foetus into Man: Physical Growth from Conception to Maturity*. Cambridge, MA: Harvard University Press.

Trevarthen, C. (1993) *Play for Tomorrow*. Edinburgh University Video Production.

Vygotsky, L. S. (1978) *Mind and Society*. Cambridge, MA: Harvard University Press.

Warnock, M. (1978) *Special Education Needs: Report of the Committee of Enquiry into the Education of Handicapped Children and Young People*.

Wells, G. (1986) *The Meaning Makers*. Portsmouth: Heinemann Educational Books.

Wood, D. (1992) *How Children Think and Learn*. London: Blackwell.

Index